Doing Their Bit

The British Employment of Military and Civil Defence Dogs in the Second World War

Kimberly Brice O'Donnell

Helion & Company

Helion & Company Limited
Unit 8 Amherst Business Centre
Budbrooke Road
Warwick
CV34 5WE
England
Tel. 01926 499 619
Fax 0121 711 4075
Email: info@helion.co.uk
Website: www.helion.co.uk
Twitter: @helionbooks
Visit our blog http://blog.helion.co.uk/

Published by Helion & Company 2018
Designed and typeset by Mach 3 Solutions Ltd (www.mach3solutions.co.uk)
Cover designed by Paul Hewitt, Battlefield Design (www.battlefield-design.co.uk)
Printed by Hobbs the Printers, Totton, Hampshire

Front cover image: Mine detection dog and handler of No. 1 Dog Platoon in France, July 1944 © Imperial War Museum (B 6499) Rear cover image: Rob, a patrol dog attached to the SAS, receives his Dickin Medal. (PDSA)

Every reasonable effort has been made to trace copyright holders and to obtain their permission for the use of copyright material. The author and publisher apologize for any errors or omissions in this work, and would be grateful if notified of any corrections that should be incorporated in future reprints or editions of this book.

ISBN 978-1-912390-68-7

British Library Cataloguing-in-Publication Data.
A catalogue record for this book is available from the British Library.

For details of other military history titles published by Helion & Company Limited contact the above address, or visit our website: http://www.helion.co.uk.

We always welcome receiving book proposals from prospective authors.

Contents

List of Illustrations

List of Tables

List of Acronyms, Abbreviations and Translations

AFHQ	Allied Forces Headquarters
ARP	Air Raid Precautions
ASU	aircraft storage unit
ATS	Auxiliary Territorial Service
AVRS	Army Veterinary and Remount Services
BAOR	British Army of the Rhine
BBC	British Broadcasting Corporation
BEF	British Expeditionary Force
CMP	Corps of Military Police
DAC	Defence Animal Centre
DAVRS	Director, Army Veterinary and Remount Services
ERO	Essex Record Office
FARELF	Far East Land Forces
GHQ	General Headquarters
HM	His/Her Majesty's
IED	improvised explosive device
IWM	Imperial War Museum
LDV	Local Defence Volunteers
LMA	London Metropolitan Archives
LST	tank landing ship
Luftwaffe	German Air Force
MAAF	Mediterranean Allied Air Forces
MAF	Ministry of Agriculture and Fisheries
MAP	Ministry of Aircraft Production
MELF	Middle East Land Forces
MOD	Ministry of Defence
NAA	National Archives of Australia
NAM	National Army Museum
NARA	National Archives and Records Administration (United States)
NATO	North Atlantic Treaty Organization
OAC	Obstacle Assault Centre
PDSA	People's Dispensary for Sick Animals
POW	prisoner of war

QMC	Quartermaster Corps (United States)
QMGF	Quartermaster General to the Forces
RAF	Royal Air Force
RAMC	Royal Army Medical Corps
RASC	Royal Army Service Corps
RAVC	Royal Army Veterinary Corps
RCE	Royal Canadian Engineers
RDC	Royal Defence Corps
RE	Royal Engineers
REME	Royal Electrical and Mechanical Engineers
RFA	Royal Field Artillery
RMP	Royal Military Police
RSPCA	Royal Society for the Prevention of Cruelty to Animals
SAS	Special Air Service
SIB	Special Investigation Branch
SOE	Special Operations Executive
S-mine	*Schrapnellmine*
Schu-mine	*Schutzenmine*
TNA	The National Archives (United Kingdom)
TNT	trinitrotoluene
UKFSSART	United Kingdom Fire Services Search and Rescue Team
USAAF	United States Army Air Force
USAF	United States Air Force
VC	Victoria Cross
Wehrmacht	German Armed Forces
V-E Day	Victory in Europe Day
VP	vulnerable point

Acknowledgements

I am grateful for the many people who provided encouragement, assistance and support during the research, writing and publication process. Thank you to Professor David McLean, Professor Abigail Woods, Dr Daniel Todman and Dr Graham Winton for their comments and suggestions on what was then my doctoral thesis. Thank you also to Dr Michael Kandiah, whose feedback and encouragement I am grateful to have received during my time as a student at the Institute of Historical Research and King's College London.

While a doctoral student, I was fortunate to receive comments on seminar and conference papers delivered at King's College London, the University of Manchester, the World Association for the History of Veterinary Medicine Congress, the International Society of Military Sciences Conference, Imperial College London, the Institute of Historical Research, the University of Birmingham, Senate House Library and Royal Holloway. Thank you, in particular, to Neil Pemberton, Julie-Marie Strange and the organisers and participants of the Dogs in History and Culture Conference at the University of Manchester in February 2013.

I would also like to express my appreciation for the countless archivists and staff at the archives, libraries and museums visited during the course of this project. I owe enormous gratitude to the staff at the National Archives at Kew, the Imperial War Museum, the Museum of Military Medicine, the Essex Record Office, the London Metropolitan Archives, the RAF Museum and Archive, the RSPCA, the PDSA, the British Library, the National Archives and Records Administration at College Park, Maryland, the Airborne Assault Museum at Duxford, the National Archives of Australia, the National Army Museum, the Mass Observation Archive at the University of Sussex, the Nuffield College Library at the University of Oxford, the UK Data Service, the Library of Congress in Washington, D.C. and the National Library of Scotland for their prompt responses to inquiries, assistance in assessing holdings and permission to quote, reference, or reproduce archival, photographic and published material. Thank you, in particular, to Gill Hubbard and Amy Dickin of the PDSA, Rob McIntosh of the Museum of Military Medicine, Elizabeth Martin of Nuffield College Library, Chris Reed of the RSPCA, Peter Devitt of the RAF Museum, Sam Stead of the Airborne Assault Museum and Kate Swann, Rebecca Newell, Robert Fleming, Emma Mawdsley and Pip Dodd at the National Army Museum. Mass Observation records are reproduced with permission of Curtis Brown Group Ltd,

London on behalf of The Trustees of the Mass Observation Archive. I am similarly grateful to the individual copyright holders who generously gave their permission to quote or reference their private papers, unpublished memoirs and recorded interviews.

I would also like to extend my thanks to Major Steve Leavis, the Officer Commanding of the Canine Training Squadron, Animal Defence Centre. In June 2013, I had the privilege of attending a presentation by Major Leavis and a demonstration by military working dog Diesel at the Fusilier Museum, Tower of London. I am enormously grateful for the invitation extended by Major Leavis to visit the Defence Animal Centre in July 2013. The private tour of the Canine Training Squadron was both informative and intriguing, as was the opportunity to observe and interact with military working dog Cassie on a detection exercise.

Thank you also to my family, Daniel and Barbara Brice and Kathy O'Donnell, for their constant encouragement and support. I am truly indebted to my husband, Frank O'Donnell, who has remained by my side during the researching and writing of this book. I am deeply grateful for his love, encouragement and support. Lastly, thank you to my late dog, Rebel, to whom this book is dedicated. He was my constant companion for nearly 16 years and his presence helped inspire this study of military dogs.

Introduction

In a letter to the Chairman of the Royal Society for the Prevention of Cruelty to Animals (RSPCA) in 1946, Field Marshal Bernard Law Montgomery acknowledged the contributions of animals to the Allied war effort in the Second World War. Montgomery noted: "The lot of animals who have helped us to win the War has not been forgotten."[1] Horses, mules, dogs, elephants and pigeons were among the animal species utilised by the British Armed Forces during the Second World War. Montgomery was not alone in recognising the work carried out by Britain's animals in the six year conflict. A few years after hostilities ended, Field Marshal William Slim remarked that animals had "served well and faithfully."[2] Military dogs were not the only trained canines to garner attention in Britain during and after the Second World War. In 1947, former London Civil Defence Regional Commissioner Admiral Edward Evans lauded the "praiseworthy" canines which had "acted as official rescue dogs and helped save many lives" in the British capital.[3]

The Second World War is often portrayed by historians as a conflict in which technology took centre stage. In *The Bombing War*, the historian Richard Overy argued: "Technology shapes the nature of all wars but the Second World War more than most."[4] Similarly, David Edgerton stressed the importance of technological innovation during the war by arguing that the British "wage[d] a devastating war of machines" in which "the machines were so many, the change so rapid: everywhere there were new devices of war, large and small."[5] The emphasis on technology and scientific innovation in Second World War historiography has tended to obscure other methods utilised by the British Armed Forces, including the employment of

---

1   FM Bernard Law Montgomery to Sir Robert Gower, 24 September 1946, in Arthur W. Moss and Elizabeth Kirby, *Animals Were There: A Record of the Work of the R.S.P.C.A. during the War of 1939-1945* (London: Hutchinson, 1947), p. 12.
2   FM Sir William Slim, Foreword to Lt. Col. J.H. Williams, *Elephant Bill* (London: The Reprint Society, 1951).
3   Admiral of the Fleet Lord Mountevans, Introduction to Dorothea St. Hill Bourne, *They Also Serve* (London: Winchester, 1947), p. vii.
4   Richard Overy, *The Bombing War: Europe 1939-1945* (London: Penguin, 2013), p. xxiii.
5   David Edgerton, *Britain's War Machine: Weapons, Resources and Experts in the Second World War* (London: Penguin, 2012), pp. 2, 293.

military dogs. While the significance of wartime technology should certainly not be disregarded, it should also be recognised that the conflict which witnessed the use of radar, jet aeroplanes and the atom bomb also allowed for the utilisation of an unprecedented number of dogs for military duties both internationally and among the British Armed Forces. Between 1939 and 1945 the belligerent nations likely utilised some 250,000 dogs.[6] While the British Army relied upon far fewer equines in the Second World War than in the First World War,[7] the number of dogs employed by the British Armed Forces in the 1939-1945 war was nearly double that of 1914-1918. Throughout the course of the Second World War, the British Army and the Ministry of Aircraft Production (MAP) utilised between 3,300 and 5,000 dogs.[8] Canines were instructed at the Army's War Dogs Training School or the MAP Guard Dog Training School prior to their deployment to units on the Home Front or overseas.

Despite the contributions of military and Civil Defence dogs, historians have paid little attention to their employment by the British Armed Forces and on the British Home Front in the First and Second World Wars. Military dogs, in particular, were omitted from or largely ignored in official histories prior to the 1960s. In the 1921 publication *Army Veterinary Service in War*, for example, Major General Sir John Moore dedicated an entire section to "the merits and demerits of the various breeds of animals used in war"[9] yet made no mention of the canines employed by the British Army in the First World War. Neither was sufficient attention devoted to the use of British military and Civil Defence dogs in the official history of the Second World War series produced by the War Office. Brigadier A.D. Magnay, in

6   Headquarters, Department of the Army, *Field Manual No. 20-20, Basic Training and Care of Military Dogs* (Washington, D.C.: U.S. Government Printing Office, 1972), p. 4, online <https://archive.org/details/FM20-20MilitaryDogTrainingandEmployment> (accessed 5 November 2013).

7   War Office, *Statistics of the Military Effort of the British Empire during the Great War, 1914-1920* (London: His Majesty's Stationery Office, 1922), pp. 396, 862 and Hansard: HC Deb 22 October 1946 vol 427 cc1452-3.

8   The National Archives (TNA): WO 32/14999, War Dogs: Awards of Royal Society for the Prevention of Cruelty to Animals, 17A, J.C. Bennison to A.W. Moss, 2 October 1945. According to Bennison, the Army and the MAP utilised some 2,000 and 1,500 canines, respectively. Brigadier A.D. Magnay, in *The Second World War, 1939-1945 Miscellaneous 'Q' Services* (London: War Office, 1954) placed the figure slightly lower at 3,300 (p. 62). It is unclear, however, if this figure was inclusive of the 400 military police dogs utilised by the CMP in the Middle East (p. 72). See also: Hansard: HC Deb 22 October 1946 vol 427 cc1452-3. In the House of Commons, MPs were informed that the Army utilised an estimated 5,000 canines. For approximate figures from the First World War, see Colonel E.H. Richardson and Blanche Richardson, *Fifty Years with Dogs* (London: Hutchinson, 1950), p. 107 and Imperial War Museum, London (IWM) 69/75/1: Private Papers of Major A.S. Waley, Messenger Dog Service (France), July 1917 to April 1919, p. 116 and Bryan D. Cummins, *Colonel Richardson's Airedales: The Making of the British War Dog School, 1900-1918* (Calgary: Detselig, 2003), Appendix A, pp. 171-182.

9   Maj. Gen. Sir John Moore, *Army Veterinary Service in War* (London: H&W Brown, 1921), pp. 98-160.

the volume entitled *Miscellaneous 'Q' Services*, concentrated on the importance of the Army Veterinary and Remount Services (AVRS) in recruiting and caring for British military dogs and other animals but neglected to discuss in any detail canine performance on operations or the advantages and disadvantages of their use.[10] Similarly, the official history of British Civil Defence in the war included an entire chapter on the V1 and V2 attacks, yet the author Terence H. O'Brien devoted just a single sentence to the use of dogs in London.[11]

The publication of Brigadier John Clabby's *The History of the Royal Army Veterinary Corps 1919-1961* in 1963 partly redressed the imbalance. His detailed account of the Royal Army Veterinary Corps (RAVC) in the mid-20th century included an entire chapter on the use of dogs during and after the Second World War.[12] Similarly, *RAF Police Dogs on Patrol: An Illustrated History of the Deployment of Dogs by the RAF 1942-2004* by Royal Air Force (RAF) Police veteran and instructor Stephen R. Davies served as an illuminating account of the employment of canines by the MAP and the RAF Police during and after the Second World War.[13] Although not an official or academic history, Davies' work was a welcome addition to the historiography on the subject of military dogs and an important source for this study.

While numerous books on the use of animals in war have been published over the last 30 years, most are popular histories intended for a general audience.[14] Such works have tended to emphasise the advantages of utilising dogs and other animals while largely overlooking their limitations and have generally failed to examine in great detail the effectiveness of animals on military operations. Moreover, publications such as Isabel George's *Beyond the Call of Duty: Heart-warming Stories of Canine Devotion and Wartime Bravery* emphasise the notion of military dogs as "real life hero[es]" and are intended to evoke emotion and feelings of gratitude towards animal participants in war.[15] Such titles, and the works themselves, anthropomorphise dogs and other animals by assigning human characteristics to those engaged in war.[16] In this way,

---

10   Magnay, *Miscellaneous 'Q' Services*, pp. 62-63, 72.

11   Terence H. O'Brien, *Civil Defence* (London: Her Majesty's Stationery Office, 1955), p. 669.

12   Brig. J. Clabby, *The History of the Royal Army Veterinary Corps, 1919-1961* (London: J.A. Allen & Co., 1963).

13   Stephen R. Davies, *RAF Police Dogs on Patrol: An Illustrated History of the Deployment of Dogs by the RAF 1942-2004* (Bognor Regis: Woodfield, 2005).

14   Examples include: Jilly Cooper, *Animals in War* (London: Corgi, 2000) and Juliet Gardiner, *The Animals' War: Animals in Wartime from the First World War to the Present Day* (London: Portrait, 2006) and Ernest A. Gray, *Dogs of War* (London: Robert Hale, 1989).

15   Isabel George, *Beyond the Call of Duty: Heart-warming Stories of Canine Devotion and Wartime Bravery* (London: Harper Element, 2010), p. 3.

16   For similar examples, see: Evelyn Le Chêne, *Silent Heroes: The Bravery and Devotion of Animals in War* (London: Souvenir, 1994) and Blythe Hamer, *Dogs at War: True Stories of Canine Courage Under Fire* (London: André Deutsch, 2006) and Clare Campbell and Christy Campbell, *Dogs of Courage: When Britain's Pets Went to War 1939-45* (London: Corsair, 2015).

they are similar to contemporary publications which also sought to portray military animals as heroic.[17]

As animals facilitated and took part in military operations, it follows that they should be included among the topics advanced by military historians. Yet few military historians have examined the strategic significance of animals in war.[18] Outside of military history, however, several scholars have considered the impact of war on military dogs, pets and other animals. In an effort to shed light on the environmental repercussions of the Second World War, Martin S. Alexander investigated the ways in which pets and other animals were affected by the Battle of France in the first year of hostilities.[19] Similarly, the cultural historian Hilda Kean touched upon the employment of military dogs and other animals in an animal welfare context in *Animal Rights: Political and Social Change in Britain since 1800*.[20] More recently, Kean examined the reasons why so many Britons opted to euthanize their canine and feline pets in the days surrounding the onset of the Second World War and how the mutual hardships of war generally led to an improved and enhanced relationship between remaining household pets and their civilian owners.[21] In addition to his work on military dogs and agency,[22] Chris Pearson touched upon the employment of dogs and other animals in the First World War in *Mobilizing Nature: The Environmental History of War and Militarization in Modern France*. Apart from military animals, Pearson considered the significance of canine and other animal companions on the Western Front.[23]

Other historians have considered the perception of military dogs within scientific circles or wider society. Robert Kirk, for example, drew attention to the employment of mine detection dogs during and after the Second World War. Kirk focused

17   Examples of contemporary publications in Britain include: James Gilroy, *Furred and Feathered Heroes of World War II* (London: Trafalgar, 1946) and St. Hill Bourne, *They Also Serve*. As shown in Chapter 2, British newspapers and periodicals also used similar language when referring to military animals.

18   A notable exception is Graham Winton, whose recent work *Theirs Not to Reason Why: Horsing the British Army 1875-1925* (Solihull: Helion & Company, 2013) explored the significance of horses to the British Army in the late 19th and early 20th centuries and the logistical concerns associated with acquiring and providing for such animals during the Anglo-Boer War and the First World War.

19   Martin S. Alexander, 'War and its Bestiality: Animals and their Fate during the Fighting in France, 1940', *Rural History*, 25:1 (2014), pp. 101-124.

20   Hilda Kean, *Animal Rights: Political and Social Change in Britain since 1800* (London: Reaktion, 1998), pp. 165-179, 191-197.

21   Hilda Kean, 'The Dog and Cat Massacre of September 1939 and People's War', *European Review of History*, 22:5 (2015), pp. 741-756 and Hilda Kean, *The Great Cat and Dog Massacre: The Real Story of World War Two's Unknown Tragedy* (Chicago: The University of Chicago Press, 2017).

22   Chris Pearson, 'Dogs, History, and Agency', *History and Theory*, 52 (2013), pp. 128-145.

23   Chris Pearson, *Mobilizing Nature: The Environmental History of War and Militarization in Modern France* (Manchester: Manchester University Press, 2012).

not on the significance of mine detection dogs on military operations but on attitudes towards such dogs in Britain and the United States, especially in the post-war period.[24] Similarly, in *Empire of Dogs: Canines, Japan, and the Making of the Modern Imperial World*, Aaron Skabelund devoted a chapter to the use and perception of military dogs prior to and throughout the Second World War. While Skabelund concentrated on dogs utilised by Imperial Japan, he also discussed the use of military dogs by other nations, including Britain and the United States.[25] Like Kirk, he emphasised the significance of contemporary representations of canines more so than their effectiveness on operations.[26]

This study examines the employment of canines by the British Armed Forces and the London Civil Defence Region in the Second World War. It traces the development of the British military dog in the first half of the 20th century, examines why and how military and Civil Defence dogs were trained and employed, analyses canine performance in training and on operations during the 1939-1945 conflict and considers the legacy of the Second World War military dog scheme. It is hoped that this study, as the first comprehensive scholarly account of British military and Civil Defence dogs in the Second World War, allows for a greater and more nuanced understanding of the British Armed Forces and British society in the Second World War. While accepting that technology played an increasingly important role in the waging of war by the British Armed Forces between 1939 and 1945, attention is drawn to a lesser known aspect of the conflict. It thus seeks not to diminish the significance of technology both during the war and in Second World War historiography but to highlight the ways in which the employment of military and Civil Defence dogs supplemented human and technological methods relied upon by the British Armed Forces and the London Civil Defence Region.

Although this study focuses on the British military dog scheme, it is not studied in isolation. An examination of the use of dogs by foreign militaries, particularly the United States, allows for a comparative approach. Apart from an Alsatian presented to the British Army by the French early in the war,[27] the available records show no evidence the British and French collaborated to any extent when developing their respective military dog schemes. The lack of Anglo-French co-operation as it pertained to military dogs is unsurprising given the surrender of France to Germany

24   Robert G.W. Kirk, 'In Dogs We Trust? Intersubjectivity, Response-Able Relations, and the Making of Mine Detector Dogs', *Journal of the History of the Behavioral Sciences*, 50:1 (2014), pp. 1-36.
25   Aaron Herald Skabelund, *Empire of Dogs: Canines, Japan, and the Making of the Modern Imperial World* (Ithaca: Cornell University Press), pp. 130-170.
26   In addition, Skabelund considered the perception of the Alsatian police and military dog in Germany and Japan in the first half of the 20th century in 'Breeding Racism: The Imperial Battlefields of the "German" Shepherd Dog', *Society and Animals*, 16 (2008), pp. 354-371.
27   'War Dog', *Our Dogs*, 5 September 1941, p. 836.

in June 1940 occurred several months before the opening of a British military dog training facility and likely precluded the further use of French military dogs during the war. Co-operation between Britain and the Soviet Union related to the training and use of military dogs appears to have been non-existent. This is also to be expected considering that even the War Office lacked detailed information regarding the Soviet employment of dogs during the war.[28]

Among the major Allied powers, it was the United States with which Britain seemed to collaborate most concerning the training and employment of military canines in the Second World War. The sharing of military dog training and employment prac- tises between the British and United States militaries during the Second World War constituted a lesser acknowledged aspect of what the historian David Reynolds has described as "the closest and most successful alliance in modern history."[29] Moreover, the British and American military dog schemes were similar in that, unlike most of the major Allied and Axis powers, they were both instituted after the outbreak of the Second World War.

This study utilises a range of primary sources, including war diaries, reports, memoirs, contemporary newspapers, periodicals and personal and official correspond- ence. War Office and Home Office records held at the National Archives at Kew were instrumental in tracing the development of the British military dog scheme and establishing a comprehensive history of the employment of dogs by the British Armed Forces and the London Civil Defence Region. Private papers and oral accounts from the Imperial War Museum (IWM) Department of Documents and the Sound Archive provide insight into the experiences of dog trainers and handlers, while the IWM photography collection allows for a glimpse of dogs in training and on opera- tions in the First and Second World Wars. As a repository for records produced by the RAVC, the Museum of Military Medicine holds a myriad of archival material related to the use of dogs by the British Army, including the war diary for the DAVRS[30] and correspondence and reports produced or received by the officer commanding of No. 2 Mine Detection Dog Platoon.[31] Digitised records made available online by the National Archives of Australia (NAA) were also instrumental in forming a more complete picture of the organisation and functioning of the British Army's War Dogs Training School and the British mine detection dog platoons.[32] While the majority

28   TNA: WO 32/14142, Guard Duties: War Dogs, 60A, War Office Policy Statement No. 16, 30 April 1948.

29   David Reynolds, *Rich Relations: The American Occupation of Britain, 1942-1945* (New York: Random House, 1995), p. 14.

30   Museum of Military Medicine, Aldershot: Box 14, War Diary of DAVRS, September- October 1939, June 1941-June 1946.

31   Museum of Military Medicine: Box 14, File of Capt. James Rankin Davison, including Reports on No. 2 Dog Platoon and Box 14, War Diary, No. 2 War Dog Platoon, Monthly Reports, August 1944- October 1945.

32   National Archives of Australia (NAA): General and Civil Staff Correspondence Files and Army Personnel Files, MP742/1, 240/6/324, Training of Dogs for Use in War and

of records concerning the employment of dogs by the London Civil Defence Region are held by the National Archives at Kew, additional archival material related to their use is located at the London Metropolitan Archives (LMA) and the Essex Record Office (ERO). Other records were accessed at the United States National Archives and Records Administration (NARA) in College Park, Maryland.

Qualitative and quantitative data compiled by the research institutions Mass Observation and the British Institute of Public Opinion (Gallup) in the years leading up to and during the Second World War have allowed for greater insight into British attitudes towards dogs and the perceived impact of the war on dog owners and their pets. Surveys conducted in the early 1940s cast light on the reasoning behind the decision made by many British dog owners to donate their pets to the Army's War Dogs Training School and the MAP Guard Dog Training School during the war.

Printed material utilised for this study included the 1952 and 1962 editions of *Training of War Dogs*, a training manual produced by the War Office. Although published after the Second World War, the manual provides details of the training methods utilised by the British Army during that conflict and in the post-war period.[33] A contemporary publication which served as a rich source of information for this study was Dorothea St. Hill Bourne's *They Also Serve*.[34] As secretary of the PDSA Allied Forces Mascot Club,[35] St. Hill Bourne had access to numerous letters penned by servicemen and rescue dog trainers during and shortly after the Second World War.

A number of persons associated with British military dogs produced works related to their experiences during the First and Second World Wars. E.H. Richardson, the commandant of the British Army's War Dog School in the First World War, wrote multiple autobiographical accounts based on his work with canines prior to, during and after the First World War. *British War Dogs: Their Training and Psychology* and *Forty Years with Dogs*, in particular, provide insight into Richardson's role in the development of the British military dog scheme of the First World War.[36] H.S. Lloyd, the chief instructor of the British Army's War Dogs Training School in the Second World War, also documented his experience with military dogs in Brian Vesey-Fitzgerald's 1948 publication *The Book of the Dog*.[37]

---

1 Australian Dog Platoon Royal Australian Engineers.

33   War Office, *Training of War Dogs* (1952) and War Office, *Training of War Dogs* (1962).

34   St. Hill Bourne, *They Also Serve*.

35   Ibid, pp. vii. The Allied Forces Mascot Club was established by the PDSA to recognise trained military animals, as well as "mascots on all the battle fronts whose presence played an important part in maintaining morale."

36   Lt. Col. E.H. Richardson, *British War Dogs: Their Training and Psychology* (London: Skeffington & Son, 1920) and Lt. Col. Edwin Hautenville Richardson, *Forty Years with Dogs* (London: Hutchinson, 1929).

37   H.S. Lloyd, 'The Dog in War', in Brian Vesey-Fitzgerald (ed.), *The Book of the Dog* (London: Nicholson & Watson, 1948), pp. 177-193.

Newspapers, magazines and periodicals published prior to and during the Second World War contain a wealth of information and relevant contemporary news related to the employment and treatment of British military dogs, as well as the impact of hostilities on non-military canines on the Home Front. Furthermore, such publications shed light on the feelings and experiences of British dog owners and the public at large during a period of uncertainty and patriotic fervour. The digital archive of *The Times*, as well as that of the *Guardian* and *Observer*, has allowed for the inclusion of a wide breadth of newspaper articles as primary source material. Several local publications were accessed through the British Newspaper Archive, a digital collection of newspapers curated by the British Library. The *Gloucestershire Echo* was particularly valuable, as its reporters produced several articles on the nearby MAP Guard Dog Training School during the war.

Contemporary periodicals, such as the dog-related publications *Our Dogs, Dogs' Bulletin, Kennel Gazette* and *Tail-Wagger Magazine*, helped to gauge the extent of influence and participation of dog breeders and trainers in the British military dog scheme of the Second World War and the perception of military canines and pet dogs outside the military. The RSPCA publication *Animal World*, as well as the *Journal of the Royal Army Veterinary Corps*, provided numerous details related to the recruitment, training and employment of military dogs.

Chapter 1 examines the employment of dogs by foreign militaries prior to and during the First World War and considers the role of dog breeder and trainer Major E.H. Richardson in the development of the British military dog scheme of the First World War. It then turns to the interwar period, a point in British history which witnessed an upsurge in dogkeeping, breeding, showing and the use of police dogs. The two decades following the First World War also saw the emergence or continuation of foreign military dog schemes, several of which are considered in this chapter.

Chapter 2 begins by considering the impact of the Second World War on canine pets, as concerns over rationing and air raids prompted many dog owners to donate their animals. The British declaration of war also resulted in the "figurative mobilization"[38] of British dogs. This chapter then traces the development of the British military dog scheme of the Second World War. Focusing on the efforts of Lloyd and Baldwin, it explores the reasons behind the establishment of the British Army's War Dogs Training School and the MAP Guard Dog Training School. Furthermore, Chapter 2 examines the recruitment and training of dogs for the British Armed Forces and highlights the anthropomorphic perception of military and Civil Defence dogs perpetuated by handlers, dog owners and the press.

---

38   Chapter 2 of this study builds upon Skabelund's work, borrowing his term to further demonstrate how British military and Civil Defence dogs and canine pets were "figuratively mobilized" throughout the Second World War.

Chapters 3, 4 and 5 examine the employment of dogs in specific military and Civil Defence roles during the Second World War. Chapter 3 focuses on the training and employment of guard, military police and patrol dogs. Chapter 4 opens with a brief history of landmines before turning to the reasons behind the British Army's decision to employ canines as mine detectors. By considering the advantages and disadvantages of dogs compared to human operators and electronic mine detectors, it analyses the performance of British mine detection dogs in northwest Europe in the last two years of the Second World War. Chapter 5 considers the use of dogs to locate casualties during the V1 and V2 attacks in and around London. It examines the performance and perception of rescue dogs trained at the MAP Guard Dog Training School and employed in the London Civil Defence Region in 1944-1945.

Chapter 6 examines the demobilisation of British military dogs in the months surrounding the end of the Second World War in September 1945. This chapter considers the challenges faced by the Army's War Dogs Training School and the MAP Guard Dog Training School stemming from both the employment of pets and the blurred distinction between military dogs and pets.

Lastly, Chapter 7 considers the legacy of the wartime Army's War Dogs Training School and the MAP Guard Dog Training School and the significance of the Second World War military dog scheme as a turning point in the history of the British military dog. This chapter thus examines the employment of guard, military police, patrol, tracker, detection and rescue dogs, as well as the use of canines by civil police, in the immediate post-war period through the early 21st century to demonstrate how the war influenced the future employment of military and police dogs.

1

Towards a Permanent British Military Dog Scheme: The First World War and the Interwar Period

In an address to the Royal United Services Institution in 1889, British Army veterinary surgeon E.E. Bennett expressed his belief in the usefulness of canines in military roles. Bennett noted that several European nations had instituted military dog training schemes and outlined the ways in which dogs could be utilised by the British Armed Forces.[1] His words were echoed by British Army veteran Major E.H. Richardson, who gave a similar speech to the Royal United Services Institution in 1912. Richardson made clear that while nations such as Germany and Belgium had instituted police and military dog training schemes and would therefore have trained dogs available upon the onset of a war, the case for a similar scheme in Britain had been largely ignored. He went on to suggest the creation of a military dog training facility where dogs could be trained to accompany human sentries and locate casualties on the battlefield. It would be nearly impossible, he warned, to amass a considerable amount of trained dogs in a short period of time if Britain became involved in a war.[2] Richardson repeated his concerns in an article published in the *Journal of the United Services Institution of India* the following year, arguing that as "foreign armies are all likely to adopt [the use of dogs] in time of war, we [British] cannot afford not to do so also."[3]

---

1   E.E. Bennett, 'Employment of Dogs for Military Purposes', *Journal of the Royal United Service Institution*, 33 (1889), pp. 499-503.
2   Major E.H. Richardson, 'The Employment of War Dogs, with Special Reference to Tripoli and Other Recent Campaigns', *Journal of the Royal United Service Institution*, 56:418 (1912), pp.1649-1659.
3   Major E.H. Richardson, 'Dogs in War', *Journal of the United Services Institution of India*, 42 (1913), p. 273.

E.H. Richardson, the War Dog School and the Messenger Dog Service

The concerns expressed by both Bennett and Richardson were justified considering that several European nations had begun training canines for military roles in the 19th and early 20th centuries. In Germany, for example, the widespread training of military dogs began in the late 19th century. Sheepdogs and Collies were taught to relay messages, escort human sentries and search for casualties.[4] During the course of the First World War, Germany was believed to have mobilised more than 30,000 canines.[5] The nation benefited from an extensive police dog system, which served in part to furnish the German Army with trained dogs when hostilities began in 1914.[6] Messenger dogs were also present in significant numbers within the German Army, as each division managed its own kennel of canine message carriers.[7]

As a result of training carried out by French civilians prior to the war, the French Army enlisted a substantial number of ambulance dogs in 1914.[8] By 1917, *The Times* was able to report the employment of French dogs for guard, sentry, messenger, ambulance and draught duties.[9] An American journalist attached to the French Army reported in August 1917 that canines had "become of such a general and important use throughout the entire French Army" and despite the efforts of French dog clubs to maintain a steady flow of dogs, the Army required several thousand more canines, particularly to serve as messengers.[10] Eventually, the French Army included an estimated 1,500 canine messengers, as well as an additional 4,500 dogs used in other roles.[11]

As in Germany, the Belgian use of police dogs allowed the Belgian Army to deploy trained dogs in 1914.[12] As a nation with a history of utilising dogs for draught work in peacetime, Belgium continued the practice during the First World War. According to one wartime estimate, the Belgians employed some 180,000 canines by 1916. In addition, Belgian dogs were utilised for sentry, ambulance and messenger work.[13]

4   Major E. Hautonville Richardson, 'War Dogs', *Nineteenth Century and After*, 57:337 (1905), pp. 473-479.
5   Headquarters, Department of the Army, *Field Manual No. 20-20*, p. 4.
6   Richardson, 'Employment of War Dogs', p. 1658.
7   IWM: 69/75/1, Waley, Messenger Dog Service, p. 106.
8   Ian Malcolm, *War Pictures Behind the Lines* (London: Smith, Elder & Co., 1915), p. 210.
9   'The Dogs of War and Blue Cross Service', *The Times*, 22 August 1917, p. 4.
10   'Soldier Dogs', *The Times*, 15 August 1917, p. 5.
11   TNA: WO 95/123/7, General Headquarters Troops: Carrier Pigeon Service Messenger Dog Service, War Diary of O.C. Carrier Pigeon and Messenger Dog Services, May 1918.
12   Richardson, 'Employment of War Dogs', p. 1658.
13   Ignatius Phayre, 'War Duties for the Dog', *Windsor Magazine*, 44 (1916), p. 69. It seems this figure, the veracity of which is unclear, referred to the number of Belgian canines utilised as draught dogs. Thus, it likely included draught dogs utilised by civilians in addition to military dogs. According to Phayre, such dogs were "conscript[ed]" into the Belgian Armed Forces to perform draught or other military roles.

In Britain, by contrast, the training of dogs for police and military use existed on a small scale and remained largely in the hands of Major E.H. Richardson,[14] who as a May 1914 article in *The Times* put it, was "the chief authority on the subject in England."[15] Richardson, a British Army veteran and dog trainer,[16] commenced the training of military dogs from his home in Scotland around the turn of the 20th century. The dogs, which were primarily Collies, were instructed for guard, messenger and ambulance roles. An army training camp close to Richardson's home afforded him multiple opportunities to conduct training exercises with British soldiers. As a result, a number of British Army officers developed an interest in trained dogs and recommended their use to the War Office.[17]

The Royal Navy also utilised guard dogs provided by Richardson in the years preceding the First World War. Beginning in 1909, at least 12 naval stations in the United Kingdom acquired trained dogs. The following year, the Admiralty made plans to extend the employment of canines to other sites.[18] Several of Richardson's dogs also saw action abroad, as other nations made use of canines instructed at his kennel.[19] During the Russo-Japanese War, for example, ambulance dogs furnished by Richardson served with the Russian Red Cross in Manchuria.[20]

Due in part to pressure from Richardson, the number of dogs utilised by British police forces rose in the years preceding the First World War. Glasgow added canines to its police force in 1910 when multiple trained dogs were obtained from Richardson.[21] Similarly, the Liverpool City Police, which first acquired police dogs in 1911, employed 17 of Richardson's dogs by 1914.[22] That same year, the procurement of 60 police dogs was authorised in Cumberland. Bolton followed suit one month later when its Watch Committee voted to obtain four dogs.[23] Despite growing interest, however, the number of police dogs in service throughout Britain remained small, especially in comparison to the extensive employment of police dogs in Germany and Belgium.

14   Richardson, *British War Dogs*, p. 50. Richardson claimed he "was the sole person who took any interest in trained dogs for the army and police, and the outflow from [his] kennels constituted the only source of supply."
15   'Police Dogs: Their Use in England and Abroad', *The Times*, 5 May 1914, p. 5.
16   Cummins, *Colonel Richardson's Airedales*, p. 11. See *Colonel Richardson's Airedales* for more information on Richardson's background.
17   Richardson, *Forty Years*, pp. 32-34.
18   'Admiralty Watch Dogs', *Glasgow Herald*, 7 February 1910, p. 3.
19   Richardson, *Forty Years*, pp. 38, 46-47.
20   'Major Richardson's Dogs', *Dundee Courier*, 16 August 1906, p. 7.
21   'Police Dogs for Glasgow', *Western Times*, 1 July 1910, p. 6.
22   'Police Dogs for Liverpool', *Manchester Guardian*, 14 February 1911, p. 12 and 'Police Dogs: Their Use in England and Abroad', *The Times*, 5 May 1914, p. 5.
23   'The Police Dog: Airedale Terriers for Bolton', *Manchester Guardian*, 29 May 1914, p. 7.

E.H. Richardson with ambulance dogs, c. 1915. (Library of Congress, LC-B2-3487-3)

In an attempt to garner further interest in police and military dogs, Richardson gave speeches and held demonstrations throughout Britain.[24] He also penned several letters and articles for *The Times*.[25] Richardson made several attempts to convince the War Office of the need for an official military dog training centre but to no avail. Thus, when Britain entered the First World War in August 1914, the British Army was without trained dogs save a single sentry dog employed by the Norfolk Regiment that had been provided by Richardson.[26]

Although the War Office initially opposed the establishment of a military dog scheme, the British Red Cross sought to utilise Richardson's ambulance dogs. In Belgium, however, Richardson discovered that ambulance dogs were not suited to static warfare, and their employment was discontinued. The next opportunity for Richardson came in late 1916, when the officer commanding, 56th Brigade, Royal

---

24 'Police Dogs: The Advantage of the Airedale', *Manchester Guardian*, 17 May 1914, p. 11 and Richardson, 'Employment of War Dogs', pp. 1649-1659 and Richardson, *Forty Years*, pp. 34, 39 and 'Ambulance Dogs in War', *The Times*, 22 November 1904, p. 13.

25 For examples, see: 'Police Dogs Abroad and at Home', *The Times*, 9 February 1909, p. 4 and 'The Houndsditch Outrage', *The Times*, 19 December 1910, p. 9 and 'Police Dogs', *The Times*, 27 December 1910, p. 3 and Maj. E.H. Richardson, 'Dogs in Warfare', *The Times*, 29 December 1914, p. 3.

26 Richardson, *British War Dogs*, pp. 51-55 and Richardson, *Forty Years*, pp. 36-37, 225.

Field Artillery (RFA) approached Richardson with a request for messenger dogs.[27] From his home in southeast England, Richardson taught two dogs to complete runs from various locations. In *Forty Years with Dogs*, Richardson acknowledged that the training of the dogs was hastened by additional requirements for messenger dogs at the front: "As the demand was urgent, my wife and I worked night and day... Those first dogs were not easy to train, as we did not know until the War progressed what were all the difficulties which would have to be overcome."[28] His comment suggests that the belated establishment of the British military dog scheme led to improvisation on the part of trainers and may have been partly to blame for problems with messenger dogs on operations.

On 31 December 1916, the two dogs were deployed to the Western Front, where they served with 56th Brigade. At Wytschaete Ridge, near the Belgian town of Ypres, the dogs covered nearly four kilometres to deliver messages to brigade headquarters.[29] According to the brigade's officer commanding, one of the dogs was responsible for conveying "the first message which was received, all visual communication having failed."[30] The dogs were also relied upon to maintain contact during the fighting at Vimy Ridge near Arras, France in April 1917 as other forms of communication were unavailable. On a separate occasion that spring, the dogs traversed nearly four kilometres over unfamiliar terrain to deliver messages near the French town of Bucquoy, despite having spent less than 24 hours in the area.[31]

As a result of the effective employment of messenger dogs by 56th Brigade, the War Office authorised the creation of a military dog training centre. The War Dog School was established in Shoeburyness, Essex in early 1917 with Richardson as commandant.[32] The dogs utilised by the British Armed Forces were primarily strays or pets. Dogs' homes, including the Battersea Dogs' Home in London, as well as police forces throughout Britain, provided strays to be trained.[33] Furthermore, in the spring and summer 1918, British newspapers published appeals which encouraged Britons to donate pet dogs to the Army. Breeds sought by the War Dog School included Airedale Terriers, Collies, Lurchers, Mastiffs and Great Danes.[34] The officer commanding, Messenger Dog Service regarded crossbred Lurchers as the best messengers,[35] while

27   Richardson, *British War Dogs*, pp. 54-56.
28   Richardson, *Forty Years*, p. 227.
29   Richardson, *British War Dogs*, p. 56. For consistency, metric units are used throughout this study.
30   Quoted in Richardson, *British War Dogs*, p. 56.
31   Richardson, *British War Dogs*, pp. 56-57.
32   Richardson, *British War Dogs*, p. 57 and 'Dogs in Battle', *The Times*, 9 December 1918, p. 3. The War Dog School remained in Shoeburyness until late 1918, when it relocated to Lyndhurst in Hampshire.
33   Richardson, *British War Dogs*, p. 60.
34   'Dogs for Army Use', *The Times*, 12 April 1918, p. 6 and 'Dogs for the Army', *The Times*, 1 July 1918, p. 5 and 'War Office Request for Dogs', *Observer*, 30 June 1918, p. 5.
35   IWM: 69/75/1, Waley, Messenger Dog Service, p. 124.

Richardson preferred the Airedale.[36] Large breeds, including Mastiffs and Great Danes, were generally nominated as guards. As for sentry dogs, Richardson favoured Airedale Terriers, Collies and Retrievers, although he emphasised that pedigree was less important than "acute hearing and scent, sagacity, fidelity, and a strong sense of duty."[37]

By July 1917, 74 messenger dogs had completed training and were employed by the British Army on the Western Front. Major Alec Waley, the officer commanding, Carrier Pigeon Service, maintained that the scheme "was in no way an organised Service." According to Waley, a lack of regulation meant that several dogs "became nothing more or less than regimental pets" upon deployment to France.[38] A keeper whose dogs were utilised in 1917 observed that, although the canines had performed well, "keep[ing] the lads from making a fuss of them" was a consistent problem.[39]

Moreover, as noted in a November 1917 report by XVII Corps, some dogs were distracted by other animals. The report concluded that, although dogs could deliver messages at a faster pace compared to human runners, "the results do not justify any great confidence in the reliability of the dogs as message carriers."[40] Several years after the end of the First World War, Richardson admitted that training at the War Dog School was rushed and imperfect:

> To a certain extent we were always working at a disadvantage. The need for the [messenger] dogs was so urgent and we were always being pressed for more and yet more from France so that the training was very often done under a great strain… Many of them went with their soldier keeper straight into the front line from the ship on which they crossed the Channel.[41]

Such problems prompted the Army Council, in January 1918, to authorise the creation of a centralised Messenger Dog Service with Major Waley as officer commanding.[42]

The first dogs to be trained as part of the Messenger Dog Service were deployed to the Nieppe Forest in France in April 1918. In the official report, Waley maintained that the "exceptionally good work" by messenger dogs in April 1918 encouraged their

---

36   Richardson, 'Employment of War Dogs', p. 1653. In this speech, Richardson described the Airedale as "the best of all those [breeds] we have in this country" and noted the Airedale's intelligence and loyalty, as well as physical attributes such as the breed's build and olfactory ability. In *British War Dogs* (p. 67), however, Richardson advocated the use of a range of breeds, including Collies, Lurchers, Airedale Terriers and Irish Terriers, as messengers.

37   Richardson, *British War Dogs*, pp. 191, 215, 218.

38   IWM: 69/75/1, Waley, Messenger Dog Service, p. 91.

39   Quoted in Richardson, *British War Dogs*, p. 84.

40   IWM: 69/75/1, Waley, Messenger Dog Service, p. 92.

41   Richardson, *Forty Years*, p. 233.

42   IWM: 69/75/1, Waley, Messenger Dog Service, pp. 91, 99-100 and Richardson, *British War Dogs*, p. 58.

Central Kennel, Messenger Dog Service in France. (© Imperial War Museum (Q 7345))

A British messenger dog is equipped with a message in France, August 1918.
(© Imperial War Museum (Q 9276))

further use in the months to come.[43] During the course of the First World War, between 325 and 346 messenger dogs trained at the War Dog School and the Central Kennel in northern France.[44]

The available records revealed that at times dogs provided the initial or only contact between units and headquarters. For example, when the German Army launched an offensive in the spring of 1918, a messenger dog was responsible for delivering the daily situation reports near Kemmel Hill, Belgium for a 10-day period during which "all other communications were broken."[45] In a report on two British messenger dogs employed by his battalion, an officer in the New Zealand Expeditionary Force wrote:

> Owing to the broken nature of the ground we were holding and the bad weather which was experienced, communication between the Company and Battalion Headquarters was exceptionally difficult, and the dogs on several occasions proved of great value in conveying messages when other means of communication failed, being far more rapid than runners, who in some cases were unable, owing to heavy shell-fire, to deliver their messages.[46]

Moreover, in May 1918, French troops came to the aid of 18th Division after a messenger dog relayed a demand for reinforcements. The dog's keeper surmised that "Amiens would be in the hands of the Germans" if not for the dog.[47]

A chief advantage of messenger dogs was the speed at which they relayed messages. The importance of speed was emphasised early on by Waley, who noted in the Messenger Dog Service war diary that the first dogs utilised as part of the service in April 1918 "in all cases had returned in excellent times."[48] Although the distances messenger dogs travelled varied, records indicate that dogs generally carried out journeys of between two and six kilometres.[49] The dogs employed by 29th Division and 1st Australian Division in the spring of 1918 completed runs of over three kilometres in around 20 minutes, although one dog clocked in at just 12 minutes.[50] *British War*

43   IWM: 69/75/1, Waley, Messenger Dog Service, pp. 102-103.
44   Ibid, p. 116. The first number, provided by Waley, refers to the "reinforcements for the Messenger Dog Service... received from England through the War Dog School." Thus, it likely excluded the messenger dogs already employed by the British Army on the Western Front at the inception of the Messenger Dog Service. See also: Cummins, *Colonel Richardson's Airedales*, Appendix A, pp. 171-182. According to the GHQ Central Kennel Register of Dogs and Men, held by the Imperial War Museum and reprinted in *Colonel Richardson's Airedales*, nearly 350 canines were deployed to France prior to May 1919.
45   Quoted in Richardson, *Forty Years*, p. 240.
46   Quoted in Richardson, *British War Dogs*, p. 118.
47   Quoted in Ibid, p. 97.
48   TNA: WO 95/123/7, War Diary, April 1918.
49   IWM: 69/75/1, Waley, Messenger Dog Service, pp. 93-115 and Richardson, *British War Dogs*, pp. 83-125 and TNA: WO 95/123/7, War Diary, August 1918.
50   IWM: 69/75/1, Waley, Messenger Dog Service, p. 107.

A British messenger dog relays a message in France. (The National Library of Scotland (N.411))

Dogs included two time sheets submitted by a messenger dog keeper. The time sheets revealed that during a seven day period in July and August the keeper's three dogs made journeys of three and four kilometres in times spanning between 13 and 45 minutes, with an average time of 24 minutes. The same dogs recorded an average time of less than 14 minutes while relaying messages over a distance of one to two kilometres between 8 and 16 September.[51] In some instances, dogs turned up with messages before the same information was received by telegraph or telephone. For example, when a dog detected poison gas in the trenches, he was sent by his keeper to alert headquarters of the impending threat. The dog completed the run some 45 minutes before the same message was transmitted via telegraph.[52]

Due to their swiftness and small size, dogs could move over the war-torn landscape of the Western Front, as well as avoid shellfire, more effectively than human runners.[53] One keeper reported that his dogs were particularly advantageous while relaying messages amid shellfire near Ypres, as "there was always a heavy bombardment on, and it would not be safe for a man to bring the messages."[54] Similarly, another keeper

---

51   Richardson, *British War Dogs*, pp. 126-127. Richardson did not specify the year in which the runs took place.
52   Ibid, pp. 87, 107-108.
53   Ibid, pp. 69, 102, 114.
54   Quoted in Richardson, *British War Dogs*, p. 114.

was adamant that, save his dog, "no one else could have delivered such dispatches under such terrific and heavy shell-fire without meeting with bodily harm."[55]

Furthermore, several accounts produced by messenger dog keepers referenced the ability of dogs to carry out journeys despite exposure to poison gas. While serving with 34th Division in 1918, two dogs handled by Keeper Macleod were exposed to gas in the Nieppe Forest. According to Macleod, the dogs "were badly gassed, but carried on... during the gas bombardment they never failed to give the greatest satisfaction."[56] Dogs were not immune from the effects of gas, however. The British Army publication *Instructions for the Use of Messenger Dogs in the Field* included information as to how keepers could reduce the risk of canine gas poisoning.[57] During inspections of the section kennels in the spring of 1918, Waley discovered that several dogs had been taken off operations as a result of gas.[58] When the Germans released substantial amounts of mustard gas on 22 April 1918, every dog serving with 1st Guards Brigade in the Nieppe Forest was impaired by its effects. Nonetheless, the effects proved only temporary. In fact, only four dogs in the Messenger Dog Service had to be destroyed or were rendered permanently out of action as a result of gas during the war.[59]

The Messenger Dog Service was not devoid of problems. The accounts of both Richardson and Waley made reference to problems encountered by keepers on operations. Two principal difficulties persisted throughout the existence of the Messenger Dog Service. First, the effective performance of messenger dogs was contingent on the actions of the officers and soldiers whose units employed canines. In the opinion of Waley, the successful employment of messenger dogs by some British Corps in 1918 was the result of the officers' confidence in and willingness to utilise canines.[60] However, some servicemen treated messenger dogs as pets, a problem noted by keepers prior to the inception of the Messenger Dog Service and which persisted throughout the war. One keeper maintained: "One of our greatest troubles [was] troops feeding and fussing about the dogs."[61] *Instructions for the Use of Messenger Dogs in the Field*, released in April 1918, warned: "The best trained dogs will... be quickly rendered unreliable by injudicious handling." To counter such problems, the instructions prohibited the feeding of messenger dogs while on operations and also stipulated that soldiers, apart from messenger dog keepers, "should not make friends with [the dogs], and the dogs should on no account be petted or made much of."[62] In his account of

55   Quoted in Ibid, p. 87.
56   Quoted in Ibid, p. 89. For similar examples, see: pp. 85-90, 101-103, 113, 120 in *British War Dogs* and IWM 69/75/1, Waley, Messenger Dog Service, p. 111.
57   IWM: EPH 171, S.S. 211, *Instructions for the Use of Messenger Dogs in the Field* (Army Printing and Stationery Services, April 1918), p. 6.
58   TNA: WO 95/123/7, War Diary, April-June 1918.
59   IWM: 69/75/1, Waley, Messenger Dog Service, pp. 103, 117.
60   Ibid, p. 111.
61   Quoted in Richardson, *British War Dogs*, p. 124.
62   IWM: EPH 171, *Instructions for the Use of Messenger Dogs*, pp. 4-5. The instructions made clear that messenger dogs were to receive one meal per day to be dispensed solely by the

A British messenger dog recovers from exposure to poison gas in France.
(The National Library of Scotland (N.405))

the Messenger Dog Service, Waley acknowledged that such advice was often ignored, as "it was nearly impossible to stop the men in the trenches petting the dogs and to enforce the rule that dogs were not to be fed when forward." Although he noted that such occurrences became less frequent as the war continued, Waley nonetheless concluded: "Most of the faults in the dogs' running were assuredly caused through the rules laid down not being adhered to."[63]

Second, numerous stray dogs on the Western Front proved a distraction for many messenger dogs. Reports submitted by XV Corps and Australian Corps underscored the frustration caused by the presence of strays. The reports maintained that when strays were encountered by messenger dogs, the delivery of messages was often delayed.[64] "Until these [stray] dogs can be removed or destroyed," concluded an officer in Australian Corps, "the Messenger Dog Service will be severely hampered."[65] Bitches, in particular, were a major temptation for some dogs. Although the British Army utilised bitches as messengers prior to the creation of the Messenger Dog Service, their employment was discontinued in 1918 owing to problems with the dogs.

keepers upon the dogs' return.
63   IWM: 69/75/1, Waley, Messenger Dog Service, pp. 105, 111.
64   Ibid, pp. 107-111.
65   Quoted in Ibid, p. 108.

Waley surmised: "No matter how trustworthy a dog might be, he could never be counted on" when bitches were in close proximity.[66]

Of the nearly 350 messenger dogs employed in France prior to May 1919, approximately 180 were reported as casualties. This represented a casualty rate of 52 percent.[67] As Bryan D. Cummins has pointed out, several messenger dogs were destroyed at the behest of commanding officers.[68] The reasons behind these decisions undoubtedly varied, and in some cases, were likely due to dogs having sustained injuries while on operations. Nonetheless, records compiled during the war revealed that a significant proportion of dogs were destroyed upon having been found to be "useless" or "no use to the service."[69] In explaining the prevalent destruction of messenger dogs, Cummins pointed to the numerous "prejudice[d]" commanding officers opposed to the employment of military dogs.[70] While it is recognised that several commanding officers remained against the employment of military dogs throughout the war, that more dogs perished at the hands of commanding officers than were killed while on operations[71] is more significant than Cummins let on. The high number of canines destroyed during the war was no doubt also a reflection of the belated establishment of the War Dog School, which resulted in the hasty instruction of dogs referred to by Richardson, as well as the haphazard nature of the fledgling Messenger Dog Service highlighted by Waley.

The work of Britain's messenger dogs came to an end shortly after the Armistice, when all dogs were withdrawn from the section kennels. The Messenger Dog Service was formally disbanded in the spring of 1919.[72] The contributions made by messenger dogs were acknowledged by Field Marshal Douglas Haig, who noted in his wartime dispatches that such dogs "did good work on a number of occasions."[73] Waley rightly maintained that the employment of messenger dogs by the British Army in the First World War was successful insofar as it supplemented other forms of communication, such as wireless telegraphy, telephony and human runners. Nonetheless, as Waley himself acknowledged, the service "was still in the experimental stage" when the war ended.[74] The Messenger Dog Service was never used to its full advantage. In part, this was the result of its belated establishment in the final year of the war.

In addition to turning out messenger dogs, the War Dog School trained canines as guards and sentries. The impetus, according to Richardson, was the widespread

---

66   Ibid, pp. 105-106.
67   Cummins, *Colonel Richardson's Airedales*, Appendix B, pp. 183-193.
68   Ibid, p. 119.
69   Ibid, pp. 183-193.
70   Ibid, pp. 119-121, 183.
71   Ibid, pp. 183-193.
72   IWM: 69/75/1, Waley, Messenger Dog Service, p. 114.
73   *Sir Douglas Haig's Despatches, December 1915–April 1919*, ed. Lt. Col. J.H. Boraston (London: J.M. Dent & Sons, 1919), p. 334.
74   IWM: 69/75/1, Waley, Messenger Dog Service, p. 124.

mobilisation of human guards and the consequent realisation by the War Office that dogs could be utilised at vulnerable points on the British Home Front. Dogs were deployed to factories, magazines and military camps on the British Home Front. As the Royal Defence Corps (RDC) oversaw the defence of vulnerable points in Britain, officers from RDC units which utilised guard dogs attended a brief training course at the War Dog School. Guard dogs were charged with protecting specified locations, to which they were usually secured by cables measuring up to 91 metres. As evidenced by the accounts provided by Richardson, however, the actual use of dogs varied by location. At some sites, such as military camps, guard dogs were allowed to roam the premises at night, while at other locations, dogs assisted human guards on patrols.[75]

The War Dog School turned out some 2,000 canine guards during the course of the First World War.[76] On the Home Front, they helped defend some 800 vulnerable points.[77] Richardson, in *British War Dogs*, provided several excerpts from officers concerning the use of guard dogs. From these accounts, it is clear that canines could locate trespassers sooner than their human counterparts. In one account, an officer commanding whose unit employed dogs remarked:

> The three guard dogs which have been used at [ammunition dumps in] Stalham, Martham, and North Walsham [in Norfolk] have, in each instance, carried out their duties in a very satisfactory manner… It has been found that these dogs will scent a stranger approaching at night a very considerable time before their presence was known by the soldier on his post, and, in my opinion, these dogs have quite justified their employment in ammunition dumps.[78]

Similarly, Captain James Brand of 151st Protection Company (RDC) noted that the guard dogs at a hay storage facility in Newcastle "almost invariably gave warning of an approach before the [human] sentries heard it themselves."[79]

As indicated in multiple first-hand accounts, the ability of guard dogs to detect trespassers inspired confidence among the officers and soldiers who employed them. Corporal Bring of 156th Protection Company (RDC), for example, noted that the human guards at an explosive store in Leicestershire "felt more secure with the dogs than without them."[80] Similarly, the dogs employed at ammunition stores in Ipswich were described by the officer commanding as "a source of security to the [human] guards and patrols."[81] In a similar vein, it was believed that the use of canine

---

75   Richardson, *British War Dogs*, pp. 59, 191-192, 203-211 and Richardson, *Forty Years*, p. 255.
76   Richardson and Richardson, *Fifty Years*, p. 107.
77   Lt. Col. E.H. Richardson, 'Alsatians as Army Dogs', *The Times*, 17 January 1927, p. 8.
78   Quoted in Richardson, *British War Dogs*, p. 195.
79   Quoted in Ibid, pp. 201-202.
80   Quoted in Ibid, p. 206.
81   Quoted in Ibid, p. 207.

guards deterred potential criminals from trespassing at vulnerable points. The officer commanding, 261st Protection Company (RDC) considered that "the moral effect [of guard dogs] was great, as the general impression prevailed in the neighbourhood that it would be preferable to encounter an armed sentry than one of the dogs."[82] Similarly, Captain B.S. Ball of the 416th Ammunition Column (RFA) commented on the perceived effectiveness of a guard dog at a vulnerable point in Norfolk: "The dog was posted outside the entrance to the Main Ammunition Dump... It had become well known that the dog was on the spot, and I think that this fact prevented would-be intruders from attempting to gain admission to the dump."[83] Lieutenant Colonel Sykes of the Royal Army Service Corps (RASC) indicated that the employment of dogs at a supply depot in Wiltshire brought an immediate halt to criminal activity at the site. "On two occasions stores had been tampered with," Sykes noted in a report, "and it is evident the persons attempting the entry of the stores had thought better of it, on discovering the canine occupants."[84]

Finally, the use of guard dogs also allowed for a decrease in the number of human guards at many sites. At multiple vulnerable points on the Home Front, officers greatly scaled down the proportion of human personnel as canine guards became available. Prior to the introduction of a single guard dog at a magazine in Berkshire, for example, the officer commanding, 6th Battalion, City of London Regiment relied upon 29 soldiers to protect the facility. The addition of a dog, by contrast, allowed for the employment of just seven human guards.[85] A similar situation unfolded at a site near Glasgow. According to Lieutenant P. Forrest of 202nd Protection Company (RDC):

> We have had twenty-one dogs, which were employed by night only on the lone-liest and most dangerous posts to accompany the sentries, and relieve them of as much strain as possible... Had there been no dogs, it would have been necessary on many of the posts to have employed double sentries, so that the saving in man-power has come to about twenty men per night.[86]

The Royal Navy and the RAF also employed guard dogs, albeit on a smaller scale than the Army. The Royal Navy utilised dogs at some of its installations, including a wireless station in Lincolnshire. Initially, the dogs were acquired from the War Dog School, but the Admiralty eventually opted to buy its own canines, which were trained by servicemen at each site.[87] While little information is available concerning

82   Quoted in Ibid, p. 206.
83   Quoted in Ibid, p. 196.
84   Quoted in Ibid, p. 209.
85   Ibid, pp. 195-203, 207.
86   Quoted in Ibid, p. 198.
87   TNA: AIR 2/80, Provision of Watch Dogs for Aerodromes, 4A, Letter from C. Mansel, 4 May 1918 and 8B, Letter from C. Mansel, 25 May 1918.

the use of canines at naval installations, records compiled by the Air Ministry in 1918 revealed numerous problems. According to an RAF representative who consulted with Admiralty officials during the war, the latter considered the use of dogs "extremely difficult and disappointing."[88] At the aforementioned wireless station, for example, multiple dogs strayed from the station or were killed by passing trains. In addition, the officer commanding noted that the dogs regularly attacked one another, which in some cases led to the deaths of new charges. Nonetheless, an RAF report concluded: "The difficulties experienced by the Admiralty appear to a large extent to arise from conditions peculiar to that Service."[89]

At Richardson's insistence, the RAF adopted the use of dogs in 1918. By the end of the war, guard dogs were present on at least three airfields in Wales.[90] Moreover, in July 1918, the General Officer Commanding of the RAF in Ireland reached out to Richardson in an effort to obtain trained dogs.[91] The fear of rabies, however, ultimately prevented the deployment of guard dogs to Ireland.[92]

In contrast to guard dogs, which were taught to protect physical structures or locations, dogs trained as sentries escorted units while on guard duty or on patrol in order to protect the soldiers themselves. While the employment of sentry dogs in France was limited due to the static nature of the Western Front, their use was somewhat successful in other theatres of war. During the First World War, sentry dogs were deployed to Italy, the Balkans, Egypt and Mesopotamia.[93] While Richardson's works contain few accounts from British servicemen who employed sentry dogs, the sparse evidence available suggests that such dogs augmented the security of the units and locations they served. In an account of the use of a sentry dog on the Western Front, a British officer noted:

> One dark night, I took out the sentry dog on patrol duty in front of our trenches near the German wire... We moved along for some time, and saw nothing. Suddenly the dog... stopped dead, pointed, and gave a low growl... Two Germans rose up as if out of the ground in front of us, and they were immediately bayoneted by our men. The dog had discovered two German sentries in a new sap of which we knew nothing, and, except for the dog, we would never have known the Germans were there.[94]

---

88   TNA: AIR 2/80, 4A, Letter from Mansel, 4 May 1918.
89   TNA: AIR 2/80, 8B, Letter from Mansel, 18 May 1918.
90   TNA: AIR 2/80, Policy Re: Use of Watch Dogs for Aerodromes, Maj. E.H. Richardson to Home Forces, 17 February 1918 and AIR 1/619/16/15/354, Watch Dogs for R.A.F. Stations, Ireland, H. McAnally to the Secretary, War Office, 28 November 1918.
91   TNA: AIR 1/619/16/15/354, Lt. Frank Dance to Col. Richardson, 29 July 1918.
92   TNA: AIR 1/619/16/15/354, 20A, Capt. F. Gidney to Col. Richardson, 19 October 1918.
93   Richardson, *British War Dogs*, pp. 214-216, 221-222 and Richardson, *Forty Years*, pp. 266-267.
94   Quoted in 'German Sentries Detected by a Dog', *The Times*, 2 April 1915, p. 11.

Yet, in *Forty Years with Dogs*, Richardson cited problems with the employment of sentry dogs during the war. While acknowledging that their use in Italy was aided by a British officer who expressed confidence in his canines, he noted that the situation in the Balkans suffered as a result of the soldiers' lack of experience with sentry dogs.[95] Moreover, in *British War Dogs*, Richardson remarked that the employment of sentry dogs in Salonika was limited owing to the cessation of hostilities not long after the dogs landed in Greece.[96] Thus, although some units likely benefited from sentry dogs, their overall contribution to the British war effort appears to have been less significant than that of messenger and guard dogs.

The War Dog School did not survive the interwar period. It is unclear why or when the War Dog School was disestablished. The training facility, which had already moved to the New Forest during the war, relocated to Bulford in the spring of 1919.[97] The school remained open until at least June 1919 but was ultimately closed within one year of relocating to Bulford.[98] The British Army began releasing its military dogs from overseas shortly before the closure of the Central Kennel in the spring of 1919. Several canines, including those utilised as messengers on the Western Front, were restored to their owners in Britain. Others were purchased by British servicemen. Dogs whose owners did not desire their return, as well as former strays, were donated to the Royal Irish Constabulary or local police forces in the United Kingdom, while a small number were retained by the British Army of the Rhine in Germany.[99]

The assertion made by Cummins that the "War Dog School was successful is beyond question"[100] is an overstatement. While the War Dog School constituted a crucial step in the development of a permanent British military dog scheme, the school, as well as the affiliated Messenger Dog Service, was not the resounding success portrayed by Cummins. The belated establishment of a military dog training school, a hastened training scheme and the continued reluctance among some officers to employ canines limited the overall effectiveness of British military dogs in the First World War. The British employment of military dogs outside the United Kingdom was of limited

95   Richardson, *Forty Years*, p. 267.
96   Richardson, *British War Dogs*, pp. 215-216.
97   Ibid, p. 63.
98   'Police Dogs for Sutherland', *Our Dogs*, 20 June 1919, p. 729. As evidenced by this article, the War Dog School was still in operation as of June 1919. An advertisement for Richardson's kennels in the 30 April 1920 edition of *Our Dogs*, however, referred to Richardson as the "late Commandant" of the training facility (p. 660).
99   IWM: 69/75/1, Waley, Messenger Dog Service, p. 116 and 'Demobilised Dogs', *Lancashire Daily Post*, 24 April 1919, p. 2 and 'Demobilised War Dogs', *Our Dogs*, 2 May 1919, p. 522 and 'Our War Dogs', *Our Dogs*, 30 May 1919, p. 643 and 'The National Canine Defence League', *Our Dogs*, 6 June 1919, p. 666. It is unknown how or to what extent dogs were utilised by the British Army of the Rhine during the interwar period, as there is no mention of such dogs in the available archival records. It is likely these canines were either pets or employed on an unofficial basis.
100 Cummins, *Colonel Richardson's Airedales*, p. 105.

duration and existed on a relatively small scale. The Messenger Dog Service only came into being in the final year of the war, and during its brief period of existence, it never expanded beyond a few hundred dogs.

In a 1940 letter to the Commander-in-Chief, Home Forces, Richardson lamented that while he had been "anxious that a nucleus training school would be always kept in action for the [British] Army" in the years following the First World War, "nothing was done" in regards to the training of military dogs in the United Kingdom.[101] While Richardson was correct that the British Armed Forces lacked a military dog training scheme in the interwar period, his assertion that "nothing was done" in the years preceding the Second World War overlooked the contributions made by dog breeders and trainers, some of whom acquired experience with military dogs during the First World War. The interwar period saw an upsurge in the keeping and showing of canines and the employment of police dogs, as well as the emergence of the Alsatian in the United Kingdom. These developments, which were spurred in part by veterans of the First World War, are crucial to understanding the British military dog scheme of the Second World War and the reasons why Britons donated their pets during the latter conflict.

The Dog in Interwar Britain and Foreign Military Dog Training Schemes Prior to and During the Second World War

"Dogs," a 1941 Mass Observation report suggested, "play a prominent part in British life."[102] Indeed, in the decade preceding the Second World War, the United Kingdom was home to between 3,000,000 and 4,000,000 canines[103] with dogs present in around 25 to 30 percent of British households.[104] An article in the May 1935 edition of *Tail-Wagger Magazine*, a monthly publication devoted to the care of canine pets produced for dog-owning members of the similarly named Tail-Waggers' Club, referred to the early 20th century as "the greatest era in the history of dogdom" owing to a rise in dog ownership and a growing enthusiasm for the selective breeding of canines.[105]

101 TNA: WO 199/416, 17A, Lt. Col. E.H. Richardson to Gen. Edmund Ironside, 11 June 1940.
102 Mass Observation Archive, University of Sussex (MOA): File Report 804, Dogs in London (Pilot Survey), 29 July 1941, Explanatory Note (Background).
103 'The Tail-Waggers' Club', *Tail-Wagger Magazine*, February 1929, p. 2 and 'The Most Wonderful Dog in the World', *Tail Wagger Magazine*, June 1932, p. 182 and 'Dogs and International Crises', *Dogs' Bulletin*, June-July 1939, p. 7.
104 MOA: File Report 804 and British Institute of Public Opinion (BIPO), Survey #53, December 1938, online <http://doc.ukdataservice.ac.uk/doc/3331/mrdoc/ascii/3812.txt> (accessed 29 September 2016). This poll, conducted in late 1938, put the percentage of British dog-owning households slightly higher (30.68%) than Mass Observation.
105 Howard Park, 'Royal Dog Lovers', *Tail-Wagger Magazine*, May 1935, p. 170.

As opinions towards dogs undoubtedly varied among individuals and over time, it is difficult to accurately gauge the attitudes and feelings of the British public towards dogs in the years preceding the Second World War. Nonetheless, some understanding of how dogs were perceived in interwar Britain can be gleaned from contemporary newspapers, dog-related publications and polls and reports carried out or compiled by Mass Observation and the British Institute of Public Opinion (Gallup) prior to and during the Second World War.

Applications for dog licences climbed steadily throughout the 1920s,[106] resulting in an annual increase of between 200,000 and 250,000 licenced canines by the middle of that decade.[107] Even in the late 1930s, when war with Germany loomed, British dog owners requested annual licences for some 3,000,000 dogs.[108] This figure also represented a striking contrast to the eve of the First World War, when during a 12 month period in 1913-1914, fewer than 1,980,000 dog licences were granted.[109] Certainly, not all dog owners obtained licences for their pets. According to one contemporary source, an additional 1,000,000 British canines were without licences during the interwar period.[110]

The reasons Britons possessed canines prior to and during the Second World War were unquestionably varied. Mass Observation, in a 1941 report, identified a number of explanations cited by Londoners as to why they owned dogs. The most oft-cited reason for owning a dog, according to the report, was for "company, companionship, [or as a] member of family."[111] Gender and socio-economic status also played a part, for it was found:

> Men, especially better-off men, stress the importance of the dog as an animal, pet, ornament, a piece of property or prestige, or appearance. Women of all classes stress the value of the dog as a companion or as a member of the family… Men stress the usefulness of a dog… and poorer people mention usefulness quite frequently whereas better-off people hardly mention it at all… One man in ten mentions the sportin (sic) value of a dog, but women practically never mention this point at all.[112]

106 Hansard: HC Deb 20 July 1926 vol 198 cc1042-3 and HC Deb 24 December 1929 vol 233 cc 2130-1W. Between 1920 and 1929, dog licence applications rose by more than 55%.
107 'Ever More Dogs', *Dogs' Bulletin*, December 1925.
108 'Dogs and International Crises', *Dogs' Bulletin*, June-July 1939, p. 7 and 'What of the Night?', *Tail-Wagger Magazine*, December 1941, p. 266.
109 Hansard: HC Deb 30 January 1930 vol 234 cc1206-7W.
110 'Ever More Dogs', *Dogs' Bulletin*, December 1925 and 'Dogs and International Crises', *Dogs' Bulletin*, June-July 1939, p. 7.
111 MOA: File Report 804, p. 8.
112 Ibid, p. 7. See also: File Report 838, Provincial Dogs (Second Survey), pp. 7-8. The explanations provided by dog owners in Worcester mirrored those in the capital and were also divided along gender lines.

While many wealthy British dog owners preferred Alsatians, Retrievers and Spaniels in the years prior to and during the war, mongrels predominated, particularly among working class Britons.[113]

That Britons appreciated and acted humane towards dogs was often presented by dog-related publications in the interwar period as both uniquely British and as an innate rather than learned quality. *Tail-Wagger Magazine*, for example, claimed in 1931: "The love of animals, and especially of dogs, is inherent in nearly all British people."[114] Three years later, the same publication insisted that the selective breeding of canines and other animals was "implanted in the blood of the British race."[115] Similarly, in a 1934 article on the importance of dogs and other pets in British society, a writer for the *Manchester Guardian* described a "national love of animals" and alleged: "Foreigners do not carry their attachment to domestic pets to the same pitch of devotion as Englishmen."[116] Thus, like the *Tail-Wagger Magazine* articles of the same period, the *Manchester Guardian* piece portrayed the British, or the English in this case, as uniquely committed to and compassionate towards animals.

While such accounts were exaggerations, they were not completely devoid of truth. The end of the First World War and the interwar period witnessed the establishment of new animal welfare organisations in the United Kingdom, and training instructions circulated by a number of British dog trainers at the time advised against corporal punishment in favour of positive reinforcement. The PDSA was established by the humanitarian Maria Dickin towards the end of the First World War in an effort to "relieve [animal] sufferings, due to injury, sickness, and ignorance."[117] In contrast to the RSPCA, the PDSA did not investigate or report crimes involving animals; its chief purpose was to offer complimentary veterinary care for dogs and other animals. Thus, personnel combed the streets of East London and elsewhere in search of pets in need of veterinary treatment, which was then carried out at one of the PDSA's facilities.[118] During the interwar period, the animal welfare organisation expanded to include a sanatorium in East London, as well as several dispensaries outside the capital.[119]

---

113 MOA: File Report 804, Appendix 1, Information about Dogs Owned by People in Sample. This study, conducted in London, found that around 50% of Londoners who kept dogs possessed mongrels. See also: File Report 838, Appendix 1, Information about Dogs Owned by People in the Sample. Per this follow-up study, carried out one month after the initial study in London, mongrels also outnumbered any specific breed in Worcester and Oxford. Although the studies in London, Worcester and Oxford were conducted nearly two years after the onset of the war, many of those questioned had possessed the same pets prior to September 1939. In the London study, for example, 64% of dog owners had obtained their dog at least two years earlier.
114 'Tail-Waggers' Club Doings', *Tail-Wagger Magazine*, May 1931, p. 17.
115 'Occupation with Interest', *Tail-Wagger Magazine*, March 1934, p. 93.
116 Freya Godfrey, 'The Family Pets', *Manchester Guardian*, 22 August 1934, p. 6.
117 Maria Dickin, *The Cry of the Animal* (London: PDSA, 1950), pp. 2-4, 73.
118 Ibid, pp. 73-74.
119 Kean, *Animal Rights*, p. 184.

The interwar period gave rise to another animal welfare organisation when in 1928 the Tail-Waggers' Club was established to bring "enlightenment to the dog-owning public as shall make for the general health and happiness of the canine race."[120] The club, which rapidly expanded to include some 400,000 members by early 1931, donated membership dues to organisations such as the Royal Veterinary College and the Battersea Dogs' Home.[121] The Tail-Waggers' Club sought to appeal to all "dog-lovers" regardless if their pets were purebred.[122]

In a 1932 article printed in *Tail-Wagger Magazine*, author and dog trainer A. Croxton Smith recommended "kindly methods of training" over the outdated form of instruction known as "breaking":

> Breaking at one time often implied a good deal of severity. If the pupil did wrong... he was rated or chastised. To-day the majority of trainers recognise that the most satisfactory way of educating a dog in his life's work, is by constant repetition of one lesson at a time until he becomes perfect... The worst way of attaining that object is to frighten [the dog] by punishment.[123]

Croxton Smith, who served as Chairman for both the Directors of the Tail-Waggers' Club and the Kennel Club during the interwar period,[124] advised readers to utilise a "kindly" approach when training canine pets, as well as herding and sporting dogs, for in all cases the "confidence [of the dog] must be gained" by the trainer.[125]

H.H. Forrester Primrose, another trainer whose article appeared in the same publication five years later, called for a similar approach. He recommended "creat[ing] an association of ideas in the canine mind" by "show[ing] the dog what you want him to do, coax[ing] him into the desired action, and associat[ing] in his mind its correct performance with something pleasant—a pat and special word of approval, perhaps a tit-bit."[126] The "associative process," he contended, formed "the basis of all successful [dog] training."[127]

The methods of Croxton Smith and Forrester Primrose were in accordance with other training techniques of the same time period. *Tail-Wagger Magazine* ran several articles on dog training prior to the Second World War, nearly all of which emphasised kindness and patience. The majority advised against physical discipline, and

---

120 'Tail-Waggers' Club Doings', *Tail-Wagger Magazine*, May 1931, p. 17.
121 Ibid.
122 'The Tail-Waggers' Club: A Great Canine Union', *Tail-Wagger Magazine*, February 1929, p. 1.
123 A. Croxton Smith, 'Training by Kindness', *Tail-Wagger Magazine*, September 1932, p. 303.
124 'The New Chairman of the Kennel Club', *Tail-Wagger Magazine*, May 1937, p. 152. Croxton Smith was already Chairman of the Directors of the Tail-Waggers' Club and a constant presence at dog shows when he was made Chairman of the Kennel Club in 1937.
125 Croxton Smith, 'Training by Kindness', *Tail-Wagger Magazine*, p. 303.
126 'H.H. Forrester Primrose, 'Ingenuity in Dog Training', *Tail-Wagger Magazine*, January 1937, p. 16.
127 Ibid, p. 16.

some encouraged the use of food as a reward.[128] Like the aforementioned authors, Major R.F. Wall, a veterinary surgeon and the author of the 1933 publication *Keeping a Dog: Its Training and Care in Health and Sickness*, also emphasised the importance of patience and positive reinforcement:

> Let your lessons be those of *inducement*… It may take a long time to get him to do as you wish, but stick to it doggedly until he does it and then reward him… It will be found that the quickest and best results will be achieved by getting the pupil to *like* doing what you wish him to do.[129]

In 1934, a journalist writing for the *Observer* noted that while "Britain ha[d] always been doggy," there had emerged over time "a wider appreciation of dogs" among the public due in large part to more extensive breeding and showing of canines. It was, as he put it, "the day of the dog."[130] For the Kennel Club, the interwar period was an era of unprecedented expansion. Annual registration figures peaked at more than 59,000 in 1927.[131] The dog fancy, as the selective breeding and showing of purebred dogs was known, involved an unprecedented number of human and canine participants in the interwar period. The *Observer* reported "an enormous influx" of dog fanciers in the years following the First World War which resulted in shows being held on an increasingly large scale.[132]

Perhaps the most significant event for dog fanciers was Cruft's Show, an annual display of purebred canines which in 1936 brought together nearly 4,400 dogs through an unprecedented 10,650 entries.[133] By contrast, no Cruft's Show prior to the First World War had attracted more than 4,200 entries.[134] Other competitions, such as the Home Pet Show in London, allowed Britons whose dogs were without

128 For examples, see 'Training the Puppy', *Tail-Wagger Magazine*, June 1929, p. 11 and 'The Well-Trained Dog', *Tail-Wagger Magazine*, June 1931, p. 3 and 'The Elementary Education of the Dog', *Tail-Wagger Magazine*, April 1933, pp. 117, May 1933, p. 155 and June 1933, p. 188 and Capt. H.E. Hobbs, 'The Value of Imagination in Dog Management', *Tail-Wagger Magazine*, February 1935, p. 49 and 'Professional Dog-Training', *Tail-Wagger Magazine*, July 1937, p. 220 and 'Scrap the Dog Whip!', *Tail-Wagger Magazine*, September 1937, p. 301 and Bella Gold, 'Think Before You Train Your Dog!', *Tail-Wagger Magazine*, August 1939, p. 255-257.

129 Maj. R.F. Wall, *Keeping a Dog: Its Training and Care in Health and Sickness* (London: A & C. Black, 1933), p. 49. For examples of training advice from other contemporary authors, see: John Woodward, *You and Your Dog* (London: C. Arthur Pearson, 1933), pp. 67-73 and R. Sharpe, *Dog Training by Amateurs* (London, 1938), pp. 1-2. Like the authors whose articles were included in *Tail-Wagger Magazine*, Wall, Woodward and Sharpe encouraged dog owners to use food as a reward.

130 'The Day of the Dog in the Home and at Shows', *Observer*, 7 October 1934, p. 30.

131 'The Kennel Club: Increase of Registrations', *Our Dogs*, 24 January 1936, pp. 243, 252.

132 'The Day of the Dog', *Observer*, 7 October 1934, p. 30.

133 'All Records Smashed by Cruft's Golden Jubilee International Championship Show', *Our Dogs*, 14 February 1936, p. 481.

134 'The World's Greatest Dog Show', *Tail-Wagger Magazine*, February 1934, p. 50.

pedigrees to exhibit their animals. The 1935 show, as *Tail-Wagger Magazine* pointed out, succeeded in involving "pet lovers of all classes" who together displayed some 3,000 dogs.[135] By the early 1930s, the United Kingdom hosted approximately 2,000 dog shows per year.[136]

During the interwar period, the Alsatian became increasingly popular among British dog fanciers. In the six years following the end of the First World War, the number of Alsatians registered with the Kennel Club increased from 15 to some 6,000. That the number of Alsatians in Britain skyrocketed during the interwar period seems to have been largely the result of the exposure of British servicemen to French and German-owned Alsatians in the First World War.[137] Recalling his experience with Alsatian guard dogs in the First World War, the chairman of the Alsatian League of Great Britain described the Alsatian as "the most faithful, the most reliable, and the easiest [breed] to control."[138] The Alsatian Wolf Dog Club, another organisation devoted to perpetuating the breed in Britain, emphasised that the Alsatian was:

> Obviously capable of endurance and speed, and of quick and sudden movement... The whole dog and its expression give the impression of perpetual vigilance, strong fidelity, lively and ever watchful, alert to every sight and sound, nothing escaping its attention, showing no fear, but with a decided suspiciousness towards strangers.[139]

In his autobiography, John Moore-Brabazon, an RAF veteran and the Minister of Aircraft Production for a time during the Second World War, made the largely accurate claim that he had "introduced the Alsatian into this country."[140] Brabazon returned from the First World War with an Alsatian and began breeding his own dogs. In early 1919, less than three months after Germany surrendered to end the First World War, he became the founding secretary of the recently-established Alsatian Wolf Dog Club, a position he retained until joining the Air Ministry the following year.[141]

For some Britons, however, the entire Alsatian breed was suspect owing to its German ancestry. The chairman of the Bristol and West of England Bulldog Club, for example, urged his countrymen to disregard the "bosch" Alsatian in favour of "all-British" canines. The Alsatian, he argued, was:

---

135 '"The People" Pet Show at Olympia', *Tail-Wagger Magazine*, January 1935, p. 37.
136 'The Dog and the Show', *Tail-Wagger Magazine*, May 1933, p. 146.
137 'The Alsatian Wolf Dog', *The Times*, 7 January 1920, p. 5 and 'Prince of Wales at Dog Show', *The Times*, 4 February 1925, p. 16 and 'Alsatians', *Western Daily Press*, 27 February 1928, p. 11.
138 'The Alsatian Wolf-Dog', *The Times*, 5 October 1926, p. 6.
139 Quoted in 'The Alsatian Wolf Dog', *The Times*, 7 January 1920, p. 5.
140 Lord Brabazon of Tara, *The Brabazon Story* (London: William Heinemann, 1956), p. 147.
141 'J.T.C. Moore-Brabazon', Supplement to *Our Dogs*, 12 December 1919 and 'Foreign Dog Fancies', *Our Dogs*, 24 January 1919, p. 94 and 'Foreign Dog Fancies', *Our Dogs*, 30 April 1920, p. 648 and 'Alsatian Wolf Dog Anglicisms', *Our Dogs*, 16 July 1920, p. 94.

German in origin, 'bosch' to the core. The name Alsatian is only camouflage, his real name is the German shepherd dog... It has amazed me that so many people should have adopted this alien breed... In these days of Empire and all British products, let us start with an all-British dog.[142]

Even Richardson doubted the usefulness of Alsatians over British breeds. In a letter to *The Times*, Richardson argued against the training of Alsatians for military roles because "dogs always reflect the temperament of their nationality."[143]

In response to the vitriol directed at Alsatians by some Britons in the months following the First World War, *Our Dogs* attempted to draw attention away from the controversy over the breed's birthplace by reminding readers that the Alsatian was respected among British veterans of the 1914-1918 conflict:

British officers, who form such a large percentage of Alsatian admirers at the moment, [have] become so captivated by the Alsatian and its work, by seeing the animal and its deeds during the war years... The men who went over the top can surely be trusted to be quite as patriotic, as severely anti-German, as any of us who stayed at home.[144]

For its part, *The Times* assured readers that "the Alsatian may be an enemy alien, but he has too much intelligence to be a Nazi."[145]

Such distrust was reminiscent of the ways in which Dachshunds were perceived by some Britons during the First World War. Although Alison Skipper has cast doubt on the pervasiveness of such incidents,[146] at least some Dachshunds were harassed or physically harmed on account of their German heritage, and markedly fewer were enrolled in the Kennel Club before and during the First World War.[147] Unlike the Dachshund, however, the Alsatian remained a favourite among British dog fanciers prior to and after the Second World War.[148] The disparity is likely explained by the Alsatian's perceived usefulness as a military dog. In 'Breeding Racism: The Imperial Battlefields of the "German" Shepherd Dog', the historian Aaron Skabelund exam-

---

142 'Alsatians', *Western Daily Press*, 16 October 1926, p. 4.
143 'Alsatians as Army Dogs', *The Times*, 17 January 1927, p. 8. Richardson further opined: "It is always better for each country to utilize its own native breeds, as the people understand the handling of them better."
144 'Foreign Dog Fancies', *Our Dogs*, 3 October 1919, p. 411.
145 'Dogs of War', *The Times*, 6 May 1942, p. 5.
146 Alison Skipper, 'The Dog as a National Symbol: All "British Bulldogs" and "German Sausages on Legs"', Paper delivered at the World Association for the History of Veterinary Medicine and the UK Veterinary History Society, 12 September 2014.
147 Philip Howell, 'The Dog Fancy at War: Breeds, Breeding, and Britishness, 1914-1918', *Society and Animals*, 21 (2013), pp. 547-551.
148 'Our Friend the Dog', *Bucks Herald*, 7 October 1938, p. 3 and 'Popular Dogs', *Hull Daily Mail*, 25 July 1947, p. 3.

ined how in the 20th century several nations adopted the use of Alsatians in military roles even though the breed represented German military prowess and colonialism. In Germany, as well as in nearly every nation which utilised military dogs, Alsatians were seen as an estimable breed known for several positive behavioural attributes, including loyalty and courage.[149] Britain was no exception. By emphasising the breed's physical and behavioural traits, many Britons were able to overlook the Alsatian's German heritage.

As in the First World War, the Germans already possessed a substantial number of military dogs prior to the outbreak of the Second World War. By 1939, several thousand canines had completed training at a facility in Frankfurt.[150] With around 50,000 dogs at the start of the Second World War, the German Army possessed, as one researcher later described it, "probably the largest, the best-trained, and best-equipped canine army in the world."[151] Contemporary reports on the German employment of military dogs put the number of canines at between 100,000 and 200,000, although the source of such figures is unclear.[152] The Germans utilised dogs on patrols, to locate casualties and to deliver messages. Following the German invasion of Belgium and the fall of France, dogs assisted German police and customs personnel in the surveillance and defence of German-controlled territory, including the French demarcation line. On the Eastern Front, dogs delivered medicines to German positions which were inaccessible to medical personnel.[153] In addition, the Germans relied upon dogs to hunt down enemy agents in German-controlled territory.[154] The British suspected the *Wehrmacht* taught dogs to parachute from aircraft, an idea supported by the findings of a veterinary examination carried out on a German military dog in early 1945.[155] As

149 Skabelund, 'Breeding Racism', pp. 355-357, 361.
150 Clayton G. Going, *Dogs at War* (New York: Macmillan, 1940), p. 2.
151 Charles F. Sloane, 'Dogs in War, Police Work and on Patrol', *The Journal of Criminal Law, Criminology, and Police Science*, 46:3 (1955), p. 386.
152 Henry R. Ilsley, 'Drastic Order Issued in Germany', *New York Times*, 14 July 1940, p. 67 and 'More Dogs are Sought for Service in War', *New York Times*, 23 August 1942, p. 28 and Going, *Dogs at War*, p. 2. The latter figure, cited in *Dogs at War*, was inclusive of canines instructed "in a ten-year period" and thus likely referred to those obtained by the German Armed Forces prior to the onset of the Second World War.
153 National Archives and Records Administration, College Park, Maryland, USA (NARA): Notes on Use of Dogs by German Army, Enclosure A, 3 April 1943 (Use of Dogs by German Army); #14 Information on War Dogs: Combat Reports and Training, 1943-1945 (#14 Information on War Dogs); Reports, Studies, and Plans Relating to World War II Military Operations, 1918-56 (Reports, Studies, and Plans-Military Operations); Records of the United States Marine Corps, Record Group 127 (RG 127); National Archives Building, College Park, MD (NACP).
154 Lloyd, 'Dog in War', p. 192 and TNA: WO 32/14142, 59A, War Office Police Statement No. 16 (Revise), 26 February 1952.
155 Maj. D.C.E. Danby, 'German War Dog No. 603', *Journal of the Royal Army Veterinary Corps*, 16:2 (1945), pp. 154-155. Upon examining the dog, which was brought to Britain by servicemen, Danby considered that the canine was likely injured "from jumping from

Skabelund has shown, canines also served "as an instrument and symbol of [Nazi] terror" at concentration camps, where they were relied upon to surveil and harass those held captive.[156]

Like Germany, Japan instituted a military dog training scheme prior to the Second World War. In the early 1930s, the Japanese employed dogs to defend railways in Manchuria. Having witnessed the employment of several Alsatians in China, a British military attaché in Japan noted in 1933 that "considerable interest is being taken in the training of dogs for use in the [Imperial Japanese] Army."[157] Messenger dogs were present among Japanese infantry units in China in the years immediately preceding the Second World War.[158] In December 1941, the Imperial Japanese Army possessed between 10,000 and 25,000 canines provided by her German ally.[159] The Japanese set up dog training centres in China and Japan and employed canines as guards, messengers, mine detectors and on patrols.[160] Contemporary reports from Burma and New Guinea suggest that the Japanese also taught locally-obtained dogs to uncover enemy soldiers.[161]

In the Soviet Union, the training of military dogs continued during the interwar period, so that within the first years of the Second World War, the Red Army was believed at the time to have amassed some 50,000 dogs. The Soviets utilised canines in a myriad of military roles, including guard, draught, messenger, mine detection and ambulance duties.[162] On the Eastern Front, draught dogs were hitched to sledges to move weapons, ammunition and other provisions across the snowy terrain. While the Soviets preferred Alsatians, dogs white in colour were relied upon to convey Russian snipers over the wintry landscape.[163] In 1942, the *New York Times* revealed that the Soviet Union also employed dogs to immobilise German tanks.[164] "Explosive dogs," as they were designated in an American report, bore explosives and were taught to chase after enemy tanks. According to the report:

an aeroplane as a 'parachutist'." Although Danby specified that the dog was imported in January 1944, he described the dog as "the first German war dog to arrive in this country following the invasion of Normandy." Thus, the date provided by Danby is most likely an error and should read January 1945.

156 Skabelund, *Empire of Dogs*, p. 139.
157 TNA: WO 208/1337, Signals: Messenger Dog Units, Military Attaché, Tokyo to Director of Military Operations and Intelligence, 16 June 1933.
158 TNA: WO 208/1337, Extract from C.S.I. Shanghai No. 16/101/2, 27 March 1940.
159 Going, *Dogs at War*, p. 3. See also: Skabelund, *Empire of Dogs*, p. 138. It is more likely the Imperial Japanese Army had around 10,000 canines in total.
160 TNA: WO 208/1337, ATIS Serial 528, Page 7, undated.
161 TNA: WO 208/1337, Extract from Tactical and Technical Trends No. 37, 4 November 1943 and 'Japanese Copy U.S. in Use of War Dogs', *New York Times*, 7 October 1944, p. 5.
162 Going, *Dogs at War*, pp. 168-170. The same figure was cited in 'More Dogs are Sought for War Service', *New York Times*, 23 August 1942, p. 28 and War Office, *Training of War Dogs* (1952), p. 2.
163 Going, *Dogs at War*, pp. 168-170.
164 'Soviet Using Dogs to Blow Up Tanks', *New York Times*, 24 June 1942, p. 7.

Troops of dogs, each encircled by a powerful explosive charge fitted with a delayed action fuse, flung themselves against the armored (sic) vehicles. These dogs were trained to attack the tank by running alongside it without being run over... After a certain length of time the animal blew up right alongside the armored (sic) vehicle, which would normally be at least damaged.[165]

On one occasion in May 1942, Soviet dogs accounted for the immobilisation of 11 armoured vehicles, most of which were tanks. Ilya Ehrenburg, a journalist who witnessed an encounter between dogs and multiple German tanks on the Eastern Front, recounted how the mere presence of the dogs prompted the withdrawal of the Germans.[166] Appendix I considers the veracity of Ehrenburg's claim and responses in the United Kingdom to his article in the *New York Times*.

In France, the training of military dogs waned during the interwar period. As war became increasingly likely in the late 1930s, however, a group of French Army veterans who had worked with military dogs in the First World War instituted a dog training scheme.[167] The decision to employ dogs on an official basis came just one month after the French declaration of war.[168] The French Army employed canines to relay messages, locate casualties and escort soldiers on patrols.[169] French civilians donated their pets, and as in several other nations, Alsatians were among the breeds specifically requested by the French Army.[170]

Less populous nations, such as Switzerland and Finland, also employed dogs in military roles. The Swiss formed a dog training centre during the 1920s. Located in Valais, the facility prepared dogs for message carrying and ambulance work. During the Second World War, the Swiss Army also employed guard dogs to augment security at the Swiss border. In addition, draught dogs conveyed *matériel* over the rugged landscape.[171] The Finnish Army, in its fight against Soviet forces, utilised canines as messengers and on patrols.[172] In early 1940, the Finns began importing trained sledge dogs from Sweden and North America. The dogs, which were primarily Huskies, hauled weapons during the winter months and could travel at a much greater speed

---

165 NARA: Use of Dogs by German Army; #14 Information on War Dogs; Reports, Studies, and Plans-Military Operations; RG 127; NACP. The author of this report had not personally witnessed the employment of "explosive dogs;" he made clear that insight into their use came from the German media.
166 'Soviet Using Dogs', *New York Times*, 24 June 1942, p. 7.
167 'Dogs of War', *Sunderland Echo and Shipping Gazette*, 17 June 1938, p. 11.
168 'French Dogs of War', *Manchester Guardian*, 2 October 1939, p. 7.
169 'War Dogs', *Animal World*, November 1939, p. 195 and 'Dogs in No Man's Land', *Lincolnshire Echo*, 11 January 1940, p. 1.
170 'French Recruiting Dogs for the Army', *Lancashire Daily Post*, 28 November 1939, p. 4.
171 Going, *Dogs at War*, pp. 174-175.
172 'Aid for Finnish War Animals: R.S.P.C.A. Sends Support of Various Kinds', *Animal World*, March 1940, pp. 21-22 and 'Aid for Finnish Animals–An Urgent Task', *Animal World*, April 1940, p. 30.

than horses.[173] In addition, the Finns taught dogs to hunt down Soviet paratroopers.[174] Although Norway was occupied by the Germans after 1940, the Norwegian Air Force instructed a number of sledge dogs in Ontario, Canada prior to the Allied invasion of Normandy. The dogs, which were Huskies obtained in Canada, were taught to convey equipment and deliver wounded servicemen to safety.[175]

Although the United States Army had utilised a small number of military dogs provided by the British and French Armies during the First World War, an official military dog training scheme put forward in early 1918 was ultimately rejected by the General Headquarters, American Expeditionary Forces.[176] Before the American declaration of war in December 1941, the employment of trained dogs by the United States Army was limited to some 90 sledge dogs which performed transport and rescue work in Alaska and other icy regions where the Army operated.[177] In contrast to the British War Office, however, the United States War Department seems to have had less hesitation in commencing a military dog training scheme following the American declaration of war. Less than four months after the attack on Pearl Harbor, the United States Army Quartermaster Corps (QMC) launched a guard dog training scheme to protect vulnerable points on the American Home Front.[178] In May 1942, eight canines began working alongside human sentries at a United States Army fort in New Jersey.[179] The effective employment of these dogs prompted the War Department to call for trained canines in additional military roles. Thus, in July 1942, the QMC unveiled a more extensive training scheme which involved preparing dogs for messenger and patrol duties.[180] Shortly thereafter, the QMC founded the

---

173 'Dog Team Corps for Finland', *Aberdeen Press and Journal*, 2 February 1940, p. 4.
174 'Chasing Parachute Jumpers', *Nottingham Evening Post*, 9 February 1940, p. 1.
175 'Norse Commando Dogs', *Dog World*, 30 April 1943, p. ii.
176 Michael G. Lemish, *War Dogs: A History of Loyalty and Heroism* (Washington, D.C.: Brassey's, 1996), p. 23. The United States Congress had also voted against an official military dog scheme the previous year. See also: NARA: Report #4248, *Dogs and National Defense*, p. 2; Department of the Army, Office of the Quartermaster General, 1958 (Report #4248, *Dogs and National Defense*); Document No. 4243 to 4270 (4243 to 4270), Departmental Records Branch Reference Collection (DRB Reference Collection); Records of the Adjutant General's Office, Record Group 407 (RG 407); National Archives College Park (NACP). The scheme put forward in 1918 would have provided for nearly 300 canines per division, as well as training schools on the American Home Front. It is unclear why the scheme was rejected.
177 NARA: Report #4248, *Dogs and National Defense*, pp. 2-3; 4243 to 4270, DRB Reference Collection; RG 407; NACP.
178 '200 Dogs Being Trained for Sentry Duty; Army to Use Them as Supply Depot Guards', *New York Times*, 22 March 1942, p. 45.
179 'Eight Dogs Inducted as Army Sentries', *New York Times*, 3 May 1942, p. 35.
180 NARA: Memorandum, Brigadier General Ray E. Porter to Assistant Chief of Staff, G-4, 17 July 1943; 452.1 to 455.2; Security Classified General Correspondence, 3/1942-1946 (Security Classified Correspondence, 1942-1946); General Records, Office of the Director of Service, Supply, and Procurement, G-4 (General Records, G-4); Records of the War Department General and Special Staffs, Record Group 165 (RG 165); NACP.

The United States Quartermaster Corps War Dog Reception and Training Center in Front Royal, Virginia, August 1942. (National Archives and Record Administration (111-SC-140929))

War Dog Reception and Training Center at Front Royal, Virginia. By late 1943, four additional training facilities had opened in Nebraska, California, Montana and Mississippi.[181] The QMC training centres turned out some 10,420 canines throughout the course of the Second World War. Apart from sentries, other roles for which dogs were prepared included patrol, messenger, mine detection and transport.[182]

In contrast to so many foreign militaries, the British Army lacked a military dog training facility in the years prior to the Second World War. Nonetheless, there was, it seemed, an increasing realisation among police forces of the utility of the dog in interwar Britain. The Home Office, in 1934, formed a committee to investigate the employment of police dogs in the United Kingdom. After consulting with dog breeder H.S. Lloyd, the committee secured funding for the formation of a dog training facility

---

181 NARA: War Department Bureau of Public Relations Press Tour Fact Sheet, 13 October 1943; Front Royal, VA; War Department, Office of the Quartermaster General, War Dog Reception and Training Center Records,1942-1947 (War Dog Reception and Training Center Records); General Records, 1942-1947; Records of the Office of the Quartermaster General, Record Group 92 (RG 92); NACP.
182 NARA: Report #4248, *Dogs and National Defense*, p. 21; 4243-4270; DRB Reference Collection; RG 407; NACP.

in Berkshire, where Lloyd and dog trainer Reginald Hill instructed canines for the police.[183] While working for the Home Office, Lloyd trained Labradors to aid police officers on patrols and Bloodhounds to locate perpetrators and missing persons.[184] As secretary of the Cocker Spaniel Club and a regular presence at national dog shows, Lloyd was a well-known figure among British dog breeders in the interwar period.[185] His kennel in Hertfordshire produced gundogs, several of which saw success at shows in Britain and abroad. Prior to the Second World War, two of Lloyd's Cocker Spaniels each garnered two Cruft's supreme championships.[186]

In the decade before the Second World War, a small number of British police forces, including the Cheshire and the Lancashire Constabularies, adopted the use of dogs.[187] In 1938, the Metropolitan Police Service took on a pair of Labradors to serve on patrols in the capital.[188] Moreover, the London and North Eastern Railway Company turned to Alsatians to safeguard ports in northeast England.[189] Yet on the eve of the Second World War, the Home Office committee acknowledged that "the British police have lagged behind the police of a good many other countries" in the employment of police dogs.[190] As revealed by correspondence among the committee members, several chief constables expressed indifference towards the employment of dogs. By November 1939, a mere 16 of Lloyd's dogs were active among British police forces. The onset of war, a lack of funding and the modest reception among chief constables led the committee to suspend further police dog training.[191]

Thus, while the police dog was accepted by some constabularies, the potential employment of trained dogs remained largely overlooked in interwar Britain. "Very similar conditions prevailed in 1939 as Col[onel] Richardson had to face in 1914," Lloyd lamented after the Second World War.[192] Yet the decision by the War Office not to retain the War Dog School in the interwar period, as well as its refusal to establish a new military dog training facility prior to the Second World War, is perhaps unsur-

183 TNA: HO 45/21004, Police: Committee on Training of Police Dogs, Committee on Police Dogs, undated and 'Police Dogs', *The Times*, 15 January 1938, p. 11.

184 'Police Dogs', *The Times*, 15 January 1938, p. 11 and 'Dogs in Police Work', *The Times*, 11 March 1938, p. 13.

185 'Terrier No Longer the Family Dog', *Dundee Evening Telegraph*, 13 February 1930, p. 4 and 'Spaniel is Kennel Club Champion', *Dundee Courier*, 9 December 1938, p. 6 and 'Cruft's Best Dog', *Western Daily Press*, 11 February 1938, p. 11.

186 'Doyen of the Gundog World Dies', *Our Dogs*, 1 February 1963, p. 155.

187 TNA: HO 45/21004, J. Becke to H.W. Stotesbury, 13 December 1945 and A.F. Hordern to H.W. Stotesbury, 3 January 1946.

188 'Police Dogs in London', *The Times*, 13 May 1938, p. 13.

189 'Police Dogs at the Docks', *The Times*, 31 January 1938, p. 18.

190 TNA: HO 45/21004, Note on Advisory Committee on Police Regional Services, 17 July 1939.

191 TNA: HO 45/21004, H.P. Griffiths to H. Legge, 20 December 1939 and H.P. Griffiths to F.J. Lemon, 15 November 1939 and F.J. Lemon to H.P. Griffiths, 20 November 1939 and Memo by S.J. Baker, 17 October 1939.

192 Lloyd, 'Dog in War', p. 182.

prising. At the time, the British government considered a widespread conflict like that of the First World War unlikely to occur for at least a decade. Consequently, the British Army of the interwar period was relatively neglected. As a result of funds and manpower being in large part divided between the Royal Navy and the RAF during the 1930s, the British Army stagnated.[193] In the words of more than one historian, the British Army emerged as "the Cinderella of the three Services."[194]

Furthermore, it was envisioned at the time that a future military conflict would require the latest technology to overpower the enemy; thus, for the British General Staff, technology and innovative weaponry took precedence over fielding an extensive army. The emphasis on technology was in part realised by the British Army's commitment to mechanisation during the interwar period. The 1920s and 1930s saw the number of British Army horses decline as motorised vehicles became more commonplace; by the late 1930s, the British Army employed a mere fraction of the equine power it had maintained in 1914.[195] The British Army of the Second World War was, as one historian put it, "commit[ted] to fighting a war of material."[196] Yet circumstances would evolve during the war, prompting the War Office to reconsider the employment of canines.

193 H.M.D. Parker, *Manpower: A Study of War-time Policy and Administration* (London, 1957), pp. 38-39 and David French, *Raising Churchill's Army: The British Army and the War Against Germany 1919-1945* (Oxford: Oxford University Press, 2000), pp. 3, 12-15, 50, 106-108.

194 Parker, *Manpower*, p. 39 and Niall Barr, *Yanks and Limeys: Alliance Warfare in the Second World War* (London: Vintage, 2015), p. 80.

195 French, *Raising Churchill's Army*, pp. 12-16, 30-35, 110-112.

196 Ibid, p. 72.

2

The Outbreak of the Second World War and the Establishment of British Military Dog Training Schemes

In her memoirs, Eileen Cox Woods recalled the day she discovered her mother had offered the family's Labrador to the British Army:

> [Rover]… was very protective towards us and would take us to school and greet us on our return. Sometimes as a plane approached while on our way to school he would push us up to a hedge until he was sure it was 'one of ours' and so safe. One day I came home from school expecting him to come rushing out to greet me as usual but there was no sign of him… Then my mother came and broke the news to me that she had answered a call from the Ministry of Defence who were asking for people to give their dogs for army training.[1]

Woods' suggestion that Rover could recognise British aeroplanes as "one of ours" is indicative of the ways in which canines were anthropomorphised by their owners, servicemen and the British press throughout the Second World War. Moreover, her account highlights how the Second World War altered the lives of pet dogs. Britain's dogs were not immune from the hardships of war, and the impact of war on the Home Front prompted some owners to donate their dogs to the war effort.

From the "Figurative Mobilization" of Canine Pets to the Recruitment of British Military Dogs

In early 1939, several months before the war began, the *Dogs' Bulletin* grimly predicted that in a future war, animals would fare no better or even worse than their human counterparts on the Home Front. In an article entitled 'If Another Crisis Comes', the

---

1   IWM: 06/26/1, Private Papers of Miss E Cox, Evacuee Diary Fragments, 'An Evacuee Remembers Speldhurst' memoir.

National Canine Defence League publication lamented: "If a great, overwhelming onslaught were made on us we should endeavour to save our own pets, but the sufferings of animals would be unimaginable and possibly little could be done to prevent or alleviate them."[2] Similarly, in his historical account of the PDSA, Frederick Montague recalled that in 1939:

> There was considerable panic among animal owners. Anticipations concerning the effect of bombing were of the most alarming kind. Incendiaries would lay down a ring of white-hot fire round London within which millions would be trapped to be drenched in agonising gases while high explosives sucked out the City's heart in piles of reeking debris.[3]

In such an atmosphere, it is unsurprising that some dog owners opted to euthanise their pets. In what the National Canine Defence League termed the "September Holocaust,"[4] some 400,000 pets, or more than a quarter of London's canine and feline population, were euthanised in the British capital in the days immediately succeeding the onset of the war in September 1939.[5] The *Dogs' Bulletin* recalled that the League's London-based clinics became "centres of destruction" as seemingly endless numbers of owners requested their pets be euthanised rather than have them live through a war in which bombing and poison gas were expected to reach the Home Front.[6] Similarly, the president of the Animal Defence Society recounted how "the massacre" of domestic pets resulted in "piles and truckloads of dead bodies."[7]

For John Davies, the British declaration of war meant the loss of his family's Welsh Collie, Prince. "He had always been frightened in a thunderstorm and there wasn't the food for him," Davies recalled in his unpublished memoirs. "The saddest day was when we came home from school to be told that Prince had been put to sleep."[8] Indeed, as the cost of meat skyrocketed in mid-1941, many Britons found it nearly impossible to purchase unrationed meat for dogs.[9] An MP told the House of Commons in October 1941 that horsemeat had become "almost unobtainable."[10] The feeding of dogs was

2   'If Another Crisis Comes?', *Dogs' Bulletin*, February-March 1939, p. 4.
3   Frederick Montague, *Let the Good Work Go On: On the Work of the People's Dispensary for Sick Animals of the Poor* (London: Hutchinson, 1947), p. 90.
4   'September Holocaust', *Dogs' Bulletin*, December 1939, p. 2.
5   Kean, 'The Dog and Cat Massacre', pp. 741-756. Kean cast doubt on the notion propagated by the press that "panic" was the chief motivator and instead argued that for some owners, "killing a family pet was to some extent about creating some control over human (and animal) lives in a situation in which ordinary people had no control." (p. 746)
6   'September Holocaust', *Dogs' Bulletin*, p. 2.
7   L. Lind-af-Hageby, *Bombed Animals, Rescued Animals, Animals Saved from Destruction* (London: The Animal Defence and Anti-Vivisection Society, 1941), p. 19.
8   John Davies, *Recollections of John Gwylim Davies*, unpublished memoirs, p. 12.
9   'Dog Meat Ramp On', *Daily Mirror*, 15 May 1941, p. 3.
10 Hansard: HC Deb 22 October 1941 vol 374 c1786.

also impacted by the Wheaten Substances Order. Enacted in mid-1940, the order reduced the amount of milled wheat available for dog foods, forcing companies to cut dog biscuit production by one third.[11] Production was curtailed again the following year, when the Ministry of Food required that dog food companies slash output even further.[12] Just as housewives queued to purchase the family's weekly rations, it became commonplace in some areas for crowds of dog owners to gather in front of shops in an effort to obtain food for their animals.[13] According to a Mass Observation study, 36 percent of London dog owners "experienced some difficulty in keeping a dog" during the war. The proportion was greater in Worcester and Oxford, where it was nearly 50 percent and 64 percent, respectively. In all three cities, the primary concern for owners was the provision of food for their pets. It is unsurprising then that some respondents felt their pets' health had deteriorated owing to the war.[14]

As the precise number of canines in the United Kingdom prior to the Second World War is unknown, it is difficult to accurately gauge the impact of the war on the dog population. It is clear, however, that applications for dog licences fell following the commencement of hostilities.[15] Table 1 shows the war's impact on dog licences through 1942.

Table 1 Dog Licences, 1937-1942[16]

Year	Number of Dog Licences
1937-38	3,000,967
1938-39	3,021,580
1939-40	2,801,025
1940-41	2,625,686
1941-42	2,569,922

11 Hansard: HC Deb 5 June 1940 vol 361 cc840-1 and 'Flour in Cat and Dog Foods', *Animal World*, August 1940, p. 68.
12 Hansard: HC Deb 2 April 1941 vol 370 cc1003-4.
13 'Rations for the Dog', *Manchester Guardian*, 19 June 1941, p. 3.
14 MOA: File Report 804, pp. 1-4 and File Report 838, pp. 2-6. Fewer respondents felt this way in London (12%) and Worcester (17%) compared to Oxford (24%). This feeling was particularly pronounced among wealthier dog owners, who were more likely to feed their pets "special diets" prior to the war compared to working class dog owners. Thus, these results are not necessarily an accurate indication of the actual health of British dogs but provide insight into the minds of dog owners and their perception of how the war had damaged their pets' health.
15 Hansard: HC Deb 30 September 1941 vol 374 c488W and HC Deb 4 May 1943 vol 389 c33W.
16 Ibid. The figures above, which represent dog licence totals for each 12 month period, do not include licences taken out in Northern Ireland.

A 1945 Mass Observation study found that around 20 percent of English and Welsh families possessed at least one dog, a five percent decrease from before the war.[17]

As Hilda Kean has emphasised, canines in the Second World War were, prior to their use by the British Armed Forces and the Civil Defence, "employed as representations for propaganda purposes."[18] Similarly, Skabelund coined the term "figurative mobilization" to express how in Imperial Japan and other nations "government and private voices figuratively manipulated dogs and other beasts to rally human populations in the pursuit of victory."[19] The "figurative mobilization" of pet dogs in the British press commenced almost immediately after the onset of hostilities. On 8 September 1939, five days after the British declaration of war, the *Daily Mirror* published on its front page the headline: "It's This Difference We're Fighting." Situated below the newspaper's leading article on the war at sea, the brief article featured a photograph of a Dachshund cradled in the arms of the British ambassador to Germany Sir Neville Henderson. A second photograph showed another dog, which the newspaper explained was in "mourning" after being "left behind" by his owner, the German ambassador to the United Kingdom Joachim von Ribbentrop. The juxtaposition was intentional, for the purpose of the article was to demonstrate how British benevolence towards animals contrasted sharply with not just Ribbentrop's treatment of his pet but the Nazis and the values they espoused. "That's what Britain is fighting," the article claimed, "the inherent Brutality of Nazi-ism that has no justice or human feeling— even for its pets."[20] The 8 September article was not the first story on Ribbentrop's dog published by the *Daily Mirror*. The previous day the newspaper ran an article on "the Chow [Chow] forsaken by his German masters." The article, written from the imagined perspective of the dog, alleged that Ribbentrop had not only abandoned his pet but was neglectful and abusive towards the canine.[21]

In December 1939, the editor of *Tail-Wagger Magazine* sought to emphasise what he perceived as a "difference in outlook" on the part of Hitler and the German people regarding dogs and other animals. He charged that "Hitler sneered contemptuously at the British and American fondness for animals," while also suggesting that German dog owners and trainers were "not always as kind to [dogs]" compared to their British counterparts.[22] By contrast, the April 1941 edition of *PDSA News* included on its

---

17   MOA: File Report 2256, Report on Dogs and Dog-Health in Wartime, 7 June 1945, p. 2. See also: BIPO: Survey #126, October 1945, online <http://doc.ukdataservice.ac.uk/doc/3331/mrdoc/ascii/4510.txt> (accessed 29 September 2016). This Gallup poll, carried out just weeks after the end of the war, found virtually no change in the proportion (30.66%) of British families with dogs compared to the aforementioned poll conducted prior to the war.
18   Kean, 'The Dog and Cat Massacre', p. 742.
19   Skabelund, *Empire of Dogs*, pp. 130-132. He likewise referred to such acts as "rhetorical wartime deployment" (p. 131) and "metaphorical mobilization" (p. 167).
20   'It's This Difference We're Fighting', *Daily Mirror*, 8 September 1939, p. 1.
21   'By the Dog that Ribbentrop Deserted', *Daily Mirror*, 7 September 1939, p. 10.
22   'Difference in Outlook', *Tail-Wagger Magazine*, December 1939, p. 366.

cover a photograph of British Prime Minister Winston Churchill stroking the head of a canine military mascot while members of the unit looked on. The caption read: "Our great Prime Minister is, among many other things, a lover of animals."[23]

Similarly, an article featured in the January 1942 edition of *Tail-Wagger Magazine* drew attention to the numerous strays recovered by British servicemen in northwest Europe prior to and during the British Army's evacuation at Dunkirk in 1940: "What drove exhausted Tommies to add further responsibilities to their overburdened shoulders by adopting stray dogs? I can offer no explanation other than that they were British and even the horrors of war could not deaden their love of dogs; especially dogs in distress."[24] For the author of the article, a reporter who witnessed the influx of evacuated servicemen in England, the ordeal "reflect[ed] the Britishers' inherited love of animals."[25] Yet such an account clearly served not to inform but to evoke an emotional response from readers. By portraying Britons as patriotic and sympathetic towards animals, the British media emphasised a perceived moral superiority over enemy nations, which were contrastingly vilified as unsympathetic or inhumane towards dogs. The depiction of Britons as benevolent animal lovers was a tendency carried over from the interwar period intended to propagate perceived notions of Britishness. Such propaganda was one aspect of a wider campaign by the British to depict Germany and the German people as uncivilised and immoral.[26]

While the use of dogs in the United Kingdom in the opening months of the Second World War was primarily limited to their "figurative mobilization" in the press, a few dog breeders and trainers made efforts to institute their actual employment among the British Armed Forces. From his home in Surrey, Colonel Richardson continued to train dogs after the First World War. Soldiers from a Canadian regiment stationed nearby enabled Richardson to carry out trials with his dogs.[27] He again made repeated attempts to convince the War Office of the usefulness of trained dogs.[28] In June 1940, for example, Richardson expressed his frustration in a letter to Commander-in-Chief, Home Forces General Edmund Ironside: "When the [Second World] War broke out I urgently asked that I might be allowed to collect and organize the dog power of the country for use with the soldiers but could not get in touch with anyone who sufficiently understood the value of these animals to man."[29] While his advanced age prevented him from training dogs on a large scale in the Second World War,

23   *P.D.S.A. News*, April 1941, p. 1.
24   Frank Illingworth, 'Dunkirk and Dogs', *Tail-Wagger Magazine*, January 1942, p. 12.
25   Ibid.
26   French, *Raising Churchill's Army*, p. 133 and Overy, *The Bombing* War, p. 622 and Ian McLaine, *Ministry of Morale: Home Front Morale and the Ministry of Information in World War II* (London: Allen & Unwin, 1979), pp. 11, 144-147, 166.
27   Richardson and Richardson, *Fifty Years*, p. 106.
28   TNA: WO 199/416, 13A, A.H. Killick to G.G. Mears, 20 May 1940 and 17A, E.H. Richardson to Edmund Ironside, 11 June 1940.
29   TNA: WO 199/416, 17A, Richardson to Ironside, 11 June 1940.

Richardson maintained a kennel from which he provided guard dogs to British civilians.[30] In addition, he instructed canines for messenger and rescue work with Air Raid Precautions (ARP) units on the Home Front.[31]

In October 1939, representatives from the War Office met with H.S. Lloyd to examine the potential use of dogs to defend vulnerable points on the British Home Front. The attendees agreed that the Army should pursue a dog training scheme comparable to that of the First World War.[32] That same month, when an MP enquired about the lack of trained dogs in the British military, Secretary of State for War Leslie Hore-Belisha responded that their use was "being examined."[33] Yet one month later the War Office reversed its stance.[34] In *The Book of the Dog*, Lloyd reflected on the interwar period and the subsequent outbreak of the Second World War: "Whilst other countries, particularly Germany, Russia and Japan, were busily engaged on building up a dog service both England and France did nothing." He attributed the unwillingness of the War Office to pursue a dog training scheme to "true British apathy," partly due to the perceived notion that a mechanised and fast-paced conflict no longer required animal support.[35] Yet Lloyd himself expressed some concern over the usefulness of dogs shortly after the onset of the war. In a November 1939 letter, Lloyd acknowledged: "One must admit that the nature of the War at present has not lent itself very much to their use."[36]

While the British government at last recognised the need for a more sizable army in early 1939,[37] its belated decision to do so resulted in the British Army being without crucial *matériel* for the first three years of the war. Home Forces, which following the evacuation of the BEF from France in 1940 encompassed the bulk of field force units in the British Army, was particularly deprived of resources.[38] With the emphasis on technology, as well as the British Army's initial dearth of *matériel*, it should come as no surprise that the War Office remained opposed to the employment of dogs prior to and in the months following the onset of the war. Lloyd argued as much in the *Book of the Dog*. He blamed the reluctance of the War Office to seriously consider canines in part on its commitment to mechanisation and the perception that the Second World War would be vastly different than the First World War:

---

30   Richardson and Richardson, *Fifty Years*, pp. 106, 169.
31   'Dogs Trained in A.R.P.', *Our Dogs*, 28 February 1941, p. 203. It is unclear if any of Richardson's dogs were in fact employed by ARP units upon completion of training.
32   TNA: WO 199/416, 1A, Report of Meeting at War Office, 10 October 1939.
33   Hansard: HC Deb 9 October 1939 vol 352 c39W.
34   TNA: HO 45/21004, G.G. Rawson to H.S. Lloyd, 24 November 1939. Rawson provided no explanation as to why the War Office reversed its stance, only informing Lloyd that it was "decided not to create a War Dog Organization in the Army."
35   Lloyd, 'Dog in War', pp. 182-183.
36   TNA: HO 45/21004, H.S. Lloyd to J. Coke, 13 November 1939.
37   Parker, *Manpower*, p. 39.
38   French, *Raising Churchill's Army*, pp. 83, 106-110, 196, 201.

The War Office was not interested in the use of dogs… it being pointed out that there was no comparison between the two wars, that this was a mechanical age, that it was a war of movement and that for many other reasons dogs could not be usefully employed.[39]

Finally, in the spring of 1940, the War Office acquiesced and authorised the creation of an experimental training centre in Berkshire. As technical adviser, Lloyd was charged with preparing the few dogs available for a prospective "Experimental War Dog Section." According to Lloyd, the War Office was convinced of the need for dogs after multiple instances of British patrols and positions uncovered by the enemy.[40] As outlined in correspondence from the Director of Military Training Major-General A.A. Richardson, the section was raised "for the purpose of the experimental training of the handlers and dogs for patrol work at night."[41] In the following weeks, four dogs were trained to escort soldiers on patrols and posted to 43rd Division for employment on training exercises.[42] The employment of these dogs prompted the War Office to reconsider its stance on military dog training, and in early 1941, the Army's War Dogs Training School was founded in Aldershot with Lloyd as chief instructor.[43]

Like Lloyd, British Army veteran and dog breeder Major James Baldwin advocated the training of dogs in military roles. As a soldier in the First World War, Baldwin had acquired a trained Alsatian which he employed during patrols on the Western Front. Upon his return to Britain, he had begun breeding Alsatians at his private kennel, and following the British declaration of war, utilised guard dogs at an aerodrome in Gloucestershire where he served as Defence Officer.[44] Baldwin was a respected Alsatian breeder and took part in dog shows in the years preceding the Second World War.[45] He corresponded regularly with the Minister of Aircraft Production, John Moore-Brabazon, who also recognised the potential of utilising the breed in war.[46]

39   Lloyd, 'Dog in War', p. 182.
40   Ibid, pp. 182-183 and TNA: WO 199/2061, War Dog Section: Formation in Southern Command, 1A, Director of Military Training to General Officer, Commanding-in-Chief, Southern Command, 29 April 1940.
41   TNA: WO 199/2061, 9A, A.A. Richardson to General Officer Commanding-in-Chief, Eastern Command, 26 July 1940.
42   Ibid.
43   TNA: WO 199/2061, 12A, Maj. S.B. Coates to the General Officers, Commanding-in-Chief, 13 November 1940 and 'War Dogs—Fall In!, Our Dogs, 11 April 1941, p. 350.
44   'Dogs Make Splendid Guards for 'Dromes', Gloucestershire Echo, 8 February 1943, p. 3 and Patrick Hennessey, The Story of the Royal Air Force Police (undated), p. 42.
45   'Prince of Wales at Dog Show', The Times, 4 February 1925, p. 16 and 'Alsatian League Show', The Times, 30 March 1939, p. 4 and 'Alsatians', Western Daily Press, 27 February 1928, p. 11.
46   TNA: AVIA 9/15, Use of Dogs for Factory and Aerodrome Defence, J.T.C. Moore-Brabazon to J. F. Baldwin, 20 August 1941 and Baldwin to Moore-Brabazon, 27 August 1941 and Moore-Brabazon to Baldwin, 6 November 1941 and Baldwin to Moore-Brabazon, 10 November 1941.

In September 1941, Baldwin held a trial involving guard dogs at Staverton Aerodrome.[47] Baldwin emphasised the advantage of dogs over human guards, telling the *Gloucestershire Echo* that during the trial: "I proved that it was easy to get on to the aerodrome and into a 'plane despite all the guards could do. But dogs detected the presence of intruders immediately."[48] After witnessing the trial, Brigadier H.T. MacMullen, the officer commanding, South Midland Area (Home Forces), implored Southern Command (Home Forces) to approve the establishment of a dog training facility headed by Baldwin.[49] Lieutenant General H.R. Alexander, Commanding-in-Chief, Southern Command also praised the performance of Baldwin's dogs. In a letter to GHQ Home Forces, he advocated the employment of guard dogs in his command, emphasising that during the trial "in no case was the concealed saboteur able to avoid capture."[50] As a result of the trial, the MAP, in late 1941, authorised the establishment of the Guard Dog Training School in Staverton, Gloucestershire with Baldwin as commandant.[51]

Baldwin and Lloyd do not appear to have collaborated to any great extent, at least prior to the establishment of the schools.[52] That separate training facilities developed was likely in part the result of a perceived sense of urgency among those who advocated for the employment of guard dogs. MacMullen expressed a feeling of urgency in a July 1941 letter to Lieutenant General E.C.A. Schreiber of Southern Command. Although aware of the existence of the Army's War Dogs Training School, MacMullen was concerned that "months, if not years" would pass "before this [South Midland] Area will gain any benefit from" that canine training facility. He instead pressed Schreiber to consider Baldwin, who, as MacMullen pointed out, had already gathered a number of potential personnel for a training facility in Gloucestershire.[53]

Perhaps more significant, the lack of co-operation between the two schools may be explained by the shifting role of the Army's War Dogs Training School. Initially, the focus of the school was not to turn out guard dogs for the Home Front but patrol dogs for employment in the field.[54] Indeed, prior to May 1942, the MAP Guard Dog

47   TNA: WO 199/2061, 42A, Brig. H.T. MacMullen to Southern Command, 19 September 1941.
48   'Dogs Make Splendid Guards', *Gloucestershire Echo*, 8 February 1943.
49   TNA: WO 199/2061, 42A, MacMullen to Southern Command, 19 September 1941.
50   TNA: WO 199/2061, 43A, Lt. Gen. H.R. Alexander to G.H.Q. Home Forces, 27 September 1941.
51   TNA: WO 199/2061, 42A, MacMullen to Southern Command, 19 September 1941 and 'Dogs Make Splendid Guards', *Gloucestershire Echo*, 8 February 1943 and 'Notes and News of the Breeds', *Our Dogs*, 19 December 1941, p. 1263.
52   Major J.Y. Baldwin, Letter to the Editor, *Our Dogs*, 12 December 1941, p. 1211. Baldwin explained that although he was aware of the existence of the Army's War Dogs Training School, time constraints had prevented him from visiting the facility.
53   TNA: WO 199/2061, 38A, MacMullen to Schreiber, 31 July 1941.
54   TNA: WO 199/2061, 12A, Coates to General Officers Commanding-in-Chief, 13 November 1940.

Training School was expected to produce guard dogs for both the MAP and the British Army.[55] When the MAP Guard Dog Training School was founded in late 1941, it was to supply canines for MAP aircraft storage units and aerodromes, the security of which passed from the Army to the Air Ministry around the same time.[56] Thus, the confirmation that the MAP, rather than the Army, would oversee the security of MAP installations likely contributed to the raising of a separate canine training facility.

To be sure, there was increased co-operation between the Army's War Dogs Training School and the MAP Guard Dog Training School as the war progressed. The involvement of the Army Veterinary and Remount Services (AVRS) from early 1942 onwards resulted in a more streamlined military dog recruitment process. Rather than the Army and the MAP separately recruiting and vying for dogs, as appears to have been the case in 1941, the AVRS, with the assistance of animal welfare organisations, became the sole channel through which military dogs were acquired.[57] The new process meant that dogs could undergo trials at both the War Dogs Training School and the MAP Guard Dog Training School, as some canines initially turned down by the former institution were accepted by the latter.[58] Moreover, the War Dogs Training School aided the MAP Guard Dog Training School in turning out dog handlers for airfields on the British Home Front.[59]

As in other nations which utilised dogs in the war, the British Armed Forces was, for the most part, dependent upon civilian dog owners to contribute animals.[60] In May 1941, *The Times* and other newspapers called upon Britons to "lend their dogs to the Army."[61] Dog fancy publications, including the *Kennel Gazette* and *Our Dogs*,

---

55   TNA: WO 199/416, 57B, Summary of the Minutes of a Meeting to Discuss the Supply of Dogs to the Army and the Ministry of Aircraft Production, 5 March 1942. At the time, personnel at the MAP Guard Dog Training School, not their counterparts at the Army's War Dogs Training School, were considered "specialists in the matter." See also: Museum of Military Medicine: Box 14, War Diary of DAVRS, April-May 1942. That the MAP Guard Dog Training School was expected to instruct guard dogs for both the MAP and the Army was also due to a lack of training space. The more expansive location of the War Dogs Training School in Northaw, to which the school was relocated in May 1942, allowed for an increase in trained dogs, including guard dogs for the Home Front.
56   TNA: WO 199/2061, 49B, GHQ Home Forces to MAP, 23 November 1941 and 50A, Southern Command to 5 Corps, 14 December 1941 and TNA: AVIA 9/15, 351/250, Dog Scheme-Progress Report No. 1, 19 November 1941. Prior to this, the British Army was obliged to defend aerodromes and aircraft storage units. That the Army was originally tasked with guarding MAP installations explains why the push for guard dogs largely came from Home Commands.
57   Museum of Military Medicine: Box 14, War Diary of DAVRS, January-February 1942 and TNA: WO 199/416, 57B, Minutes of a Meeting, 5 March 1942.
58   Museum of Military Medicine: Box 14, War Diary of DAVRS, February 1944.
59   TNA: AIR 2/8734, Training of Police as Dog Handlers, 35A, Postagram, 1 February 1944.
60   Skabelund, *Empire of Dogs*, pp. 154-155.
61   'Dogs for the Army', *The Times*, 6 May 1941, p. 2 and 'Army Wants Dogs', *Manchester Guardian*, 6 May 1941, p. 5 and 'Army Needs More Dogs', *Yorkshire Post*, 6 May 1941, p. 5.

ran similar appeals.[62] Lloyd later recalled that the effectiveness of such requests was initially doubted since it was believed that dog owners would be unwilling to give up their pets.[63] Over the next four months, however, the Army's War Dogs Training School received several thousand canines.[64]

The following March, Brigadier C.A. Murray of the AVRS met with RSPCA Secretary Arthur Moss, Lloyd, Baldwin and the commandant of the War Dogs Training School to consider the recruitment of military dogs. They determined that some 2,500 dogs were needed for various roles with the Army and the MAP. The RSPCA and the National Canine Defence League elected to help the AVRS procure dogs from the British public, and it was resolved to continue the recruitment of dogs in newspapers.[65] In part this was a calculated decision by the War Office, as it was realised that by involving animal welfare organisations in the recruitment process dog owners would be more likely to hand over their pets.[66] The inclusion of the RSPCA was also a practical consideration. RSPCA Inspectors performed much of the groundwork by supplying registration cards to owners[67] and conducting "preliminary inspection[s]" of some canines as a means of weeding out those clearly unfit for instruction.[68]

British newspapers continued to publish periodic requests for dogs throughout much of the war.[69] Although the DAVRS reported a "dwindling supply of dogs on loan from the public" in early 1943, the situation was quickly rectified following an appeal aired by the British Broadcasting Corporation (BBC).[70] Animal welfare organisations and veterinary surgeons were directed by the DAVRS to discourage dog owners from euthanising their pets, as they could potentially be utilised in military roles.[71] As in

62   'Club and Kennel Notes', *Kennel Gazette*, April 1941, p. 66 and 'War Dogs—Fall In!', *Our Dogs*, 11 April 1941, p. 350.
63   Lloyd, 'Dog in War', p. 185.
64   'Dogs in the Army', *Animal World*, September 1941, p. 67.
65   TNA: WO 199/416, 57B, Minutes of a Meeting, 5 March 1942.
66   TNA: WO 32/10800, War Dogs: General: Provision of War Dogs, Minutes, QMGF to Army Veterinary and Remount Services, 16 March 1942.
67   TNA: WO 32/10800, Minutes, Army Veterinary and Remount Services to QMGF, 12 March 1942.
68   TNA: WO 32/10800, Minutes, Army Veterinary and Remount Services to QMGF, 18 March 1942.
69   'Lend Your Dog to the Army', *Daily Express*, 6 May 1942, p. 4 and 'Appeal to Dog-Owners', *Manchester Guardian*, 12 February 1943, p. 3 and 'Dogs for War Service', *The Times*, 14 January 1944, p. 2. In August 1944, *Animal World* informed readers that the British Armed Forces had "sufficient dogs for their needs." See: 'War Dogs', *Animal World*, August 1944, p. 61.
70   Museum of Military Medicine: Box 14, War Diary of DAVRS, February 1943 and DAVRS Report for the First Period, 3 February 1943.
71   Clabby, *History of the RAVC*, p. 41.

the First World War, the Battersea Dogs' Home provided strays.[72] Another animal welfare organisation, the Our Dumb Friends' League, also handed over strays in its possession.[73] Furthermore, police forces were offered compensation for contributing unclaimed dogs.[74]

Initially, the Army's War Dogs Training School asked for Collies, Lurchers, Retrievers and Airedale Terriers. Although early newspaper appeals did not include Alsatians,[75] the breed was popular among the first dogs provided to the War Dogs Training School.[76] Following the aforementioned meeting in March 1942, appeals expanded to include Alsatians and Bull Terriers. In addition, the appeals specified that dogs be aged 10 months to five years. The sole exception was Bull Terriers, which had to be younger than three years.[77] Beginning in early 1944, the Army also sought Labradors, presumably to serve as mine detectors.[78] While Lloyd and Baldwin sought particular breeds, they each made clear that the potential of dogs in military roles was not dependent on pedigree. In a letter published in *Our Dogs*, for example, Lloyd explained that "*intelligence and natural ability*, not breed, would be the deciding factor" when choosing canines for the Army's War Dogs Training School.[79] Similarly, in a January 1944 speech, Baldwin maintained that the MAP Guard Dog Training School admitted "any kind of dog" excepting small breeds.[80]

Apart from the Alsatian and the Labrador, the breeds sought by the British military were of British origin.[81] In the United States, by contrast, the QMC sought Doberman Pinschers, Giant Schnauzers and Belgian Shepherds in addition to Alsatians and

72   Gloria Cottesloe, *The Story of the Battersea Dogs' Home* (Newton Abbott: David & Charles, 1979), p. 129.
73   Museum of Military Medicine: Box 14, War Diary of DAVRS, April 1944.
74   Ibid, June 1944.
75   'Dogs for the Army', *The Times*, 6 May 1941 and 'Army Wants Dogs', *Manchester Guardian*, 6 May 1941 and Letter from Lloyd in 'War Dogs—Fall In!', *Our Dogs*, p. 350. It is unclear why the May 1941 newspaper appeals omitted Alsatians, particularly since Lloyd included the breed in a personal request for canine trainees published in *Our Dogs* just one month earlier.
76   'Dogs on Loan to the Army', *The Times*, 6 November 1941, p. 6.
77   TNA: WO 199/416, 57B, Minutes of a Meeting, 5 March 1942 and 'Dogs Wanted for War Service', *The Times*, 5 May 1942, p. 2 and 'Dogs and the Army', *Animal World*, November 1942, p. 83 and 'War Dogs', *Animal World*, October 1943, p. 76.
78   'Dogs for War Service', *The Times*, 14 January 1944 and 'The Need for War Dogs', *Animal World*, May 1944, p. 37 and TNA: WO 291/1048, Detection of Mines by Dogs, Military Operational Research Unit, Interim Report No. 120, April 1947.
79   Letter from Lloyd in 'War Dogs—Fall in!', *Our Dogs*, p. 350.
80   'Dogs' Great Aid in War', *Gloucestershire Echo*, 12 January 1944, p. 5.
81   'Dogs for the Army', *The Times*, 6 May 1941 and 'Dogs on Loan to the Army', *The Times*, 6 November 1941 and 'Dogs Wanted for War Service', *The Times*, 5 May 1942 and 'Dogs and the Army', *Animal World*, November 1942, p. 83 and TNA: WO 199/416, 57B, Minutes of a Meeting, 5 March 1942 and 'War Dogs', *Animal World*, October 1943, p. 76 and 'Dogs for War Service', *The Times*, 14 January 1944 and 'The Need for War Dogs', *Animal World*, May 1944, p. 37 and TNA: WO 291/1048, Interim Report No. 120, April 1947.

Collies.[82] The difference in the choice of breeds in Britain and the United States may be explained by the availability of certain pedigree dogs, as well as access to breeding studs, in each country. Although Alsatians, Schnauzers and other German breeds had become increasingly popular among British dog fanciers during the 1930s,[83] British and North American breeds continued to reign supreme at the national level. Of the 15 breeds with the most entries at the 1936 Cruft's Show, the Alsatian and the Dachshund stood out as the only German breeds.[84] Indeed, in *The History of the Royal Army Veterinary Corps*, Clabby acknowledged: "It seems not unlikely that the best specimens of the [Doberman Pinscher] breed have not been available to the [British] Army." He further pointed out that the Doberman Pinscher's fine coat and "nervous disposition" often precluded their employment.[85] In the United States the Doberman Pinscher constituted the 15th most popular breed as determined by American Kennel Club registrations.[86] In fact, American breeders had developed a number of German breeds prior to the Second World War, so that the war did not completely prevent their access to the studs required to continue breeding.[87] Furthermore, compared to Britain, the United States' greater population likely allowed for more stringent requirements when recruiting military dogs. With between 13,000,000 and 15,000,000 canines, the United States was home to more than five times the number of canines in Britain by 1942.[88]

While the reasons Britons gave up their dogs undoubtedly varied among individuals, the willingness of many owners to provide animals seems to have stemmed from two primary considerations: the feeding of pets and patriotic sentiment. It is significant that the recruitment of animals for the Army's War Dogs Training School began at a point during the war in which rationing was particularly severe. Although rationing had commenced in early 1940, it was in 1941, as the historian Angus Calder

82   NARA: War Department Bureau of Public Relations, Five Breeds of Dogs Needed by Army for Scout Duty in Pacific, 4 June 1945; May-June 1945; Press and Radio News Releases, 1921-1947; War Department Special Staff Public Relations Division Branches-News Branch; RG 165; NACP.

83   'Our Friend the Dog: A "New" Breed in Germany', *Bucks Herald*, 27 May 1938, p. 2.

84   '4,000 Dogs on Show: Labradors the Most Popular Breed', *Lincolnshire Echo*, 12 February 1936, p. 5.

85   Clabby, *History of the RAVC*, p. 179. Although Clabby largely focused on the employment of dogs in the Second World War, his chapter on military dogs covered over four decades of the 20th century. Thus, his comments on Doberman Pinschers may not apply solely to the Second World War but likely refer to the British Army's experience with the breed prior to the early 1960s.

86   Henry R. Ilsley, 'U.S. Dog Registration Mark Set by Total of 84,525 during 1937', *New York Times*, 30 January 1938, p. 72.

87   Henry R. Ilsley, 'Plans for Increase in Dog Breeding Program Here Hit by Conditions Abroad', *New York Times*, 1 October 1939, p. 96 and Henry R. Ilsley, 'Drastic Order Issued in Germany Severe Shock to Canine Circles', *New York Times*, 14 July 1940, p. 67.

88   Fairfax Downey, *Dogs for Defense: American Dogs in the Second World War 1941-1945* (New York: Trustees of Dogs for Defence, Inc., 1955), 3 and Hansard: HC Deb 4 May 1943 vol 389 c33W.

put it, "when shortages of food... began to become oppressive."[89] As imported food-stuffs declined in 1941, certain foods became more costly and increasingly scarce, and individual rations were reduced. Costs continued to mount the following year; August 1942 was, according to Calder, "the peak of rationing" in the United Kingdom.[90] In April 1941, Mass Observation found that "difficulty of feeding pets" was among the "questions uppermost in the public mind" and thus considered by Britons to be nearly as pressing a concern as bombing on the Home Front or a potential German invasion.[91]

For many dog owners, such concerns influenced the decision to give up their animals.[92] A dog breeder from Liverpool, for example, donated an entire litter of Alsatians to the MAP in an effort to ensure the dogs received enough food.[93] A private in the British Army provided his dog to the Army's War Dogs Training School in 1942 because he felt his pet "would be better fed and looked after with [the Army] while [the dog owner] was in the Services."[94] Similarly, the owners of a Collie in Shropshire cited food shortages as the reason for providing their dog for military service.[95] Realising that many Britons were concerned about feeding their animals, the National Canine Defence League encouraged those with larger breeds, such as Alsatians, to donate their dogs to the war effort.[96] Similarly, in an article written for *Our Dogs*, Baldwin sought to persuade dog owners to give up their dogs by stressing that canines would receive sufficient food and excellent treatment at the MAP Guard Dog Training School:

> The dogs will all be really well looked after and have everything of the best. You can rely upon the dogs having just as much attention and care as if you had them at home... I would particularly like Alsatians or any dog which is a good, sharp, natural guard. In fact, I shall hope to be offered *every* Alsatian in England that is capable of doing the job. The dog will not be in any more danger than in everyday life and will be perfectly looked after by people who have been devoted to the breed all their lives. The owner will have no uneasy moments with his conscience about the food that the dog is consuming, and he will know that the dog is releasing a man for the army.[97]

89   Angus Calder, *The People's War: Britain 1939–1945* (London: Pimlico, 1992), pp. 71–72, 228.
90   Ibid, pp. 228, 231, 239, 276, 380.
91   MOA: File Report 651, Questions Uppermost in the Public Mind, 9 April 1941.
92   'Hundreds of Dogs Await "Call-Up"', *Gloucestershire Echo*, 2 June 1943, p. 1.
93   Ron Brown, *Jet of Iada DM, MFV* (Liverpool, 2006), pp. 13-15.
94   Airborne Assault Museum Archive, Duxford: Shelf 3F4 Box 4/9/1, Handwritten/typed account by Private J. Barringer.
95   William Randolph, 'Demobbing the War Dogs', *Dundee Evening Telegraph*, 4 September 1945, p. 2.
96   Leonard E. Naylor, 'Soldier Dogs', *Burnley Express and News*, 11 April 1942, p. 6.
97   J.Y. Baldwin, 'War Dogs', *Our Dogs*, 12 December 1941, p. 1213.

Some owners were also prompted by a willingness to further the British war effort. Upon donating her Alsatian to the Army's War Dogs Training School in April 1941, a Briton explained the motivation behind her decision: "Although I shall hate to part with him I'd like to think he was doing his bit."[98] Another dog owner expressed a similar sentiment: "My son is in the Middle East and he would be delighted to know that his dog is doing his bit, too."[99] When volunteering her dog, a wife and mother noted: "My husband has gone, my sons have gone, take my dog to help bring this cruel war to an early end."[100] The *Yorkshire Evening Post* reported in May 1942 that 14 dog owners in Leeds had thus far donated their pets. The RSPCA inspector who enrolled the dogs found that it was patriotism which spurred each owner to provide his animal.[101]

Such beliefs, and the actions they entailed, were certainly not exclusive to British dog owners. Indeed, the explanations provided by some Americans as to why they donated their dogs strongly resembled those given by British dog owners. A dog owner from Colorado, for example, gave up her pet because she "believed it was the proper and patriotic thing to do."[102] Similarly, a young boy in California penned a letter to the United States Secretary of War in which he explained that "to do something in this war" he would give up his pet dog.[103] As Skabelund has shown, every nation which utilised dogs was dependent on its civilian population for canine trainees. He rightly pointed out that the recruitment of dogs among civilians "linked, in both actual and symbolic ways, the home front to the battlefront." By giving up their dogs, owners were able to "prove their patriotism," as well as gain "a sense of personally participating in the war effort."[104]

Similarly, in a study of the perception and commemoration of military animals, Steven Johnston discussed the complex notion of patriotism as it pertained to the willingness of British and American dog owners to "sacrifice" their dogs for employment in war. According to Johnston, in making the decision to provide their dogs, owners perceived their own patriotism and affection for their pets as mutually *inclusive*. The concept of sacrifice, therefore, extended to one's pets:

> People love their dogs. They also love their countries... These loves prove to be compatible: if we all must make sacrifices in war, including the people we love, why not our dogs, too?... We want those we love to serve, we want to be proud

98   'Training Dogs for War Duties', *Yorkshire Post*, 30 April 1941, p. 1.
99   'War Dogs May Help to Win the War', *Morpeth Herald*, 31 July 1942, p. 4.
100 Quoted in Lloyd, 'Dog in War', p. 185.
101 'Dogs Join Up', *Yorkshire Evening Post*, 28 May 1942, p. 6.
102 NARA: Mrs Marsh Hargis to Senator Edwin C. Johnson, 21 May 1944; Decimal 454.3; Decimal Correspondence Files, 1940-1945; RG 407; NACP.
103 NARA: Don Thompson to Harry Stimson, Secretary of War, 3 April 1942; Decimal 454.25; Decimal Correspondence Files, 1940-1945; RG 407; NACP.
104 Skabelund, *Empire of Dogs*, pp. 154-155.

of them, and we want them to share our love of country... Dying for country, entailing a transition from pet to soldier, would only double the love (and pride and mourning).[105]

While Johnston's argument overlooked practical concerns, such as the feeding of pets during wartime rationing, his assertion that patriotism influenced many Britons to give up their pets is supported by the comments of several dog owners. Both Lloyd and Baldwin encouraged such a perception among dog owners. In a 1941 letter printed in the dog fancy publications *Our Dogs*, *Kennel Gazette* and *Tail-Wagger Magazine*, Lloyd emphasised that by contributing their pets, Britons carried out an act of patriotism which furthered the war effort:

> There must be many patriotic owners of dogs who would feel it an honour to see them actually engaged in helping to defeat the enemies of this country... In offering dogs for this work, owners can have every confidence that they are not only fulfilling a national obligation, but that their dogs will receive skilled care and attention.[106]

Baldwin also touched upon patriotism in an effort to obtain dogs for the MAP Guard Dog Training School. In contrast to Lloyd, however, he expressed the belief that dogs were capable of possessing a sense of allegiance or duty to Britain. In *Our Dogs*, he called upon the dog owner to allow his dog to "do his job for his country."[107] He further asserted: "It is the correct thing for our dogs to give us any help in their power."[108]

That sacrifice was prominent in the minds of many dog owners who gave up their pets was in accordance with wider contemporary depictions and perceptions of the Second World War. As the historian Sonya O. Rose has demonstrated, the Ministry of Information and the British press furthered the understanding that all Britons were making sacrifices to "do their bit" in the conflict. The perceived readiness of civilians to go without while enduring hardships was depicted as a uniquely British trait which served to bond all Britons together.[109] As Rose rightly argued, the wartime media propagated the idea that Britons "should be self-sacrificing, placing the community's interests and needs above their own."[110]

---

105 Steven Johnston, 'Animals in War: Commemoration, Patriotism, Death', *Political Research Quarterly*, 65:2 (2012), p. 363.
106 Letter from Lloyd in 'War Dogs—Fall In!', *Our Dogs*, p. 350 and 'On War Dogs', *Tail-Wagger Magazine*, May 1941, p. 99 and 'Club and Kennel Notes', *Kennel Gazette*, April 1941, p. 66.
107 Baldwin, 'War Dogs', *Our Dogs*, 12 December 1941, p. 1213.
108 Baldwin, Letter to the Editor, *Our Dogs*, 12 December 1941, p. 1211.
109 Sonya O. Rose, *Which People's War?: National Identity and Citizenship in Wartime Britain 1939-1945* (Oxford: Oxford University Press, 2003), pp. 2-14, 105.
110 Ibid, p. 14.

The Training, Care and Depiction of British Military Dogs

In the spring of 1941, the Army's War Dogs Training School was, according to Captain D.C.E. Danby of the RAVC, "in a modest way with a few dogs."[111] Within a few months of opening in Aldershot, however, the school relocated to Ickenham in northwest London. Here, the school operated out of Lloyd's personal kennel with around 40 canines.[112] By May 1942, some 80 canines were in training at the War Dogs Training School.[113] That month, the school relocated again, this time to Northaw in Hertfordshire. The expansive grounds in Northaw, which encompassed the Greyhound Racing Association Kennels and more than 70 acres, allowed for an enlarged war establishment.[114] By the following November, the Army's War Dogs Training School had turned out more than 300 canines, while a further 442 dogs were in training.[115] The school continued to expand as the war progressed; by June 1944, the war establishment allowed for 750 dogs.[116] Appendix II shows the entire war establishment, including human personnel, in 1944.

Training at the MAP Guard Dog Training School, which in November 1941 comprised just 15 canines,[117] also proceeded apace. By November 1943, some 665 dogs were either in training or actively employed as guards at MAP establishments on the Home Front.[118] During the course of the Second World War, the British Armed Forces turned out between 3,300 and 5,000 canines. Of these, the majority were attached to the British Army. The Army employed around 57 percent of military dogs utilised by the British Armed Forces in the Second World War, while canines trained at the MAP Guard Dog Training School constituted the remaining 43 percent.[119]

In order to qualify for training, dogs at the Army's War Dogs Training School were first subjected to gunfire. Any dogs which displayed considerable anxiety as a result of

---

111 Capt. D.C.E. Danby, 'A War Dogs' Training School', *Journal of the RAVC*, 15:2 (1944), p. 42.

112 S.M. 'Monty' Hunt, 'The War Dogs Training School', *Chiron Calling*, Summer 1995, p. 11.

113 Museum of Military Medicine: Box 14, War Diary of DAVRS, May 1942 and Danby, 'A War Dogs' Training School', *Journal of the RAVC*, p. 43.

114 Hunt, 'The War Dogs Training School', p. 11. According to Hunt, the school had 240 canines in training shortly after arriving in Northaw. See also: Museum of Military Medicine: Box 14, War Diary of DAVRS, March-June 1942. The enlarged war establishment put the number of dogs at 450.

115 Museum of Military Medicine: Box 14, War Diary of DAVRS, November 1942.

116 TNA: WO 32/10800, 24A, War Dogs Training School Home War Establishment, 20 June 1944.

117 TNA: AVIA 9/15, 351/250, Dog Scheme, Progress Report 1, 19 November 1941.

118 Museum of Military Medicine: Box 14, War Diary of DAVRS, November 1943.

119 TNA: WO 32/14999, 17A, Bennison to Moss, 2 October 1945. The percentages above were calculated using the figures provided by Bennison. According to Bennison, the British Army and the MAP employed some 2,000 and 1,500 canines, respectively. See also: Hansard: HC Deb 22 October 1946 vol 427 c1452-3 and Magnay, *Miscealleanous 'Q' Services*, pp. 62, 72.

battle noises were eliminated from the training process and restored to their owners. The remaining dogs then underwent a course in basic obedience. As before, any dogs regarded as unfit were turned away.[120] Of the dogs provided, approximately 55 percent qualified and subsequently completed training at one of the two schools.[121] As revealed by data collected prior to November 1943, nearly 50 percent of the dogs supplied to the Army's War Dogs Training School were released as unfit or unable to perform. By contrast, the MAP Guard Dog Training School turned away less than 25 percent of the dogs provided.[122] Consequently, a number of dogs turned down by the Army's War Dogs Training School performed well as part of the MAP scheme.[123] Table 2 shows the number of canines recruited for the Army's War Dogs Training School and the MAP Guard Dog Training School, the percentage accepted for training at each institution and the number employed by the British Army and the MAP upon completion of instruction as of November 1943.

Table 2 Military Dog Training and Employment Rates by Training Institution, 1943[124]

Training Institution	Number of Dogs Recruited for Trial	Dogs Accepted for Training (%)	Number of Trained Dogs on Employment
Army's War Dogs Training School, Northaw	2,275	52.1%	919
MAP Guard Dog Training School, Staverton	1,148	76.7%	665

The training of dogs at the Army's War Dogs Training School spanned between five and eight weeks, while courses at the MAP Guard Dog Training School lasted around five weeks.[125] At the War Dogs Training School, training focused on preparing dogs for specific roles, while a subsequent period of instruction allowed dogs to become accustomed to operating alongside their newly designated handlers.[126] Both schools encouraged servicemen who had an affinity for and previous knowledge of canines to serve as trainers and handlers.[127] Baldwin, for example, sought dog

---

120 'The Dogs of War', *Hull Daily Mail*, 2 June 1943, p. 4 and NAA: MP742/1, 240/6/324, Capt. H.O. Bamford, Training of War Dogs, 3 January 1945, p. 1.
121 Magnay, *Miscellaneous 'Q' Services*, p. 62.
122 Museum of Military Medicine: Box 14, War Diary of DAVRS, November 1943.
123 Ibid, February 1944.
124 Ibid, Report for the Period 4-17 September 1943, 17 November 1943.
125 Brig.-Gen. Murray, 'War Dogs', *Animal World*, September 1944, p. 68 and 'War Dogs', *Gloucestershire Echo*, 15 June 1944, p. 3.
126 Murray, 'War Dogs', *Animal World*, September 1944, p. 68.
127 TNA: WO 199/416, 89A, Draft of Tactical Employment of War Dogs, 13 August 1942 and Murray, 'War Dogs', *Animal World*, September 1944, p. 68 and 'War Dogs', *Our Dogs*, 12 December 1941, p. 1213.

breeders and trainers for the school's training staff. Through personal connections and advertisements in *Our Dogs*, he attracted a number of well-known dog fanciers, including breeders Margaret Griffin and Dorothy Homan, as well as E. Marshall of the Southern Alsatian Training Society.[128] Similarly, a number of trainers at the Army's War Dogs Training School were dog fanciers in peacetime. Captain John Garle, an instructor at the school between 1942 and 1945, had extensive knowledge of foxhounds, while one of the school's training officers served as Secretary of the Kennel Club.[129]

According to *Tactical Employment of War Dogs*, a War Office training manual issued to Home Forces in 1942, soldiers drawn from infantry units to serve as dog handlers were expected to "have a natural love for dogs."[130] In this vein, Eastern Command (Home Forces) called upon units in the command to provide for patrol dog instruction at the Army's War Dogs Training School "only men who are fond of dogs or who have had experience in handling them."[131] Monty Hunt, a corporal in the Wiltshire Regiment who grew up with sporting and pet dogs, was one of three soldiers in his battalion to train as a handler at the War Dogs Training School when volunteers were called for in 1942. He remained a handler until the following year, when he joined the War Dogs Training School as an instructor.[132] Handlers in the RAF Police were similarly expected to be volunteers "keen to work with dogs."[133]

Lloyd, in *The Book of the Dog*, stressed the importance of the relationship between handler and dog:

> The whole success of the work depended on the suitability of the one for the other… It quickly became apparent that the temperament of both man and dog must be studied and the combination made on this alone. Dogs who were utter failures with one type of handler were in the hands of another just as conspicuously successful.[134]

Like Lloyd, several former dog handlers reflected on the significance of the handler's role during training and on operations. In an interview with the Imperial War

---

128 'War Dogs', *Our Dogs*, 12 December 1941, p. 1213 and 'Notes & News of the Breeds', *Our Dogs*, 19 December 1941, p. 1263 and 'Notes & News of the Breeds', *Our Dogs*, 26 December 1941, p. 1283.
129 D. Hipgrave, 'The Hook, Northaw, The Army War Dogs' Training School, 1942-45', *Journal of the Potters Bar and District Historical Society*, 8 (1995), p. 5.
130 TNA: WO 199/416, 89, Draft of Tactical Employment of War Dogs, 13 August 1942.
131 TNA: WO 199/2537, Employment of Guard Dogs, 33A, General Staff, Eastern Command, 9 November 1942.
132 IWM: 94/1219, S.M. Hunt, 'A Brief Look into the Life of the War Dogs Training School, 1941-1946', Book 1, p. 2 and Book 2, p. 77.
133 TNA: AIR 2/8734, 19A, C.E.H. James to Air Officer, 23 December 1943 and 99A, Air Ministry Order 1058, Employment of Patrol Dogs at R.A.F. Stations, 25 October 1945.
134 Lloyd, 'Dog in War', pp. 184-185.

Museum, Monty Hunt maintained that the assignment of "the right handler to the right dog" was crucial. Echoing the point made by Lloyd, he explained: "Some dogs would work with some people and yet not with another."[135] Instructions related to the employment of mine detection dogs emphasised the combined effort required by both dog and handler and stressed "the mood of the handler is reflected in the dog."[136] Wartime training manuals emphasised that trained dogs were prone to errors if not employed according to instructions. *Tactical Employment of War Dogs*, for example, warned that "dogs cannot be treated as machines" and made clear that each dog differed in behaviour and effectiveness on operations. Thus, it was up to the humans involved, as "handlers are the only people who know each dog's peculiarities."[137] Moreover, instructions related to the employment of military police dogs in North Africa suggest that dogs were not seen as dispensable. The instructions, distributed in early 1944, urged military policemen: "Remember always – You have a valuable Dog, doing great work. We cannot afford to lose them."[138]

It is unclear if Lloyd or Baldwin drew upon the expertise gained by Richardson and Waley in the First World War, but as Robert Kirk has pointed out, the training scheme developed by mine detection dog instructors was remarkably similar to and seemed to emulate the training techniques promoted by Richardson a quarter of a century earlier.[139] British mine detection dog instruction closely resembled that of messenger dogs in the First World War, as both training schemes discouraged punishment while incorporating food as a means to encourage canines.[140] Similarly, directions for training military police dogs in the Middle East and North Africa recommended verbal praise and emphasised the importance of trust, patience and repetition during instruction:

> It is essential to obtain the whole confidence of your dog… Under no circum-
> stances must you ask too much of him or let him down, let him realise that he
> can trust you at all times… If you start an exercise always finish it no matter
> how long it takes you, for, once your dog has completed an exercise either rightly
> or wrongly he will do the same next time. SO MAKE SURE HE DOES IT

---

135 IWM: 16497, Interview with Silvester Montague 'Monty' Hunt, 1 February 1996, Reel 1.
136 TNA: AVIA 22/871, Detection of Mines by Dogs, Mine Detection Dogs, undated.
137 TNA: WO 199/416, 89A, Draft of Tactical Employment of War Dogs, 13 August 1942.
138 TNA: WO 204/7732, Military Police Dog Units Organisation: Correspondence, Instructions on Use and Training of Dog Police, Corps of Military Police, 20 February 1944.
139 Kirk, 'In Dogs We Trust?', pp. 4-7.
140 Richardson, *British War Dogs*. p. 70. Training carried out at the War Dog School was, in the words of Richardson, "based on appeal," as he considered "coercion [in messenger dog training] is of no avail." He also eschewed corporal punishment: "Under no circumstances whatever must [the dog] be roughly handled or roughly spoken to. If it makes a mistake, or is slack in its work when being trained, it is never chastised, but is merely shown how to do it over again." For a detailed description of mine detection dog instruction, see War Office, *Training of War Dogs* (1952), pp. 54-57.

RIGHT AT ALL TIMES. Remember dogs are creatures of habits repeating what they have been taught.[141]

Moreover, guidance provided to Deputy Provost Marshals of airfields where dogs instructed at the Army's War Dogs Training School were attached urged personnel to "always praise the dog for a job well done" and recommended giving "a piece of meat as a reward" when dogs successfully finished patrols.[142] To be sure, such methods were not unique to the Second World War or to military dog training but had been utilised by dog trainers prior to the war. As shown in Chapter 1, a number of dog-related publications and training manuals in the interwar period favoured the use of repetition and reward over physical punishment or the "breaking" of dogs.

This was in stark contrast to the United States, where trainers did not use food as an incentive. The QMC training manual recommended that instructors refrain from "reward[ing] a military dog by feeding him tidbits, as he will become accustomed to this form of reward and expect it… in the field."[143] Furthermore, while British trainers generally eschewed corporal punishment,[144] American training practices allowed, and in some instances recommended, that dogs experience mental or physical discomfort as part of the training process. Although the training manuals of both the QMC and the Marine Corps emphasised that trainers and handlers "must never lose patience or become irritated" with their dogs, the same instructions acknowledged:

> It is seldom necessary to resort to physical punishment to teach a lesson to a sensitive dog. Withholding of praise, a rebuking tone, or even 'No' said reprovingly, are usually sufficient punishment for him. If the dog is callous or insensitive, punishment in his case must be more severe… Real punishment should be inflicted as a last resort and only for deliberate disobedience, stubbornness, or defiance when the dog has learned better.[145]

141 TNA: WO 204/7732, Instructions on Use and Training, Appendix H and Appendix I.
142 TNA: AIR 2/8734, 28A, Instructions for the Handling of V.P. Dogs from the War Dogs Training School and Advice by the Head Trainer and Veterinary Officer for Commanding Officers Upon Completion of Dog Handlers' Course Held at the War Dogs Training School, 15 January 1944.
143 NARA: War Department Technical Manual No.10-396, War Dogs, 1 July 1943 (TM 10-396), p. 58; Decimal 300.7; Decimal Correspondence Files, 1940-1945; RG 407; NACP.
144 War Office, *Training of War Dogs* (1952), p. 33. According to the training manual: "Physical violence, even for wilful disobedience, must never be resorted to as the dog may become sullen, stubborn or cowed. If it is necessary to administer a rebuke, a gruff word or a sharp tap on the hind quarters should suffice." See also: TNA: WO 291/2673, 37B, Outlines of Training of Various Types of War Dogs at the War Dogs Training School, British Army of the Rhine (BAOR) Training Centre, undated. Although the training of guard dogs called for instructors to "bait" canines, the instructions made clear that the use of a rod was "calculated to annoy and not hurt."
145 NARA: TM 10-396, pp. 57-58; Decimal 300.7; Decimal Correspondence Files, 1940-1945; RG 407; NACP and 1130/1, U.S. Marine Corps War Dog Training

As shown in Chapter 4, the contrast in British and American training methods was particularly evident when it came to preparing canines for mine detection.

Following a tour of the MAP Guard Dog Training School in late 1942, an RSPCA inspector told *Animal World* that he felt "very satisfied to know that all the animals were so happy and comfortable."[146] RSPCA chairman Sir Robert Gower reached a similar conclusion upon touring the Army's War Dogs Training School.[147] Although it is likely the RSPCA sought to assuage dog owners whose pets were in training at the schools, the available evidence suggests that the RAVC and staff at the War Dogs Training School took many steps to maintain the health and welfare of dogs. Prior to the Army's War Dogs Training School relocating to Northaw, the DAVRS assigned a Veterinary Officer to supervise veterinary care and monitor canine health at the training facility.[148] Additional RAVC staff, known as dressers, completed a range of tasks, including monitoring the dogs' temperatures, cleaning their teeth and administering vaccinations and medications.[149] The site in Northaw already included several permanent kennels, as it was recently home to the Greyhound Racing Association and was only vacated in the days prior to the arrival of the Army's War Dogs Training School. The kennels, the majority of which were brick structures, were shared quarters with space for two dogs apiece.[150]

Beginning in 1942, members of the Auxiliary Territorial Service (ATS) assumed responsibility for the maintenance of the school's kennels. Like the male trainers and handlers at the school, several of the ATS servicewomen had worked with dogs or other animals prior to the Second World War.[151] Two female privates, for example, worked with various animal species at the Liverpool Zoo before joining the ATS,[152] while another servicewoman worked at a civilian dog kennel earlier in the war.[153] By

Manual, pp. 52-53; 1130 Animal to 1130/1 War Dog Training Manual; General Correspondence, 1 January 1939 to 30 June 1950; Correspondence Files of the Office of the Commandant and Headquarters Support Division Central Files Section, 1939-1950; RG 127; NACP.

146 'War Dogs', *Animal World*, December 1942, p. 91. The article indicated that the RSPCA inspector toured "another War Dog School." Thus, the training centre which he toured was likely the MAP Guard Dog Training School.

147 Ibid. The article referred to the school inspected by Gower as "one of the War Dogs Training Schools."

148 Museum of Military Medicine: Box 14, War Diary of DAVRS, January and March 1942 and Danby, 'A War Dogs' Training School', *Journal of the RAVC*, pp. 42-44.

149 Danby, 'A War Dogs' Training School', *Journal of the RAVC*, pp. 43-44.

150 Museum of Military Medicine: Box 14, War Diary of DAVRS, April 1942 and Murray, 'War Dogs', *Animal World*, September 1944, p. 67. Newly-arrived dogs and casualties, however, were kept separately in individual kennels.

151 Danby, 'A War Dogs' Training School', *Journal of the RAVC*, pp. 42-43 and J. Vernon, 'A.T.S.', *Journal of the RAVC*, 18:1 (1946), p. 21.

152 'Training Dogs for the Army', *Manchester Guardian*, 3 June 1943, p. 3.

153 IWM: 94/1219, Hunt, 'A Brief Look', Book 3, p. 157.

late 1944, ATS staff at the Army's War Dogs Training School numbered 47, nearly all of whom served in the kennels.[154]

At the Army's War Dogs Training School, newly-acquired dogs were vaccinated against distemper and housed in separate kennels for up to 10 days. While in quarantine, dogs were monitored by veterinary staff who noted any changes in temperature.[155] According to the former DAVRS Brigadier-General C.A. Murray, many dogs exhibited signs of nervousness after entering the school. Such behaviours, however, were usually only temporary. In *Animal World*, Murray explained: "Personal attention and patience are very often all that are necessary to overcome this tendency."[156] Periodic sick parades allowed veterinary personnel to monitor ailing canines. In addition, the school benefited from an on-site hospital and pharmacy, as well as X-ray equipment at a laboratory in close proximity.[157]

For many military dogs, the standard of care provided by RAVC personnel at the Army's War Dogs Training School was an improvement from peacetime. According to a report compiled by the DAVRS in late 1942, several canines "require[d] a veterinary overhaul" after entering the school.[158] In 1944, the *Journal of the Royal Army Veterinary Corps* published data concerning the health of dogs at the War Dogs Training School. The data revealed that, during 12 months in 1942 and 1943, less than five percent of canines at the school died as a result of disease or injury. While diarrhoea and intestinal parasites, such as tapeworms and roundworms, were prevalent among dogs at the school, serious maladies were rare.[159] Indeed, the overwhelming majority of illnesses at the school stemmed from intestinal parasites. During warmer months, dogs were likely to suffer from skin afflictions owing to fleas and lice, although such afflictions were largely diminished when the school eliminated straw from the kennels.[160] In addition to being vaccinated against distemper, each dog was required to provide two healthy faecal samples prior to leaving the school.[161] Furthermore, while many dog owners struggled to feed their pets, dogs at the Army's War Dogs Training School and the MAP Guard Dog Training School were guaranteed a fare of meat, biscuits and vegetables.[162]

---

154 NAA: MP742/1, 240/6324, Appendix A, War Dogs Training School Home War Establishment. Seven ATS servicewomen performed administrative roles, such as answering the telephone, while the remaining 40 were listed as "kennel orderlies."
155 Danby, 'A War Dogs' Training School', *Journal of the RAVC*, p. 43.
156 Murray, 'War Dogs', *Animal World*, September 1944, p. 69.
157 RSPCA Archive, Horsham (RSPCA Archive): Animals-War Dogs, Danby, 'The Management of War Dogs', undated.
158 Museum of Military Medicine: Box 14, War Diary of DAVRS, DAVRS Report for the Second Period, November 1942.
159 Danby, 'A War Dogs' Training School', *Journal of the RAVC*, pp. 57-62.
160 Clabby, *History of the RAVC*, pp. 176-177.
161 RSPCA Archive: Danby, 'Management of War Dogs'.
162 Museum of Military Medicine: Box 14, War Diary of DAVRS, October and December 1942.

Although less information is available regarding the health of dogs following their departure from the Army's War Dogs Training School, it is clear that military dogs continued to be looked after by veterinary personnel even after their deployment to theatres of war. Each mine detection dog platoon was assigned an RAVC sergeant,[163] and in northwest Europe, RAVC personnel performed veterinary examinations and ensured canine mine detectors were vaccinated against rabies.[164] In addition, each mine detection dog platoon was provided with two veterinary chests containing an assortment of bandages, antiseptics and medicines.[165] Following the Allied invasion of Normandy, the AVRS operated a canine veterinary hospital in northwest Europe to care for the guard and mine detection dogs which deployed to France in 1944 as part of 21st Army Group.[166] The war diary of the AVRS revealed that veterinary personnel routinely examined guard and mine detection dogs in northwest Europe.[167] In correspondence with the Army's War Dogs Training School, the officer commanding, No. 2 Dog Platoon noted that the dogs had sufficient quantities of food in northwest Europe. He also made clear that RAVC personnel "visit us regularly, and have attended to our needs most carefully."[168] Similarly, in the Middle East, a small number of RAVC staff was included on the war establishments of both the CMP dog training facility and individual units.[169]

Outside of the Army's War Dogs Training School, the diets of military dogs varied according to role and the theatre of war in which they were employed. Guard dogs deployed to vulnerable points in the United Kingdom prior to March 1943 received around two pounds of meat, biscuits and vegetables each day, although the War Office advised that they consume scraps when feasible.[170] In contrast, canines utilised by the

---

163 TNA: WO 205/1173, Mine Detection by Dogs, 3C, Training Instruction on the Handling of Dogs for Mine Detection, undated.
164 TNA: WO 171/191B, War Diary of Veterinary and Remount Services, August–September, December 1944 and TNA: WO 171/3937, Veterinary and Remount, War Diary of Veterinary and Remount Services, January and August 1945.
165 NAA: MP742/1, 240/6324, Appendix F, Contents of Veterinary Chests, 15 December 1944.
166 'Administrative History of the Veterinary and Remount Branch, 21st Army Group, on the Continent', *Journal of the RAVC*, 17:2 (1946), p. 66.
167 TNA: WO 171/191B, Veterinary and Remount Services, War Diary, August–December 1944. The August 1944 war diary noted, however, that the constant redeployment of units created logistical problems for RAVC staff charged with looking after military dogs.
168 Museum of Military Medicine: Box 14, File of Capt. James Rankin Davison, Technical Report, J.R. Davison to Commandant, War Dogs Training School, 7 October 1944.
169 TNA: WO 169/13320, War Diary of Military Police Dog Training School, February 1943 and TNA: WO 169/13321, War Diary of No. 1 Military Police Dog Section, February 1943 and TNA: WO 169/13322, War Diary of 'A' Military Police Dog Section, July 1943 and TNA: WO 169/13323, War Diary of No. 3 Military Police Dog Section, October 1943 and TNA: WO 169/13324, War Diary of No. 4 Military Police Dog Section, December 1943 and TNA: WO 169/13325, War Diary of No. 5 Military Police Dog Section, December 1943.
170 TNA: WO 199/2537, 19A, Memorandum from War Office and 41B, Memorandum from War Office, 8 March 1943. The War Office, in March 1943, increased this amount by approximately four ounces while reiterating that "dogs will, however, continue to be

RAVC personnel attend to a mine detection dog in France, July 1944. (© Imperial War Museum (B 6496))

CMP in North Africa were given up to three pounds of meat, bones, bread and vegetables. Like guard dogs on the Home Front, however, military police dogs in North Africa were expected to eat scraps to supplement or replace their rations.[171] The War Office was particularly vague regarding the feeding of mine detection dogs, noting in instructions supplied to RE units:

> It is unlikely that special dog food will be available regularly when on active service, although reserve rations in the shape of dog biscuits and tinned meat should be carried whenever possible. To avoid possible shortage of dog rations, it is recommended that the dogs be included on the human ration strength.[172]

Compared to the Army's War Dogs Training School, less is known about the site of the MAP Guard Dog Training School. According to an article published in the *Gloucestershire Echo* in June 1944, the training facility in Staverton could hold some 200

subsisted, where possible, on cookhouse scraps of the unit to which they are attached." The amount prescribed in 1943 also applied to canines employed by the RAF.

171   TNA: WO 204/7732, Instructions on Use and Training, Appendix E, Notes for Personnel Responsible for Care of Dogs and Appendix G, Ration and Fuel Scale.

172   TNA: WO 205/1173, 3C, Training Instruction, undated.

canines.[173] An Alsatian breeder who toured the MAP Guard Dog Training School in 1943 noted that dogs were quartered in individual kennels "with any amount of straw for its bedding and in conditions which are completely draught-proof."[174] He further revealed that canines employed at aerodromes in the vicinity were billeted on-site in individual kennels. As was the case at the Army's War Dogs Training School, veterinary personnel at the MAP Guard Dog Training School administered distemper vaccinations to incoming dogs at the school's satellite location in Redditch. Thereafter, they underwent approximately three weeks of obedience training in Redditch prior to commencing guard dog instruction in Staverton.[175]

In contrast to the First World War, when the National Canine Defence League spoke out against the employment and treatment of military dogs and other animals, the Second World War saw less resistance from animal welfare organisations and activists over the use of canines. As the historian Hilda Kean has shown, such groups were primarily concerned with caring for animals affected by the war on the Home Front.[176] In an account of the RSPCA in the Second World War, Arthur Moss and Elizabeth Kirby acknowledged that the procurement of military dogs did ignite some controversy. In a chapter devoted to the use of dogs in the war, the authors admitted: "Criticism has been levelled at the R.S.P.C.A. for lending its powerful aid to the obtaining of war dogs. It has been contended that the Society exists to protect animals, not to expose them to danger." Moss and Kirby dismissed such claims, however, by arguing:

> What would have been the misery which all British dogs would have undergone had the Nazis won? British war dogs have saved human lives as well as those of their own kind who remained in this country, doing an equally useful war work as sheep-dogs and the like. On that ground alone, their employment in the war was fully justified.[177]

The *Animals' Defender* condemned the Soviet use of dogs to target tanks, yet hardly objected to the employment of dogs by the British Armed Forces.[178] Similarly, the *Manchester Guardian*, in an article published in May 1941, made no mention of ethical concerns related to the use of dogs in war. Perhaps in an effort to assuage British dog owners, the newspaper downplayed the seriousness of canines in war by using humour

---

173 'War Dogs', *Gloucestershire Echo*, 15 June 1944, p. 3.
174 Revered Farrar, 'Guard Dog Training School', *Our Dogs*, 17 December 1943, p. 1223.
175 Ibid.
176 Kean, *Animal Rights*, pp. 167-170, 191.
177 Moss and Kirby, *Animals Were There*, p. 133.
178 'Suicide Dogs', *Animals' Defender*, August 1942, p. 13 and 'Dogs of War', *Animals' Defender*, June 1941, pp. 81-82. While the June 1941 edition of *Animals' Defender* questioned the decision of dog owners to give up their dogs, as "separat[ing] a faithful dog from those it knows and trusts may be an act of great cruelty," the journal did not denounce the employment of dogs per se.

to emphasise the role of dogs as companions: "Seeing how greatly most dogs like soldiers and how much most soldiers like dogs a good time should be had by all."[179] An article in the *Western Daily Press* went so far as to argue that as "comrades in arms," Britain's military dogs "will revel in their work."[180]

While the press seemingly ignored the ethical implications of utilising dogs in military roles, correspondence between the DAVRS and Engineer-in-Chief Major General C.J.S. King revealed that the employment of dogs for mine detection was expected to spark controversy. Brigadier G.A. Kelly of the DAVRS explained:

> The majority [of military dogs] are loaned by the public and an undertaking has been given to return them to their owners when no longer required. If it becomes known that dogs in this category are being used for the detection of mines, I anticipate violent protests. The public may become antagonistic and offers to loan dogs to the Army and other Ministries, on which I am almost entirely dependent, will cease.[181]

Upon learning the British Army employed mine detection dogs in northwest Europe, a Briton penned a letter to the editor of the *Gloucestershire Echo* in which he argued against the use of animals in war:

> If we humans are lunatic enough to believe that bayonets, submarines, bombs, and 16-inch shells, are the only means to settle differences, surely this is no reason to drag horses and dogs into our disputes. I was horrified when Germany began to launch their 'flying bombs,' being so utterly inhuman. But is it worse, or less inhuman, less un-Christian, less un-British, to sacrifice horses and dogs for our benefit in such devilish circumstances as the modern battlefield?[182]

Yet complaints such as these seemed to have been rare. Alternatively, the press may have excluded similar letters from publication so as not to damage morale. The available records, as well as contemporary newspapers, provide no indication that an outcry such as that predicted by Kelly occurred during the war. While the employment of mine detection dogs was not concealed from the British public,[183] it is likely that most

179 'Unmechanised Warfare', *Manchester Guardian*, 6 May 1941, p. 4.
180 'Canine "Cadets"', *Western Daily Press*, 11 April 1942, p. 5.
181 Museum of Military Medicine: Box 14, Reports and Correspondence between UK and USA on Training and Trials of Use of Dogs as Mine Detectors, G.A. Kelly to Maj. Gen. C.J.S. King, 6 June 1943.
182 'Dogs on Battlefield', Letter to the Editor, *Gloucestershire Echo*, 5 July 1944, p. 3.
183 'Dog Mine Smellers Save Troops' Lives', *Citizen*, 9 August 1944, p. 2 and 'Kirkcaldy Man in Dog Platoon', *Fife Free Press*, 2 December 1944, p. 4.

owners of dogs employed by the British Army were not notified of the specific roles in which their pets were utilised until after the war.[184]

Throughout the Second World War, military dogs were portrayed by the British government and the press as willing and patriotic participants in the war against the Axis powers. Furthermore, their conduct on operations was often viewed through an anthropomorphised lens; servicemen and the press interpreted the behaviours and actions of military dogs as humanlike responses to feelings of courage or patriotism. The "heroic" feats of military dogs, and their perceived readiness to further the Allied cause, were reported in national and provincial newspapers and perpetuated by the British military. The purpose behind such "figurative mobilization," as the historian Aaron Skabelund has shown, was "rallying people for total war."[185]

National and local newspapers frequently employed terms and phrases, such as "recruits" and "join up," in articles on military dogs, while also comparing their employment to that of soldiers. By referring to dogs in such terms, the press encouraged the perception of military dogs as combatants like their human counterparts. The *Hull Daily Mail*, for example, emphasised similarities between military dogs and human servicemen, acknowledging that trained dogs were "like any other recruit to the Army."[186] Similarly, the *Daily Mirror* published an article entitled "Dogs as Soldiers," in which it referred to canines as "recruits."[187] In another article, the newspaper featured a photograph of a dog described as "one of the first dogs to 'join up' for war service."[188] A similar photograph appeared in the 18 May 1942 edition of the *Citizen*. The dog was shown standing on hind legs next to a table as an RSPCA inspector completed the relevant paperwork. The accompanying caption asserted that the Alsatian was "Gloucester's first dog recruit."[189] Descriptions and photographs such as these suggested that dogs possessed agency. The dog was depicted as a willing and able participant with the capacity to "join up" of his own volition. Dog owners, too, seemed to believe that dogs understood the complexities of war. A dog owner who gave her Airedale Terrier to the Army's War Dogs Training School told the *Daily Mirror* that the canine "seemed to know what was expected of him."[190]

Contemporary tributes by animal welfare organisations also encouraged the anthropomorphic treatment of dogs. The RSPCA introduced a medal for military canines and sent certificates to owners whose dogs had performed "special acts of bravery and

184 Randolph, 'Demobbing the War Dogs', *Dundee Evening Telegraph*, 4 September 1945, p. 2.
185 Skabelund, *Empire of Dogs*, p. 167.
186 'The Dogs of War', *Hull Daily Mail*, 2 June 1943. For additional examples, see 'Hundreds of Dogs Await "Call-Up"', *Gloucestershire Echo*, 2 June 1943 and 'War Dogs May Help to Win the War', *Morpeth Herald*, 31 July 1942 and 'War Dogs', *Western Daily Press*, 11 April 1942.
187 'Dogs as Soldiers', *Daily Mirror*, 6 May 1941, p. 1.
188 'Your Dog is "Called Up" for War Job', *Daily Mirror*, 5 May 1942, p. 5.
189 'Gloucester's First Dog Recruit', *Citizen*, 18 May 1942, p. 4.
190 'Her Dog Has Joined Army to Avenge her Brother', *Daily Mirror*, 24 April 1943, p. 5.

devotion to duty in hazardous circumstances."[191] The PDSA established the Allied Forces Mascot Club to honour animals employed by or otherwise associated with the militaries of Allied nations. In addition, the animal welfare organisation introduced the Dickin Medal, an honour described by the Secretary of the Allied Forces Mascot Club as "the supreme award for animal heroism."[192] The Dickin Medal was already recognised as "the Animals' V[ictoria] C[ross]" by the mid-1940s.[193] When the first canine Dickin Medal recipient was honoured in 1944, the citation referenced the dog's "constant devotion to duty."[194] Appendix III, which lists every canine Dickin Medal recipient decorated for work carried out during the Second World War, provides additional examples of such anthropomorphised language as applied to military and Civil Defence dogs. By assigning esteemed traits and behaviours generally used to venerate humans to animals, animal welfare organisations such as the PDSA and RSPCA encouraged the perception that the same attributes were valued and expected in animals. Such recognition further blurred the line between human and animal, while also suggesting that military animals possessed agency.

191   TNA: WO 32/14999, 1A, Acting Chief Secretary, RSPCA to Brig. C. Kelly, 19 April 1945 and 2A, Acting Chief Secretary, RSPCA to Lt. Col. J.C. Bennison, 15 June 1945.
192   St. Hill Bourne, *They Also Serve*, pp. 1-4.
193   Ibid, p. 3.
194   'PDSA Dickin Medal', online <https://www.pdsa.org.uk/what-we-do/animal-awards-programme/pdsa-dickin-medal> (accessed 29 January 2018).

3

Guard, Military Police and Patrol Dogs

During one month in 1944, the dogs of No. 1 Military Police Dog Section of the Corps of Military Police (CMP) led to the arrests of 32 trespassers at vulnerable points in Egypt. The arrests prevented the loss of more than £1020 in British equipment and supplies.[1] Jerry, a dog employed by the section, earned a "reputation of never missing his man" during his tenure with the CMP. By August 1945, the Boxer had garnered 21 arrests, and along with his handler, recovered a total of £764 in War Department *matériel*.[2] Jerry was one of many dogs employed by the British Armed Forces to protect vulnerable points, supplies or servicemen during the Second World War. Guard or military police dogs were utilised by the British Army, the MAP and the RAF to defend aerodromes and other vulnerable points, as well as equipment and supplies. The CMP and the RAF Police also established training schools outside the United Kingdom. In addition, dogs trained at the Army's War Dogs Training School were employed on infantry patrols.

Archival material concerning the use of guard and patrol dogs, although plentiful, is primarily concerned with the establishment and administration of the Army and the MAP dog schemes rather than the performance of canines. As a result, an incomplete picture has emerged regarding the employment of guard and patrol dogs on the Home Front and abroad. A further consequence of the lack of archival material concerning the performance of guard and patrol dogs is that the relevant sections of this chapter must rely on anecdotal evidence. By contrast, meticulous records kept by the dog sections of the CMP provide for a more in-depth study regarding the performance of military police dogs in the Middle East, North Africa and Italy.

---

1   TNA: WO 169/17751, 1 Dog Section, War Diary, October 1944.
2   TNA: WO 32/14999, 16A, J.W. Scott to DAVRS, 14 August 1945.

The Demand for and Employment of Guard Dogs on the British Home Front

As war became increasingly likely in the late 1930s, the British government took steps to ensure the security of military installations and other sites throughout the country. Prior to the Second World War, a Vulnerable Points Sub-Committee was formed to operate under the aegis of the Defence Committee. In June 1939, the sub-committee submitted an inventory of military installations and other sites thought to be "vulnerable" to sabotage if Britain became involved in a war. At that time, the accepted definition of a vulnerable point was broad so as to include sites deemed "necessary for the conduct of military operations," as well as those considered "essential for the maintenance of the life of the community."[3]

Following the British declaration of war in early September 1939, several thousand servicemen were called upon to guard the sites recommended by the sub-committee. By November 1939, some 37,500 troops had been posted to vulnerable points on the British Home Front. As Britain prepared for a German invasion following the fall of Belgium and the Netherlands in May 1940, additional servicemen were posted to aerodromes and other vulnerable points. By late July 1940, over 70,000 British Army personnel, including some 60,000 soldiers drawn from Field Force and Home Defence, were tasked with guarding vulnerable points in Britain. The incessant need for more servicemen at numerous vulnerable points prevented the adequate training of the Field Army. Thus, the government, in the summer of 1940, created the role of Vulnerable Points Adviser to coordinate the defence of significant installations on the Home Front.[4]

The Vulnerable Points Adviser was ordered to make "every effort... to release troops of the Field Army and to replace them by other formations."[5] He was further tasked with reassessing the government's inventory of vulnerable points to determine which sites were "of first priority for vital production or for national security."[6] In this vein, a new classification scheme for vulnerable points was introduced the following year. Vulnerable points were grouped by importance; those accorded VP1 status were of primary concern, as they were deemed "vital to [the British] War Effort or which, by virtue of their location, represent[ed] to the enemy likely targets and objectives for air-borne attack."[7] Sites designated VP2, VP3 or VP4 were believed to be less susceptible to sabotage and thus relied more heavily on the Home Guard and civil police as guards.[8]

---

3   TNA: CAB 112/1, Protection of Vulnerable Points, History, Item 1: History of Vulnerable Points, p. 1.
4   Ibid, pp. 2-4.
5   CAB 112/26, Extracts and Copies of Chiefs of Staff Committee Memoranda on Vulnerable Points, 2B, Instructions for the Vulnerable Points Adviser, 30 September 1940.
6   CAB 112/26, 2B, Instructions for the Vulnerable Points Adviser, 30 September 1940.
7   CAB 112/26, 85A, Revised Memorandum by the Vulnerable Points Adviser, 8 July 1941.
8   Ibid.

In addition to canines, the War Office utilised a number of human means to conserve manpower during the Second World War. In May 1940, the War Office allowed for the creation of the Home Guard, a paramilitary force composed of volunteers devoted to protecting the British Home Front from invasion. Known as the Local Defence Volunteers (LDV) until July 1940, the Home Guard undertook varying responsibilities at different points during the war. As more servicemen were deployed outside the United Kingdom, the Home Guard became increasingly significant in the eyes of the War Office and GHQ Home Forces and its members were further relied upon to augment British Army personnel on the Home Front.[9] Like the military dog scheme, the Home Guard was viewed by the War Office prior to and shortly after the outbreak of the Second World War as a somewhat frivolous or unnecessary endeavour. A similar organisation developed during the First World War had not survived the interwar period, and although some civilians and MPs in the 1930s expressed the need for a volunteer defence scheme, the War Office made no move to institute such an organisation in the months surrounding the onset of the Second World War.[10] Yet, as the historian S.P. MacKenzie rightly noted, changes in the course of the war meant that by early 1940, the Home Guard "appeared so urgently necessary."[11]

Then, in early 1941, the CMP established a VP Wing specifically "to police selected military establishments and V.Ps. in order to release infantry units for other duties."[12] Composed of servicemen considered unfit for combat, CMP (VP) units were expected to patrol military installations and other sites in part to detect and apprehend trespassers.[13] By August 1941, nearly 3,700 CMP (VP) guards were charged with defending vulnerable points on the Home Front, thus enabling more than 7,350 soldiers to resume training.[14] The number of military policemen continued to increase, so that by late 1943, over 350 vulnerable points were defended by approximately 7,200 CMP (VP) servicemen.[15]

Government records indicate that the War Office contemplated the employment of dogs to defend vulnerable points shortly after the outbreak of the Second World War. In October 1939, Army officials consulted with H.S. Lloyd regarding the potential use of dogs on the Home Front. Representatives from the War Office showed interest in Lloyd's recommendation that canines be utilised at aerodromes and other military

9   S.P. MacKenzie, *The Home Guard: A Military and Political History* (Oxford: Oxford University Press, 1996).
10   Ibid, pp. 16-26.
11   Ibid, p. 17.
12   TNA: WO 199/2168, Corps of Military Police (V.P.), 1A, Southern Command to 5 Corps, 25 January 1941.
13   TNA: WO 199/2168, Series of Lectures for Recruits C.M.P. (V.P. Wing), undated and TNA: CAB 112/1, History of Vulnerable Points, p. 6.
14   TNA: CAB 112/1, History of Vulnerable Points, pp. 5-6.
15   TNA: CAB 112/26, Summary of Personnel Employed in Protective Duties, 6 November 1943.

installations.[16] With the permission of the War Office, Lloyd provided a trained dog for a seven day trial at RAF Northolt in west London.[17] Major John Shanson, who oversaw the defence of the direction finding station at RAF Northolt, noted in correspondence with Eastern Command Headquarters that the canine was "friendly with all men at the Guard Post and although occasionally barking during the night, it did not appear that he would do so on the approach of any human being." The dog's lacklustre performance led Shanson to conclude that "it would appear to be unsafe to rely upon [dogs] in place of a [human] sentry."[18] Lieutenant Colonel Cox of Eastern Command (Home Forces) concurred with Shanson's assessment. Thus, the War Office, in November 1939, abandoned plans to utilise dogs as guards or in other war-related roles.[19]

As the war continued, however, military officials expressed increasing concern over the defence of vulnerable points on the Home Front. The defence of aircraft, in particular, posed problems for units charged with protecting aerodromes and aircraft storage units. In Britain, as in other belligerent nations, the war fuelled the demand for aircraft. Between 1939 and 1945, nearly 131,550 aircraft were manufactured in Britain.[20] This upsurge in aircraft necessitated the establishment of several hundred additional airfields in the United Kingdom.[21] Following its establishment in May 1940, the MAP assumed authority from the Air Ministry over the procurement and maintenance of aircraft for the RAF. The MAP also oversaw the storage of aircraft in the interim between manufacture and receipt by RAF units. Prior to reaching the RAF, aircraft were housed at airfields or factory aerodromes designated aircraft storage units (ASUs). Per MAP policy, aircraft were scattered or "dispersed" in an attempt to minimise potential damage or destruction from enemy bombing.[22] Dispersal became increasingly important in late 1940, when the *Luftwaffe* launched air raids specifically intended to obliterate aircraft factories.[23]

In a February 1940 letter to Home Forces Headquarters, the General Officer Commanding-in-Chief of Western Command (Home Forces) proposed the use of guard dogs at aerodromes to help defend the "large numbers of Aircraft [which] are standing in open fields by copses and hedgerows where intending saboteurs would lie up at night and remain undetected."[24] The situation was further complicated by a

---

16   TNA: WO 199/416, 1A, Report of Meeting at War Office, 10 October 1939 and TNA: HO 45/21004, Memo by Baker, 17 October 1939.
17   TNA: WO 199/416, 7A, L.G.M. Nash to A.H. Killick, 31 October 1939.
18   TNA: WO 199/416, 9B, John K. Shanson to Lt. Col. Cox, 16 November 1939.
19   TNA: WO 199/416, 9A, Lt. Col. Cox to Home Forces, 17 November 1939 and TNA: HO 45/21004, Rawson to Lloyd, 24 November 1939.
20   Richard Overy, *The Air War: 1939-1945* (London: Europa, 1980), p. 150.
21   Reynolds, *Rich Relations*, p. 116.
22   J.D. Scott and Richard Hughes, *The Administration of War Production* (London, 1955), pp. 291, 338, 359.
23   Calder, *The People's War*, p. 161.
24   TNA: WO 199/416, 11A, General Officer Commanding-in-Chief, Western Command to Headquarters, Home Forces, 27 February 1940.

shortage of manpower, which meant that human guards had to defend vast sections of airfields.[25]

The danger posed to aircraft was not limited to areas under Western Command. In July 1941, South Midland Area (Home Forces) Commander Brigadier H.T. MacMullen also advocated the use of dogs at ASUs and maintenance units in the South Midlands at which "the number of machines is now so great as to make present efforts to guard them little better than a farce."[26] Two months later, he again implored the General Officer Commanding-in-Chief, Southern Command (Home Forces) to approve the employment of guard dogs:

> It is requested that the necessary authority to push forward with this [guard dog] scheme may be obtained at an early date. I feel considerable apprehension of my responsibility to protect the aircraft which are being assembled in ever increasing numbers… and I am sure it will be agreed that it is absurd to assume that a guard of one and a half Platoons is at present anything but a guard in name only.[27]

In September 1941, Lieutenant General Harold Alexander, then serving as Commanding-in-Chief, Southern Command (Home Forces), also expressed apprehension for the security of ASUs:

> In this Command there is a large number of Aircraft Storage Units where aircraft are held widely dispersed around woods and other cover. These aircraft have to be protected against sabotage. A very large number of men are tied-up on this duty, but in spite of the number, the protection of these aircraft is far from satisfactory. However alert and active patrols may be it is almost impossible for them to detect and thwart the determined saboteur, especially at night.[28]

Recalling the use of guard dogs in northwest Europe following the cessation of hostilities in 1918, Alexander called for the employment of canines on the British Home Front: "At the present time when commitments are very heavy, and the man power situation is acute it is recommended that dogs be once more called upon to perform the duty of guarding such places as A[ircraft] S[torage] U[nit]s."[29]

Following the successful performance by trained dogs at Staverton Aerodrome in September 1941, MacMullen petitioned Southern Command (Home Forces) to institute a guard dog scheme. He reasoned that under the direction of Major Baldwin the

25   Ibid.
26   TNA: WO 199/2061, 38A, MacMullen to Schreiber, 31 July 1941.
27   TNA: WO 199/2061, 42A, MacMullen to Southern Command, 19 September 1941.
28   TNA: WO 199/2061, 43A, Lt. Gen. H.R. Alexander to GHQ, Home Forces, 27 September 1941.
29   Ibid. Perhaps Alexander was referring to the canines attached to the British Army of the Rhine mentioned in Chapter 1.

scheme would offer an ancillary means of security at a number of ASUs in Oxfordshire and the surrounding areas.[30] As Defence Officer of Staverton Aerodrome, Baldwin was keenly aware of the struggles involved in defending aircraft. In a February 1943 interview with the *Gloucestershire Echo*, he recalled how the use of guard dogs augmented security at the aerodrome:

> When this war came and I was Defence Officer at an aerodrome, I found that it was impossible to protect it properly with men guards because if anyone wanted to get on to the airfield they could easily avoid the [human] sentries. But dogs can detect anybody at 200 yards at night and give the alarm.[31]

At the March 1942 meeting attended by Baldwin and Lloyd, the MAP and the Army called for nearly 1,600 guard dogs to defend vulnerable points.[32] The training of guard dogs and handlers was carried out at both the Army's War Dogs Training School and the MAP Guard Dog Training School. CMP policemen, each paired with a dog, completed a period of training at the War Dogs Training School prior to recommencing duty at vulnerable points on the Home Front.[33] The MAP Guard Dog Training School hosted training courses for aircraftmen, while members of the RAF Police undertook training at either school.[34] Canines trained to protect vulnerable points were employed alongside handlers on patrols or confined to a specific location to alert human guards to trespassers.[35]

Unlike the Home Guard, which until 1942 was primarily focused on protecting the British Home Front from invading forces or parachutists,[36] the use of guard dogs largely came about to counteract *internal* subterfuge. Their role, as set out in a letter from Southern Command (Home Forces), was to "enable the [anti-sabotage patrols] to be carried out with increased efficiency, without the necessity of drawing upon additional manpower." The use of guard dogs, therefore, allowed for a shift in manpower, as servicemen previously tasked with defending aircraft from "anti-sabotage" at

30   TNA: WO 199/2061, 42A, MacMullen to Southern Command, 19 September 1941.
31   'Dogs Make Splendid Guards, *Gloucestershire Echo*, 8 February 1940.
32   TNA: WO 199/416, 57B, Minutes of a Meeting. Of these, the majority were requested by the MAP. The MAP called for 1,200 canines, while the Army sought to acquire 370 guard dogs in addition to 920 dogs for other military roles.
33   TNA: WO 199/2537, 21A, V.P. Dog Handlers' Course, 27 July 1942.
34   TNA: AIR 2/8734, 1A, O.W. de Putron, 28 October 1943 and 35A, Postagram from Provost Marshal, Air Ministry, 1 February 1944.
35   TNA: WO 199/416, 89A, Draft of Tactical Employment of War Dogs, 13 August 1942.
36   MacKenzie, *The Home Guard*, pp. 41-45, 102-124, 179-180, 184. As MacKenzie has shown, the precise purpose of the Home Guard was ill-defined and unclear throughout much of the war. Nonetheless, as the possibility of invasion subsided in 1941-1942, the Home Guard focused less on resisting enemy troops and took on other tasks, including bomb disposal, medical assistance and the operation of anti-aircraft guns.

vulnerable points "could form more adequate bodies for dealing with airborne and parachute troops."[37]

The training and use of dogs employed by the Army differed from that of canines instructed at the MAP Guard Dog Training School. At the Army's War Dogs Training School, guard dogs were taught to work with multiple handlers, while dogs at the MAP Guard Dog Training School learned to recognise a single handler. While the procedure maintained by the War Dogs Training School hastened the training process for handlers,[38] allowing dogs to work with multiple handlers could lead to problems. Instructions distributed by the Army's War Dogs Training School acknowledged that "most V[ulnerable] P[oint] dogs have to be handled by inexperienced men who have not attended a course of training." Thus, the instructions made clear that "the handling of the dogs should be confined to as few men as possible."[39] In late 1943, the Assistant Provost Marshal, Eastern Command (Home Forces) reported that the performance of dogs employed by units in his command suffered if worked by several handlers. For this reason, the four CMP companies in Eastern Command which utilised guard dogs ensured that each canine was handled by no more than three military policemen.[40] Similarly, correspondence between General Staff (Operations) and Southern Command (Home Forces) acknowledged: "In some cases… too many men handle the dogs, and in such cases the dog will not work to maximum efficiency."[41] While such criticism reflected the importance of proper handling, the available records suggest that the mismanagement of guard dogs on the Home Front was not a widespread issue.

Prior to the establishment of the Army's War Dogs Training School, Lloyd favoured the use of crossbred Labradors for guard work, although he stressed that temperament was more important than pedigree.[42] Baldwin, on the other hand, preferred Alsatians, as he considered the breed "the easiest to train."[43] The MAP Guard Dog Training School also sought a number of other breeds, including Mastiffs, Bull Terriers and

---

37 TNA: WO 199/2061, 50A, Southern Command to 5 Corps, 14 December 1941. See also: 54A, Commander-in-Chief, Home Forces to Under Secretary of State, 22 December 1941, in which it was stated that CMP units were to utilise canines "for anti-sabotage work on vulnerable points."

38 TNA: AIR 2/8734, 1A, de Putron, 28 October 1943. To qualify as a handler at the MAP Guard Dog Training School, aircraftmen and RAF Police personnel were required to undergo eight weeks of training. By contrast, the training of handlers at the War Dogs Training School lasted less than two weeks.

39 TNA: AIR 2/8734, 28A, Instructions for the Handling of V.P. Dogs from the War Dogs Training School, 15 January 1944.

40 TNA: WO 199/2537, 45A, Assistant Provost Marshal, Eastern Command to G(Ops), Eastern Command, 4 November 1943.

41 TNA: WO 199/2061, 91A, Letter from J.A. Hickman, 3 November 1943.

42 TNA: WO 199/416, 1A, Report of Meeting at War Office, 10 October 1939.

43 'Dogs Make Splendid Guards', Gloucestershire Echo, 8 February 1940.

Trained Alsatians at RAF Brize Norton. (© Imperial War Museum (CH 10287))

Airedale Terriers.[44] As Baldwin made clear during the war, stature was of prime importance. "We take in any kind of dog provided it is of a fair size," he explained in early 1944.[45] By the end of the Second World War, however, the Alsatian had emerged as the preeminent guard dog breed at the MAP Guard Dog Training School and the Army's War Dogs Training School.[46] Moreover, photographic evidence suggests that during the war the Alsatian was the favoured breed at some airfields, including RAF Brize Norton in Oxfordshire and RAF Langley in Buckinghamshire.[47] Training instructions drawn up by the Army's War Dogs Training School following its relocation to Germany in 1945 cited the breed's "naturally suspicious nature" and "formidable appearance" as reasons for the widespread use of Alsatians as guards.[48]

By late July 1942, 40 guard dogs had completed training at the Army's War Dogs Training School and had been deployed to vulnerable points throughout Britain.[49] Training proceeded apace, so that by November 1943, the War Dogs Training School

44   Ibid.
45   'Dogs' Great Aid', *Gloucestershire Echo*, 12 January 1944.
46   TNA: WO 291/2673, 37B, Outlines of Training. See also: Royal Air Force Museum Archive and Library, London (RAF Museum): 007253, *Royal Air Force Police Dog Training*, May 1974.
47   IWM: CH 10287, Royal Air Force Flying Training Command, 1940-1945 and IWM: H 28928, The Royal Air Force in Britain, 1939-1945.
48   TNA: WO 291/2673, 37B, Outlines of Training.
49   TNA: WO 199/2537, 19A, Memorandum from War Office, 18 July 1942 and Museum of Military Medicine: War Diary of DAVRS, July 1942.

and the MAP Guard Dog Training School had turned out some 1,000 trained guard dogs.[50] Of the dogs employed by the British Armed Forces in the Second World War, most were trained as guards.[51]

Dogs guarded a range of VP1 and other installations on the Home Front, including ammunition dumps and wireless stations. By late 1943, guard dogs were in use at 42 vulnerable points in Southern Command alone, including wireless stations in Leafield, Thornhill, Burnham-on-Sea and Portishead, the pumping station at the Severn Tunnel and a power station near St Ives, Cornwall. The Ordnance Survey similarly relied upon a trained dog to help protect its facility at Crabwood House near Southampton.[52] In Eastern Command, trained dogs assisted military policemen in the protection of Special Operations Executive (SOE) stations and other clandestine installations, such as the Radio Security Service in Hanslope Park. By November 1943, Eastern Command had guard dogs operating as part of CMP (VP) units at 23 vulnerable points stretching from Northamptonshire to Norfolk.[53] As the war continued, canines were also utilised at prisoner of war (POW) camps in Britain.[54]

In addition, dogs helped defend aircraft at airfields and ASUs. At RAF Brize Norton, for example, dogs were relied upon to defend a number of Horsa gliders intended for use in the Allied invasion of Normandy.[55] The available evidence indicates that the use of dogs at airfields led to an enhanced sense of security among officers who oversaw the protection of aircraft. For example, in an account of the use of dogs at RAF St Brides in Wales, the officer commanding reported:

> The team of eight dogs have been with us for ten days, time enough for me to render a report as to the absolute success of the scheme from one who for months past has been worried over the painfully inadequate anti-sabotage patrol consisting of a handful of really good men.[56]

Similarly, in a report on the dogs at his station, another officer surmised:

> Their efficiency cannot be too highly commended and by the employment of dog patrols it has been proved that much greater security is obtained than would be possible by using men alone. This is particularly so during hours of darkness

---

50   Museum of Military Medicine: War Diary of DAVRS, November 1943. The figure provided by the MAP Guard Dog Training School was inclusive of guard dogs currently in training.
51   Murray, 'War Dogs', *Animal World*, September 1944, p. 68.
52   TNA: WO 199/2061, 93B, Appendix 'A' to SC Z/5702/G(Ops), 5 November 1943 and 51A, 5 Corps to Southern Command, 17 December 1941.
53   TNA: WO 199/2537, 45A, Assistant Provost Marshal to G(Ops), 4 November 1943.
54   Museum of Military Medicine: War Diary of DAVRS, October 1945.
55   Davies, *RAF Police Dogs on Patrol*, pp. 5-8.
56   TNA: AVIA 9/15, 102/2, Extract from Letter from O.C, RAF Station St. Bride's Major, 16 April 1942.

when Alsatian dogs employed are very alert and will indicate to their handlers the presence of human beings at distances of over three hundred yards. Since their arrival at the Station, no loss of equipment by theft has been reported from aircraft in dispersal fields.[57]

As noted in the aforementioned account, the dog's exceptional sense of smell enabled canine guards to detect trespassers at a considerable distance. It was generally found that guard dogs could identify trespassers from 185 to 275 metres.[58] This ability, combined with the physical presence of dogs, led some officers to consider dogs more effective guards than humans. For example, an officer commented:

During the past two and a half years, I have had two guard dog teams and with approximately three hundred aircraft at dispersal, no theft or pilfering has been reported which proves that the psychological effect of dogs carrying out patrols is far more effective than a man carrying a gun.[59]

A number of military officials also submitted favourable reports concerning the use of dogs at vulnerable points. In correspondence outlining the plan to expand the employment of dogs among RAF Station Police, the Provost Marshal, RAF concluded that teams of trained dogs and handlers "form as efficient and complete a guard as is possible."[60] Similarly, in March 1943, the Commander-in-Chief, Home Forces declared that "V[ulnerable] P[oint] dogs have proved a success" on the Home Front.[61]

In one of many instances of Anglo-American co-operation throughout the war, the MAP Guard Dog Training School provided trained guard dogs for the United States Army to defend equipment and supplies at American military installations in Britain.[62] That the MAP Guard Dog Training School went so far as to provide canines for American airfields in the United Kingdom is unsurprising considering that the wartime partnership forged between Britain and the United States involved, as the historian Niall Barr put it, "the resources of the British and American navies, armies and air forces fused into one."[63] Indeed, the United States military in the United Kingdom was not only reliant on Britain for airfields but for housing and *matériel*.[64]

57   Quoted in Moss and Kirby, *Animals Were There*, p. 121.
58   Murray, 'War Dogs', *Animal World*, September 1944, p. 68 and 'Dogs Make Splendid Guards', *Gloucestershire Echo*, 8 February 1940.
59   Quoted in Moss and Kirby, *Animals Were There*, pp. 120-121.
60   TNA: AIR 2/8734, 1A, de Putron, 28 October 1943.
61   TNA: WO 199/416, 107A, Commander-in-Chief, Home Forces to the Under Secretary of State, War Office, 18 March 1943.
62   Moss and Kirby, *Animals Were There*, p. 121.
63   Barr, *Yanks and Limeys*, p. 3.
64   Reynolds, *Rich Relations*, pp. 90, 108-109, 116, 149, 190, 294.

At the outset of 1944, more than 1,000,000 American soldiers, sailors and airmen were based in the United Kingdom. While the majority were in Britain awaiting the proposed Allied invasion of northwest Europe, many airmen of the United States Army Air Force (USAAF) were posted to one of several RAF or recently-built USAAF airfields in East Anglia to carry out bombing raids over Germany. As of late 1943, the USAAF was operating out of nearly 70 airfields in the United Kingdom. This number continued to increase in advance of the Allied invasion of Normandy.[65] The airfields and their American servicemen inhabitants constituted what one historian has described as "a vast [United States] Army Air Force empire" in the United Kingdom.[66]

Members of the United States 9th Air Force completed handler training at the MAP Guard Dog Training School.[67] An officer in the USAAF praised the performance of 29 canines instructed at the British training facility:

> Results of this program have been highly successful throughout… Previously to bringing in the guard dogs, gliders were daily being pilfered… Since the dogs were utilized, pilfering and sabotage has been completely eliminated. It is estimated that the dogs and handlers have taken the place of a guard which would normally require at least fifty or sixty men for the same protection.[68]

In addition, Major Baldwin worked with the United States Chief Quartermaster, European Theatre of Operations to further the use of guard dogs by the United States Army outside the United States. For his assistance, Baldwin earned the American Legion of Merit for "an outstanding example of co-operation of allied nations in the accomplishment of a common end."[69]

CMP and RAF Police Dogs in the Middle East, North Africa and Italy

The employment of dogs by the British Army and the RAF was not limited to vulnerable points on the British Home Front. The CMP and the RAF Police also utilised trained dogs on a large scale outside the United Kingdom. As the number of British

---

65   Ibid, pp. 89, 102, 108-109, 116, 183-184, 198, 290, 294, 394, 398, 409, 433. The number of American servicemen rose sharply in the months preceding the Allied invasion of Normandy before declining to an estimated 600,000 to 700,000 by late 1944-early 1945. Nonetheless, some 400,000 American servicemen were in the United Kingdom when hostilities ceased in September 1945.
66   Ibid, pp. 108-109.
67   Davies, *RAF Police Dogs on Patrol*, p. 4.
68   Quoted in Moss and Kirby, *Animals Were There*, p. 121.
69   Quoted in 'American Legion of Merit for Col. Baldwin', *Cheltenham Chronicle*, 1 December 1945, p. 2.

and other Allied servicemen in the Middle East skyrocketed in the early 1940s so too did the amount of War Department equipment and supplies. As one CMP officer put it, the Middle East became "a huge military base equipped not only with Depots stretching for miles, but also with manufacturing plants turning out many of the innumerable articles required by a modern army."[70] International trade was rendered difficult by the war, and as a result, a number of black markets emerged as impoverished civilians took advantage of the wartime blackout to engage in theft and other illegal activities. Furthermore, local trains utilised by the British to move *matériel* were poorly defended and vulnerable to attack.[71] Rampant stealing by civilians in the Middle East, according to the *Journal of the Royal Army Veterinary Corps*, had "reached alarming proportions" by 1942.[72]

With a shortage of human guards at their disposal, the CMP turned in part to dogs to help protect War Department *matériel*. In June 1942, the CMP established a dog training facility in Egypt.[73] By late 1943, the CMP dog scheme had expanded to include five sections, each composed of 48 dogs, spread throughout much of Egypt, Palestine, Syria and Lebanon.[74] The AVRS procured the canines, many of which were Alsatians or Boxers.[75] The *Instructions on Use and Training of Dog Police* circulated in early 1944 emphasised that while the CMP favoured Alsatians and Boxers, "any dog will do for guard purposes provided he has size," which was specified as at least 20 kilograms.[76]

Upon arrival at the Military Police Dog Training School in Egypt, dogs were divided into one of two groups: "barkers" or "combat." Barkers, as an article published in the *Journal of the Royal Army Veterinary Corps* explained, were "akin to the household guard dog," the purpose of which was to "raise the alarm by barking on the approach of an intruder." By contrast, dogs designated for combat were taught to "catch, overpower and hold a wanted man."[77] The dogs were generally worked together, so that barkers signalled to the handlers of combat dogs that a perpetrator was in the vicinity.[78] When released by their handlers, military police dogs seized and detained the

70 Quoted in Major S. Ogden-Smith, *A Record of the Activities of The Corps of Military Police in the Middle East, 1939-1944* (Printing and Stationery Services, M.E.F., 1945), p. 58.
71 Ibid, p. 58-60.
72 'The Employment of Military Police Dogs in the Middle East', *Journal of the RAVC*, 19:3 (1948), p. 91.
73 Ibid, p. 91.
74 TNA: WO 169/13321, War Diary, 1943 and TNA: WO 169/13322, War Diary, 1943 and TNA: WO 169/13323, War Diary, 1943 and TNA: WO 169/13324, War Diary, 1943 and TNA: WO 169/13325, War Diary, 1943.
75 'Employment of Military Police Dogs', *Journal of the RAVC*, p. 91.
76 TNA: WO 204/7732, Instructions on Use and Training, 20 February 1944.
77 'Employment of Military Police Dogs', *Journal of the RAVC*, p. 92. Although this article was published after the Second World War, the war diaries of the CMP Dog Sections include multiple references to "barkers" and "combat" dogs.
78 Ogden-Smith, *A Record of the Activities*, p. 78.

perpetrator so that the handler could carry out the arrest.[79] Thus, the purpose behind the employment of military police dogs, such as those attached to the CMP, differed from that of most guard dogs. As the CMP's *Instructions on Use and Training of Dog Police* pointed out, military police dogs were not intended to merely guard military installations and equipment but to take part in periodic searches at such sites alongside military policemen in an effort to locate potential burglars.[80]

In April 1944, a correspondent for the *Daily Mirror* attended a demonstration by military police dogs and their handlers in Egypt. The accompanying article provided a glimpse into the training and operational use of military police dogs:

> Across the grass arena pads a strange figure in a fencing mask and heavily-padded white canvas suit... Away on the other side of the ground a military police corporal unleashes a 'boxer' dog, which bounds ferociously across the turf towards the man in the mask. As the dog comes abreast of his victim, he deals him a terrific blow in the back of the right leg. Then, as the man topples over, the dog digs his teeth into the padding on the leg and holds on to him.[81]

Instructions distributed by the RAF Police indicate that its police dogs carried out a similar role to those of the CMP. The instructions emphasised that police dogs "are Police Raiders and not Guard Dogs."[82]

While the main function of military police dogs may have been to conduct searches as referenced above, the available records reveal that at least some dogs utilised by the CMP did in fact serve in roles comparable to those of guard dogs employed by the Army and the MAP on the Home Front. The war diary for the Military Police Dog Training School mentioned the use of police dogs for "guard duties" at a dump in Cairo in April 1943.[83] Similarly, CMP dogs were employed as guards in Alexandria upon the Prime Minister's arrival to Egypt in early 1945.[84]

The use of police dogs outside the United Kingdom grew rapidly in the last two years of the war. In October 1943, the CMP training school in Egypt was expanded to accommodate 120 dogs.[85] To deal with the increase, the CMP established a War Dog Holding Centre in Moascar, Egypt the following year.[86] Moreover, in late 1944,

---

79   RSPCA Archive: Materials Used in the Production of Animals Were There by A.W. Moss and E. Kirby, Press Cutting, 'Slaithwaite Dog-Fancier in Middle East', *Huddersfield Examiner*, 3 October 1944.

80   TNA: WO 204/7732, Instructions on Use and Training, 20 February 1944.

81   'How 'Boxer' Dogs are Taught to Hold Intruders', *Daily Mirror*, 27 April 1944, p. 2.

82   TNA: AIR 23/6002, R.A.F. Police Dogs: Administration Policy, 59A, Draft for Command Routine Orders-Dog Police, undated.

83   TNA: WO 169/13320, War Diary, April 1943.

84   TNA: WO 169/21383, 3 Dog Section, War Diary, February 1945.

85   TNA: WO 169/13320, War Diary, October 1943.

86   TNA: WO 169/17757, Military Dog Training School, War Diary, October 1944.

A military police dog in training in North Africa, August 1942.
(© Imperial War Museum (E 15659))

a new section was raised in Iraq with dogs drawn from Egypt.[87] As the war continued, the use of dogs by the CMP spread beyond the Middle East. In January 1944, the CMP founded a dog training facility in North Africa. Personnel at the 'A' Military Police Dog Training Establishment oversaw the training of dogs for a new unit known as No. 51 Military Police Dog Section.[88] No. 51 Section, which included sub-sections in Algeria and Italy, commenced operations in April 1944.[89] Although No. 51 Section and the Algiers-based training facility were disbanded in August 1944, a separate CMP dog company was raised in Italy that same month.[90] While the unit, known as 'B' Dog Provost Company, primarily operated in Italy, one section moved to Austria towards the end of the war.[91]

87   TNA: WO 169/19439, MP Dog Section, War Diary of Military Police Dog Section PAIFORCE, September 1944.
88   TNA: WO 170/3605, Dog Sections: 'A' Police Dog Training Establishment, War Diary, February 1944, Appendix 1, Formation of New Units and April 1944.
89   TNA: WO 170/3604, Dog Sections: 51 Police Dog Section, War Diary, April 1944.
90   TNA: WO 170/3604, Letter from Allied Force Headquarters, 14 August 1944 and TNA: WO 170/3606, Dog Sections: 'B' Police Dog Company, War Diary, August 1944.
91   TNA: WO 170/3606, War Diary, August-December 1944 and TNA: WO 170/7032, Provost Companies: 'B' Dog Company, War Diary, January-December 1945.

A military police dog with his handler in Algeria, April 1944. (© Imperial War Museum (NA 13611))

As the RAF Police were without a dog training facility in the Middle East, dogs attached to the RAF Police in that theatre of war were instructed at the CMP Dog Training School in Egypt. In June 1944, the Provost Marshal, Mediterranean Allied Air Forces (MAAF) asserted that the use of dogs to protect airfields and other RAF installations in the Middle East had thus far "exceeded [his] expectations."[92] In an effort to expand the use of dogs among RAF Police outside the United Kingdom, he called for the creation of a training facility in Egypt.[93] The RAF Police Dog School was founded near Cairo shortly thereafter.[94] The use of dogs by the RAF Police was not limited to the Middle East, however. In the latter half of 1944, the RAF Police also erected dog training facilities in Italy and North Africa.[95]

92   TNA: AIR 23/6002, 28B, Provost Marshal, MAAF to AOA, MAAF, 30 June 1944.
93   Ibid.
94   TNA: AIR 23/6002, 50A, Provost Marshal, MAAF to Provost Marshal, RAF, 30 July 1944 and 83B, HQ, RAF, Middle East to HQ, Mediterranean Allied Air Forces, 24 November 1944. The name of the training school was changed from RAF Police Dog Centre to RAF Police Dog School in late 1944.
95   TNA: AIR 23/6002, 50A, MAAF to RAF, 30 July 1944 and 78A, HQ, Provost & Security Unit, CMF to HQ, MAAF, CMF, 15 November 1944.

During the course of the Second World War, military police dogs worked at various sites, including ordnance depots, vehicle parks, petrol storage depots and marshalling yards.[96] The presence of dogs at such locations, it was believed, served to discourage crime.[97] Major S. Ogden-Smith, who donated his own dog to the CMP, addressed this point in the wartime publication *A Record of the Activities of The Corps of Military Police in the Middle East*. Ogden-Smith observed: "Police dogs are hated and feared by the native, [and] the native is hated by the dogs (but not feared) so the appropriate balance is struck."[98] In addition, signposts indicating the employment of military police dogs at some installations likely served to dissuade potential perpetrators.[99]

While deterrence may be difficult to substantiate, it is clear that military police dogs helped recover costly War Department equipment and supplies by assisting military policemen in the apprehension of trespassers. CMP dogs in Egypt, for example, apprehended over 300 persons and prevented the loss of approximately £3,000 of *matériel* by the end of 1942.[100] Although incomplete, the war diaries for the CMP dog sections in the Middle East, North Africa and Italy included detailed figures concerning the number of arrests, as well as the monetary value of *matériel* recovered by dogs and their handlers. In November 1943, for example, the dogs of No. 1 Section apprehended 34 trespassers at military installations.[101] During an 11 month period in 1944, the dogs of that section captured 204 persons, and in doing so, prevented the loss of War Department *matériel* worth approximately £5365.[102]

By late 1944, military police dogs in the Middle East had accounted for more than 1,000 arrests.[103] Simmi, a canine member of No. 1 Section, garnered 86 arrests prior to his death in September 1944. When reporting on the Boxer's performance to the RSPCA, the officer commanding of the Military Police Dog Training School described a specific incident in which Simmi took part:

> Whilst [Simmi was] patrolling a 'dump' with his handler… a train entered the 'dump' and whilst the unloading was in progress a native descended from the train with some articles from a broken case, the native was arrested and on the way to a truck he escaped and ran towards a train which was in motion. 'Simmi'

---

96   For examples, see: TNA: WO 169/17753, 3 Dog Section, War Diary of No. 3 Military Police Dog Section, January 1944 and TNA: WO 169/17754, 4 Dog Section, War Diary of No. 4 Military Police Dog Section, January 1944 and TNA: WO 169/17755, 5 Dog Section, War Diary of No. 5 Military Police Dog Section, August 1944 and TNA: WO 170/3604, War Diary, April 1944.

97   TNA: WO 204/7732, Instructions on Use and Training, 20 February 1944 and TNA: AIR 23/6002, 28B, Provost Marshal to AOA, 30 June 1944.

98   Ogden-Smith, *A Record of the Activities*, pp. 78-79.

99   TNA: WO 204/7732, Instructions on Use and Training, 20 February 1944.

100 'Employment of Military Police Dogs', *Journal of the RAVC*, p. 92.

101 TNA: WO 169/13321, War Diary, November 1943.

102 TNA: WO 169/17751, War Diary, February-December 1944.

103 Ogden-Smith, *A Record of the Activities*, p. 76.

was released but the native jumped onto the moving train and hung on by his hands. 'Simmi' jumped at the native and pulled him away from the train and held him until his handler arrived. The native was very violent, tried to escape twice after this, but on each occassion (sic) 'Simmi' caught him.[104]

As the report made clear, Simmi's actions enabled his handler to eventually detain the perpetrator. Similarly, the performance of Blackie, a dog in No. 51 Section, provides further evidence as to the effectiveness of military police dogs. According to an account submitted to the AVRS:

> L/Cpl. Ball, with his dog, entered a warehouse and surprised eight Italian civilians in the act of filling sacks with W[ar] D[epartment] clothing. When these civilians saw that they were being challenged only by one man and a dog, they attacked him. L/Cpl. Ball released Blackie who knocked one man down and kept him down, at the same time rendering valuable assistance to his handler by taking random bites at the other Italian civilians. Finally, L/Cpl. Ball and Blackie managed to arrest and hold five of the eight civilians and the other three were arrested as they left the warehouse by another policeman who had been brought on the scene by the noise.[105]

During the four months in which No. 51 Section was in operation in North Africa and Italy, the section amassed at least 57 arrests and prevented the loss of nearly £835 in equipment and supplies.[106]

As evidenced by Blackie's performance, military police dogs could effectively detain trespassers during an arrest, thus allowing their handlers to apprehend several perpetrators. Akeela, a dog with No. 1 Section, also aided his handler in the arrests of multiple persons. According to an account provided by the officer commanding of the Military Police Dog Training School:

> 'Akeela' picked up eight thieves, some being armed with loaded sticks. The thieves seeing as they thought only one dog and Cpl Wigley, the handler of 'Akeela', attacked both N[on] C[ommissioned] O[fficer] and Dog with their

104 TNA: WO 32/14999, 16A, Scott to DAVRS, 14 August 1945.
105 TNA: WO 32/14999, 11A, Lt. Col. J.F. Hart to DAVRS, 24 July 1945.
106 TNA: WO 170/3604, War Diary, April–August 1944. Although the war diary for April indicates that the section commenced work in North Africa that month, it does not provide information related to any arrests carried out by the section. The war diaries for June–August provide individual descriptions of arrests, including the name of the dog(s) which led to the arrest(s) and the monetary value of *matériel* recaptured. By contrast, the war diary for May 1944 indicates that the section carried out 16 arrests but does not specify in every case whether a military policeman and/or dog enacted the arrest. Thus, the figures cited for that month may include arrests carried out by military policemen in addition to dogs.

sticks. Cpl Wigley was struck and knocked to the ground, he then drew his pistol and firing, killed one of the thieves. During this battle 'Akeela' was attacking and driving off the remaining thieves, and finally secured the capture of one more thief. By the time assistance arrived, much valuable W[ar] D[epartment] property was saved and recovered.[107]

In *The History of the Royal Army Veterinary Corps*, Clabby rightly pointed out that dogs, particularly those in the Middle East, also defended the military policemen to whom they were attached.[108] An account concerning a Boxer attached to No. 1 Section highlights the significance of the military police dog as protector:

When on duty one night, five thieves entered the dump which L/Cpl. Storey and 'Ran' were guarding. 'Ran' was released, followed up by L/Cpl. Storey. Four of the thieves were armed with long loaded sticks and the fifth with a matchet... All five thieves attacked both L/Cpl. Storey and 'Ran'... 'Ran' although struck repeatedly by the matchet and loaded sticks, successfully held off the thieves from doing further harm to his handler until assistance arrived.[109]

Like Ran, several military police dogs sustained injuries while on operations. Jerry, the aforementioned Boxer of No. 1 Section, was stabbed during an arrest yet successfully managed to detain the perpetrator. In an account of the incident, Jerry was described as possessing "great devotion to duty," an attribute also ascribed to a number of other military police dogs.[110] Similarly, Prince was described as "an exceptionally good all-round Dog with a very good nose." According to a report on the Alsatian's performance in the Middle East, Prince, "on numerous occasions... pick[ed] out natives at a distance of about two hundred yards." His role as a military police dog, the same account made clear, "undoubtedly calls for great bravery and devotion in all circumstances."[111] As evidenced by the anthropomorphic language used in these accounts, the perception among some humans involved with the CMP dog scheme was that canines exhibited characteristics typically ascribed to human soldiers.

As shown in Chapter 2, staff at the Army's War Dogs Training School and the MAP Guard Dog Training School implemented a number of measures to ensure the health of military dogs. Similar veterinary procedures were instituted at the CMP Dog Training School. All canines received rabies and distemper vaccinations prior to leaving the school.[112] Despite such precautions, however, the CMP dog scheme in the Middle East was plagued by high casualty rates among its dogs. No. 1 Section,

---

107 TNA: WO 32/14999, 16A, Scott to DAVRS, 14 August 1945.
108 Clabby, *History of the RAVC*, p. 184.
109 TNA: WO 32/14999, 16A, Scott to DAVRS, 14 August 1945.
110 Ibid.
111 Ibid.
112 Ogden-Smith, *A Record of the Activities*, p. 79.

for example, lost 28 dogs in 1944.[113] When taken into consideration that the section consisted of 48 dogs, the deaths of 28 canines is remarkably high. Although the cause of death was rarely specified, the war diary for No. 1 Section reveals that the gastro-intestinal illness enteritis led to two canine deaths in February 1944.[114] Moreover, in March 1945, four dogs died after contracting nephritis at the Military Police Dog School in Egypt.[115] Laboratory tests also determined that several dogs at the training facility were infected by the bacteria haemolytic streptococci, which led to several canines running fevers. In November 1945, RAVC officer Captain A.A. Lamont surmised: "It is highly probable that a high degree of [haemolytic streptococcal] infection is present amongst all dogs at the [Military Police] Dog Training School."[116] Ethical concerns aside, the high casualty rate among military police dogs in the Middle East did not seem to hinder the scheme's effectiveness to any great extent. Moreover, the high casualty rate appears to have been limited to the Middle East, as similar rates were not reported by the CMP in North Africa and Italy. No. 51 Section, for example, lost only two dogs prior to its disbandment in August 1944.[117]

While the use of military police dogs undoubtedly augmented the security of military installations outside the United Kingdom, the employment of dogs represented just one method of defence. Thus, as was the case with all military dogs in the Second World War, military police dogs were used in addition to other methods. In the Middle East, for example, the CMP greatly enlarged its Special Investigation Branch (SIB) in an effort to curtail illegal activity. The SIB in Egypt grew from just five members in September 1939 to more than 500 by late 1944. The SIB accounted for over 46,000 arrests in 1943 and 1944. In addition to dogs, the CMP utilised horses as part of the Military Mounted Police in Egypt and Palestine. By late 1944, the Mounted Police in Egypt had apprehended nearly 650 persons.[118]

---

113 TNA: WO 169/17751, War Diary, January-December 1944.
114 TNA: WO 169/17751, War Diary, February 1944.
115 Captain A.A. Lamont, 'An Investigation Into an Outbreak of Acute Nephritis', *Journal of the RAVC*, 17:1 (1945), pp. 31-34 and TNA: WO 169/21379, Dog Training School, War Diary of the Military Police Dog Training School, March 1945.
116 Lamont, 'An Investigation', *Journal of the RAVC*, p. 33.
117 TNA: WO 170/3604, War Diary, March-August 1944. Although one of the dogs died as a result of rabies in July 1944, the war diaries for No. 51 Section contained no other reports of the disease. The other casualty's cause of death was not specified.
118 Ogden-Smith, *A Record of the Activities*, pp. 57-75. In contrast to the CMP dog sections, the SIB dealt with a number of crimes, such as rape and murder, apart from burglary. Thus, the number cited above, while inclusive of burglary, includes arrests resulting from all types of illegal activity.

Patrol Dogs for the British Army

In early 1940, a British soldier told a *Daily Express* correspondent: "We'd have got that Jerry patrol if it hadn't been for that blasted dog."[119] While on patrol in France, his unit was discovered by an Alsatian attached to a German patrol. The soldier described the way in which the dog worked:

> The Jerries were coming straight towards us. About 400 yards in front of them was one of their dogs... I saw it stop in its tracks... It had smelled us. I saw it hugging the ground as it squirmed round towards its own lines again, then it got up and ran back to the patrol. We didn't want to shoot or anything, because it would have given us away out in front.[120]

By having a dog lead the patrol, the Germans were alerted to the presence of British troops. For the aforementioned British soldier, this encounter, as well as a confrontation with another German-trained dog shortly thereafter, was enough to convince him that "those [patrol] dogs do a lot of good work for the Jerries."[121]

In addition to being witnessed by members of the BEF, the German employment of patrol dogs was reported in the British press. In late 1939, the *Daily Mirror* revealed that dogs were "being used in increasing numbers by German patrol parties" in northwest Europe.[122] Similarly, the *Yorkshire Post* described a clash between German and British troops in early 1940 resulting from the employment of a patrol dog.[123]

In Britain, the issue was broached in the House of Commons in May 1940, when Secretary of State for War Oliver Stanley was questioned about the potential use of patrol dogs in the British Army. The question of using patrol dogs, Stanley informed the House of Commons, was "still in the experimental stage."[124] Stanley was likely referring to the provisional War Dog Section established by the War Office that spring. Composed of four dogs trained by Lloyd, the section was employed by 43rd Division to escort soldiers on reconnaissance patrols.[125] An account submitted in late 1940 by 12 Corps noted:

119 Quoted in O.D. Gallagher, 'We'd Have Trapped Jerry—But for the Dog', *Daily Express*, 6 January 1940, p. 5.
120 Quoted in Ibid.
121 Quoted in Ibid.
122 T.E.A. Healy, 'Warned by War Dogs', *Daily Mirror*, 29 December 1939, p. 15.
123 'Nazi Patrol Outwitted', *Yorkshire Post*, 6 February 1940, p. 1.
124 Hansard: HC Deb 7 May 1940 vol 360 cc1022-3.
125 TNA: WO 199/2061, 1A, Director of Military Training to Southern Command, 29 April 1940 and 9A, Richardson to Eastern Command, 26 July 1940. Chapter 2 details the history behind the establishment of the "War Dog Section."

The dogs have definite value from a patrol point of view. They have been taken out on several nights with unit Battle Patrols and have proved to be of the utmost value in detecting the presence and direction of enemy personnel. On exercises they have worked well in strange country, although they have been liable to be put off the scent or to make a false point owing to the recent passage of umpires or civilians across the ground.[126]

This account satisfied the Commander-in-Chief, Home Forces, who wrote to the Under Secretary of State that the "report fully justifies the adoption of dogs for patrol work."[127] He proposed the training of 460 patrol dogs for infantry units. This figure, which translated to one pair of patrol dogs for every battalion in Home Forces, was approved at the March 1942 meeting at the War Office.[128]

Correspondence between the Director of Military Training and the Home Forces Commands also suggests that the section's performance impacted the decision by the War Office to set up an official military dog training facility. In a November 1940 letter, Major S.B. Coates told the General Officers Commanding-in-Chief: "As a result of patrol dogs experiments carried out in recent months, it has been decided to experiment further." He added: "Consideration is being given to the establishment, at an early date, of a War Dog Training School."[129]

The role of the patrol dog, as defined by the 1942 War Office guide *The Tactical Employment of War Dogs*, was to escort infantry units on "mobile patrols… in order to give warning of the presence of the enemy," as well as to serve alongside "standing patrols where they can give definite and precise indication of the direction from which the enemy is approaching."[130] The British Army's employment of patrol dogs differed from that of the German Army. Whereas German patrol dogs moved in advance of their handlers and often without leads, patrol dogs utilised by British units stayed with their handlers throughout the duration of patrols. In *The Book of the Dog*, Lloyd acknowledged that the *Wehrmacht* "had the better type and better trained patrol dogs," a development he attributed to the German Army's willingness to train dogs prior to the outbreak of war.[131]

126 TNA: WO 199/416, 38B, Commander, 12 Corps to Home Forces, 3 November 1941.
127 TNA: WO 199/416, 38A, Commander-in-Chief, Home Forces to the Under Secretary of State, 2 December 1941.
128 TNA: WO 199/416, 38A, Home Forces to the Under Secretary of State, 2 December 1941 and 57B, Minutes of a Meeting, 5 March 1942.
129 TNA: WO 199/2061, 12A, Coates to the General Officers, 13 November 1940.
130 TNA: WO 199/416, 89A, Draft of Tactical Employment of War Dogs, 13 August 1942. The role of patrol dog in the Second World War was identical to that of the sentry dog in the First World War.
131 Lloyd, 'Dog in War', pp. 184-186.

By early 1943, some 170 canines had joined infantry units as messenger or patrol dogs. Of these, the majority were attached to Home Forces.[132] Although records related to the employment of patrol dogs by the British Armed Forces are limited, a small number of written or oral accounts on patrol dogs were produced during and after the war. In an interview with the Imperial War Museum, former Army dog handler and trainer Silvester "Monty" Hunt described the performance of his patrol dog during a training exercise in 1942:

> One night when I was out with a patrol dog, the dog stopped... We thought perhaps there wasn't anyone there, so we tried to get the dog to move on, but he wouldn't move... I told the patrol commander and they went to investigate... They found that the opposing forces was only about 150 yards away.[133]

Bob, a dog attached to the Queen's Own Royal West Kent Regiment, received the Dickin Medal for his role on reconnaissance patrols with 6th Battalion. Although Bob had trained as a messenger, his assistance to 6th Battalion during a patrol in North Africa in early 1943 brought about the award.[134] According to Bob's owner, who recounted the event to the Allied Forces Mascot Club:

> The patrol... were soon in the enemy lines. Shortly after, Bob stopped and gave the warning of near enemy. The patrol leader waited for a period to try and find out how near he was. As he could not hear anything he decided to go on; but Bob would not move. A member of the patrol told his leader that perhaps Bob knew that the enemy was nearer than they thought. How true that was became clear very soon after, because a movement was seen only a few yards away.[135]

Such accounts highlight the ability of patrol dogs to detect persons when human soldiers could not.

The use of patrol dogs continued in a haphazard fashion and on a small scale in North Africa, where the Inniskilling Fusiliers employed a few dogs as messengers and on patrol. By September 1943, the unit was down to one patrol dog following the deaths of three other canines.[136] In correspondence with the Army's War Dogs Training School, the handler of the remaining dog praised their performance but admitted they "were not used much in the North African Campaign." He blamed the nature of the war in North Africa, where "conditions were seldom of any use to work

132 TNA: WO 199/416, 102A, Memorandum from War Office to G(Ops), GHQ, Home Forces, 2 February 1943 and 106A, Capt. Ashley Brannall to War Office, 11 February 1943.
133 IWM: 16497, Interview with Silvester Hunt, Reel 2.
134 St. Hill Bourne, *They Also Serve*, pp. 12-13.
135 Quoted in Ibid, p. 13.
136 Clabby, *History of the RAVC*, pp. 96-97.

Bob, a messenger and patrol dog attached to the Queen's Own Royal West Kent Regiment, with his handler. (PDSA)

A patrol dog employed by the Queen's Own Royal West Kent Regiment in North Africa, December 1942. (© Imperial War Museum (NA 289))

the dogs."[137] A similar situation seems to have unfolded for the rest of 78th Division. Twenty-five canines were employed by the division in North Africa beginning in late 1942. It is unclear to what extent these dogs were utilised on operations, but the available records suggest that their employment was restricted, as nearly all became casualties within the first months of their arrival in North Africa.[138] In a paper on the use of patrol and other military dogs, the General Staff Policy Committee on Weapons and Equipment indicated that British patrol dogs in North Africa "were of little value" owing in part to them transforming into "cook-house pets."[139]

The use of patrol dogs by the British Army during the Second World War was short-lived. In January 1943, the Commander-in-Chief, Home Forces noted in correspondence with the War Office that: "Reports from formations who have been allotted patrol and message carrying dogs... are, on the whole, unfavourable."[140] Two months later, he further concluded: "Dogs are not satisfactory for message or patrol work in the infantry battalion and accordingly it is recommended that their training and allocation for this purpose should cease."[141] As the Commander-in-Chief gave no indication as to how patrol dogs performed on operations, it is difficult to ascertain the reasons behind his argument that dogs no longer be utilised on infantry patrols. Lloyd, in *The Book of the Dog*, pointed to indifference on the part of infantry officers:

> Difficulties were experienced, even after having got an efficient dog produced by a reliable staff trainer, in handing the dog over to a member of the Field Forces who had to work him on operations... Patrol dogs were used very effectively by the British Army wherever C[ommanding] O[fficer]s were sufficiently interested to permit them to function... The other side of the story is that there existed Commanding Officers so disinterested in dogs... that they looked upon dogs sent them as just one more headache and, in these units, dogs were very infrequently used and no encouragement given their handlers.[142]

Although the reasons behind the decision are not entirely clear, the Army, in late 1943, began removing patrol and messenger dogs from Home Forces and 21st Army Group units with the intention that such dogs would be utilised as guards at

---

137   Quoted in Ibid, pp. 96-97.
138   TNA: WO 204/7732, 48A , Deputy Chief Administrative Officer to 8 Army, 6 January 1944 and 73A, 78 Division to Rear 13 Corps HQ, 31 January 1944. Although the records do not specify the role(s) in which the dogs were employed, their attachment to infantry units suggests that they were intended for use as messengers and on patrol.
139   TNA: WO 163/183, Organization and Weapons Policy Committee, General Staff Policy Committee on Weapons and Equipment, Paper No. 'BZ', Employment and Training of Dogs for War Purposes, undated. The committee also emphasised that patrol dogs in North Africa appeared "insufficiently accustomed to battle noises and explosions."
140   TNA: WO 199/416, 100A, G.R. Holt to Under Secretary of State, 20 January 1943.
141   TNA: WO 199/416, 107A, Home Forces to Under Secretary of State, 18 March 1943.
142   Lloyd, 'Dog in War', p. 185.

vulnerable points.[143] The move followed an August 1943 ruling by the General Staff, which considered there was "no requirement for any other type of dog" apart from guard dogs.[144] The General Staff upheld their previous directive on patrol dogs in early 1944, noting that such canines would not be utilised in northwest Europe following the upcoming Allied invasion of Normandy "except possibly with formations and units operating in mountainous areas."[145]

The British experience with patrol dogs was in stark contrast to that of the United States, where canines utilised in such a role were referred to as scout dogs. During the Second World War, the United States QMC turned out some 570 scout dogs, of which almost 440 were deployed outside the United States.[146] While the training and employment of American guard dogs began to subside in 1944, the training and use of scout dogs intensified as the war continued.[147] As British records pertaining to the employment of patrol dogs are sparse, it is difficult to ascertain why British and American military officials reached such dissimilar conclusions concerning their use. Considering the British Army withdrew most patrol dogs during the war, it is safe to argue the United States military experienced greater success with scout (patrol) dogs compared to the British.

Perhaps the decision to remove British patrol dogs had less to do with their performance and more to do with the guard dog's proven usefulness at defending vulnerable points. As early as February 1943, Allied Force Headquarters (AFHQ) had relayed to the DAVRS that canines in North Africa "ha[d] not been satisfactory in the forward areas;" consequently, it was recommended that "the best use can be made of them for the defence of vulnerable points."[148] Upon concluding that Home Forces should no longer employ patrol or messenger dogs, the Commander-in-Chief, Home Forces similarly proposed in a letter to the War Office that "the quantity of anti sabotage [guard] dogs under training might be increased."[149]

143 Museum of Military Medicine: War Diary of DAVRS, September–October 1943.
144 TNA: WO 32/10504, General and Warlike Stores: General Weapons Policy Committee, General Staff Policy on the Employment and Training of Dogs for War Purposes, 14 August 1943.
145 TNA: WO 32/10504, General Staff Policy on Employment and Training of Dogs for War Purposes, 1 March 1944. The General Staff suggested that patrol dogs could be utilised by the British Army in Southeast Asia, but their use was ultimately rejected by the General Staff Equipment Policy Sub-Committee of GHQ (India). See: TNA: WO 203/3126, Mine Detection Methods, T.W.J. Taylor to Brig. S.H. Persse, 12 July 1944.
146 NARA: Report #4248, *Dogs and National Defense*, p. 36; 4243-4370; DRB Reference Collection; RG 407; NACP.
147 Ibid, pp. 11, 24, 36.
148 Museum of Military Medicine: War Diary of DAVRS, February 1943.
149 TNA: WO 199/416, 107A, Commander-in-Chief, Home Forces to the Under Secretary of State, War Office, 18 March 1943.

What is clear, however, is that the use of patrol dogs by the British Army did not completely disappear. Captain B.N. Gaunt recounted the employment of patrol dogs by the Seaforth Highlanders during the final year of the war:

> The dog was trained to lie down when anything moved in front of it and wouldn't go forward until the handler told it to. In this way you knew if there was anything in front of you well before you could see it or they could see you. It was a great help especially as the dogs were also trained to take you back to our own lines along the same path which you came out on.[150]

Rob, another patrol dog, was deployed to North Africa as part of an infantry unit before joining the Special Air Service (SAS) Regiment in late 1943. In Italy, the SAS utilised the Collie on patrols. According to a report submitted to the RSPCA:

> [Rob] was used as patrol and guard over small parties who were lying up in enemy occupied territory. There is no doubt that his presence with these parties saved many of them from being discovered, and thereby captured or killed. The dog has made over 20 parachute descents.[151]

The insistence that Rob participated in parachute jumps with the regiment has since been called into question by SAS veteran Jimmy Quentin Hughes. In his 1998 autobiography *Who Cares Who Wins*, Hughes claimed that Rob's role in the regiment was primarily that of pet. Reports that the dog had participated in parachute jumps, Hughes maintained, were the result of a letter in which members of the regiment fabricated a record of Rob's involvement in an effort to convince his owners that he was crucial to the war effort.[152]

While Rob's role in the Second World War stands contested, records indicate that some patrol dogs did participate in parachute jumps with the Airborne Forces during the latter part of the war. In the *Journal of the Royal Army Veterinary Corps*, Sergeant Ken Bailey of 13th Parachute Battalion revealed that, in 1944, the battalion taught four Alsatians to parachute from aircraft. Prior to joining the battalion, the dogs had trained for patrol work at the Army's War Dogs Training School. Bailey, who handpicked the dogs, remarked on the importance of the selection process:

> It was obvious that a dog chosen for this work must have higher qualities than those of an ordinary patrol dog. It must be of reasonable size to move around

---

150 IWM: 62/346/1, Private Papers of Captain B N Gaunt, 'The last three months of the Fighting in Europe in the Second World War', pp. 23-24.
151 TNA: WO 32/14999, 17A, Bennison to Moss, 2 October 1945.
152 Jimmy Quentin Hughes, *Who Cares Who Wins: The Autobiography of a World War Two Soldier* (Liverpool: Charico, 1998), pp. 235-236.

comfortably without being unduly distressed by the weight of the 'chute and harness, of great energy, so that, by 'bottling up' and controlling this nervous energy, it could be used as an incentive to jump. The dog must also... be absolutely fearless and, if anything, of an aggressive nature.[153]

For 13th Battalion, canine parachute training was a gradual process which spanned several weeks in the months before D-Day. Upon arrival, the dogs were housed in the fuselage of a stationary aeroplane. Using food as a reward, handlers taught the dogs to exit the aeroplane on command. As Bailey explained: "This... was to be the broad pattern of training for the future—the conservation of energy, the incentive of food and, step by step, the enforcing of implicit obedience."[154] The dogs were then introduced to the sounds and motion of moving aircraft at RAF Netheravon in Wiltshire. "In a surprisingly short time," Bailey recounted, "the dogs began to show signs of excitement when the motors of the taxi-ing plane were throttled down."[155] Handlers instructed the dogs to exit from both immobile and taxi-ing aircraft. Finally, following several practice flights, the dogs joined the battalion in parachute drops over Wiltshire. Each dog was attached to its own static-line parachute and expected to exit the aircraft after his handler. Bailey recalled the initial jump, which took place in April 1944:

> The moment the aircraft throttled down to run-in for the 'live drop' the bitch began to get excited... As the green light flashed, she eagerly watched the other parachutists disappear through the 'hole', though still keeping in the position she had been taught behind the handler's heels. There was no time to observe more before it became the writer's turn to jump. She was next observed when the writer's 'chute had opened... Her 'chute had just developed and she was oscillating from side to side about ten degrees... Though she looked somewhat bewildered she showed no signs of fear... She 'touched down' completely relaxed, making no attempt to anticipate or resist the landing, rolled over once, and immediately scrambled to her feet and stood looking round.[156]

In a 1992 interview with the Imperial War Museum, former paratrooper John Bernard Robert Watson recalled that dogs "seemed to enjoy" parachute training.[157] Their employment on operations proved more problematic, however.

---

153 'Parachuting the War Dog', *Journal of the RAVC*, 20 (1950), p. 6. Although the author was listed as "Pegasus," the June 1950 edition of the journal confirmed Bailey was the author.
154 Ibid, p. 7.
155 Ibid.
156 'Parachuting the War Dog', *Journal of the RAVC*, pp. 8-11.
157 IWM: 12412, Interview with John Bernard Robert Watson, 30 January 1992, Reel 3.

Three dogs parachuted over Normandy as part of 13th Battalion on 6 June 1944.[158] According to Flight Lieutenant P.M. Bristow, the dog aboard his aeroplane on D-Day appeared reluctant to jump and was eventually forced from the aircraft by the wireless operator. A similar occurrence was noted by 296 Squadron, which also carried a dog belonging to 13th Battalion.[159] The recollections of members of 13th Battalion suggest that dogs accompanied the battalion to northwest Europe not merely as companions but for use on patrols. Major General Peter Downward, who served as commander of the scout platoon to which two canines were attached, indicated in his memoirs that the dogs participated in training exercises prior to the battalion's deployment to the Netherlands in early 1945.[160] Watson, also a member of 13th Battalion, considered the dogs "a tremendous asset" to patrols.[161]

Bing, a patrol dog which joined 13th Battalion on D-Day, was utilised by the battalion in Normandy, and along with another Alsatian, participated in a second operational jump during March 1945.[162] While in Germany, Bing was utilised on patrols. Lieutenant Ellis Dean recounted an occurrence in March 1945 during which Bing's actions led to the capture of several Germans:

> The Scout Platoon were often in the lead and at one point 'Bing' was sent to investigate a house, nearing the house he froze indicating German presence to his handler... The building was promptly surrounded and many prisoners were taken.[163]

The 9th Parachute Battalion also possessed a trained dog, an Alsatian known as Glen. According to James Baty, a member of the battalion, Glen functioned as a patrol dog.[164] However, the commanding officer of 3rd Parachute Brigade downplayed the significance of the dogs attached to the battalions. In an interview with the Imperial War Museum, he revealed that he acquired dogs in an effort to "prevent boredom" among the men. "They weren't really duly effective," he admitted in the 1991 interview, "but the chaps loved them."[165] Similarly, Baty acknowledged that

---

158 Ibid.
159 Cited in Andrew Woolhouse, *13–Lucky for Some: The History of the 13th (Lancashire) Parachute Battalion* (Amazon Createspace, 2013), pp. 94-95.
160 Peter Downward, *'Old Yourself, One Day': Personal Memoirs of Peter Downward* (Chippenham: Delworth Group, 2004), pp. 177-180.
161 IWM: 12412, Interview with John Watson, Reel 3.
162 Cited in Woolhouse, *13–Lucky for Some*, pp. 484-485 and IWM: 12412, Interview with John Watson, Reel 3.
163 Quoted in Woolhouse, *13–Lucky for Some*, p. 522.
164 IWM: 21192, Interview with James Baty, 14 April 2001, Reel 3. Baty also claimed Glen was a mine detection dog. If that was indeed the case, it is likely Glen carried out this role unofficially, as trained mine detection dogs in the British Army were confined to four mine detection dog platoons.
165 IWM: 12347, Interview with Stanley James Ledger Hill, 25 November 1991, Reel 1.

An Alsatian employed by 13th Parachute Battalion, 1945. (Airborne Assault Museum, Duxford)

Dogs attached to 13th Parachute Battalion, May 1945. (Airborne Assault Museum, Duxford)

Glen of 9th Parachute Battalion with his handler, 1944. (Airborne Assault Museum, Duxford)

despite instructions to the contrary, the men viewed Glen as a pet.[166] Other members of the battalion echoed Baty's assertion. Fred Milward, for example, commented that: "[Glen] was a beautiful Alsatian and everybody's pet; but as his training began we were told… we must not make too much fuss of the dog."[167] Such comments attest to Glen's ambiguous role as both military dog and pet.

Glen's training contrasted from that of 13th Battalion's dogs. Attached to a static-lined parachute, the Alsatian was taught to dive from a balloon at nearly 250 metres before transitioning to aeroplanes.[168] Moreover, unlike 13th Battalion's dogs, Glen learned to exit the aeroplane before his human counterparts.[169] A member of 9th Battalion recalled that during training, Glen "jumped on his own, and seemed more eager to do so than us."[170] On D-Day, however, Glen appeared hesitant and was forced from the aeroplane by his handler. "He loved jumping," Baty recalled,

---

166 IWM: 21192, Interview with James Baty, Reel 3.
167 Quoted in Laurie Goldstraw, 'The Paratrooper and his Dog', *After the Battle*, 74 (1991), 33.
168 Ibid, 33.
169 IWM: 21192, Interview with James Baty, Reel 1.
170 Quoted in Goldstraw, 'The Paratrooper and his Dog', 33.

"but… all the flak coming up… he must have had a premonition because he wouldn't jump."[171] Although Glen survived the descent, he was killed in a bombing raid shortly thereafter.[172] As Glen died not long after the battalion's descent over Normandy, the dog's effectiveness on operations cannot be ascertained.

The employment of guard and military police dogs continued even after the cessation of hostilities. The MAP Guard Dog Training School, or the RAF Police Dog Training School as it had become known, continued to rely upon numerous canines after the war. In early 1946, Baldwin told the *Gloucestershire Echo*: "We cannot begin [releasing dogs] for some time."[173] At that time, the RAF still relied upon nearly 750 canines at approximately 500 sites, including POW camps. Instead of reducing the amount of dogs in training, the RAF Police Dog Training School sought additional dogs to allow for the further demobilisation of servicemen.[174] The use of dogs by the Royal Military Police (RMP), as the CMP was designated after 1946, also persisted after the war; by mid-1948, the RMP dog sections in the Middle East had apprehended nearly 3,400 persons and prevented the loss of approximately £94,000 in War Department equipment and supplies.[175] The wartime employment of guard and military police dogs, therefore, led to the continued use of dogs in such roles in the postwar period.

The increasing number of guard and military police dogs recruited during the Second World War, as well as their continued use after 1945, suggests that dogs formed an effective adjunct to human guards and military policemen. Apart from high casualty rates among CMP dogs in the Middle East, the British guard and military police dog schemes on the Home Front and abroad encountered few difficulties as compared to other military roles performed by dogs in the war. As evidenced by War Office and Air Ministry records and accounts by servicemen, the use of trained dogs enhanced security at military installations in Britain, the Middle East, North Africa and continental Europe. In contrast to guard and military police dogs, patrol dogs were utilised on a small scale in the British Army. While reports from some servicemen attest to the usefulness of dogs on patrols, their restricted employment suggests that the overall contribution of British patrol dogs to the Allied war effort was relatively minimal.

171 IWM: 21192, Interview with James Baty, Reel 1.
172 IWM: 21192, Interview with James Baty, Reel 3.
173 Quoted in 'War Dogs "Demob" Delayed', *Gloucestershire Echo*, 9 January 1946, p. 4.
174 'Dogs to Speed Demob', *Dundee Evening Telegraph*, 7 March 1946, p. 8 and 'War Dogs "Demob" Delayed', *Gloucestershire Echo*, 9 January 1946.
175 'Employment of Military Police Dogs', *Journal of the RAVC*, p. 92.

4

"A Brain Child of World War II": The Introduction and Employment of Mine Detection Dogs

The year 1944 marked the first use of mine detection dogs in the British Army. In his historical account of the RAVC, Brigadier John Clabby described the mine detection dog as "a brain child of World War II."[1] Similarly, in *Dogs of War*, Ernest A. Gray likened the mine detection dog, which he described as "the conspicuous British war dog of World War Two," to the messenger dog of the First World War.[2] Indeed, just as the use of messenger dogs during the First World War was indicative of the static conditions of the Western Front, the introduction of mine detection dogs in the Second World War came as a result of the enemy's increasing employment of non-metallic landmines. Four British mine detection dog platoons were formed during the Second World War; the dogs and their handlers completed a period of training at the Army's War Dogs Training School in Britain prior to deploying to France in the latter half of 1944. During the final two years of the war, the platoons assisted the Royal Engineers (RE), as well as other Allied mine detection units, in northwest Europe.

War diaries, reports and correspondence held at the National Archives and the Museum of Military Medicine provide insight into the development and functioning of the British mine detection dog scheme. Records related to No. 2 Mine Detection Dog Platoon created or compiled by its officer commanding are particularly numerous and thus allow for a more detailed investigation into that platoon's role in northwest Europe.

---

1 Clabby, *History of the RAVC*, p. 186.
2 Gray, *Dogs of War*, p. 163.

The Demand for Mine Detection Dogs: The Formation and Training of Dog Platoons

The 1934 British Army publication *Military Engineering* defined landmines as "explosive charges laid in the ground with the object of delaying the advance of the enemy by impairing his morale, destroying his personnel and transport, or interrupting his communication."[3] The use of landmines began several years before the outbreak of the Second World War. Anti-personnel mines were introduced in the last half of the 19th century, and both the British and German Armies utilised landmines during the First World War. The Germans relied upon anti-personnel mines to hinder the movement of British troops as well as to keep them from recapturing ground. The arrival of the tank in 1916 led to a new type of landmine known as the anti-tank mine. As the number of British tanks rose during 1917, Germany responded by expanding anti-tank mine production. Nevertheless, the landmines of the First World War were rudimentary in design, and their use existed on a relatively small scale.[4]

In terms of the quantity of anti-tank and anti-personnel mines and the destruction they entailed, the Second World War ushered in a new era of landmine warfare. It was in the Second World War that troops first witnessed the extensive use of landmines.[5] As landmine expert Mike Croll put it: "During the war the mine came of age and its use shaped combat in every theatre from Okinawa to Normandy... Mine warfare entered the field of battle on a massive scale."[6] Every belligerent was affected by the use of landmines in the Second World War, and although the Allied and Axis forces utilised landmines, as Croll pointed out, "none mastered it like the Germans."[7] German experiments with trinitrotoluene (TNT) during the interwar period allowed for the introduction of the anti-tank *Tellermine* in 1929. German scientists continued to experiment with landmines over the following decade, so that by the outbreak of the war, the *Wehrmacht* had at its disposal one anti-personnel and two anti-tank mines.[8]

Between 1939 and 1945, the Germans planted some 35,000,000 mines.[9] The *Wehrmacht* favoured expansive minefields containing both anti-tank and anti-personnel mines set in a fixed pattern. In addition, British troops frequently discovered

---

3   Quoted in Rae McGrath, *Landmines and Unexploded Ordnance: A Resource Book* (London: Pluto Press, 2000), p. 3.
4   Mike Croll, *The History of Landmines*, (Barnsley: Leo Cooper, 1998), pp. 25-31. Croll pointed out that although Germany commenced the large scale production of anti-tank mines following the Battle of Cambrai in late 1917, few British tanks came into contact with mines during the First World War.
5   Ibid, pp. 53-81.
6   Ibid, p. 53.
7   Ibid, p. 51.
8   Lydia Monin and Andrew Gallimore, *The Devil's Gardens: A History of Landmines* (London: Pimlico, 2002), p. 48.
9   Croll, *History of Landmines*, p. 37.

German-laid mines along roads, railways and verges.[10] Early in the war, British soldiers had few means for detecting enemy mines, as the Army lacked electronic mine detectors.[11] Furthermore, prior to the evacuation at Dunkirk, few British soldiers had received even basic landmine training. As an officer observed: "The soldiers had never seen one [mine], let alone trained on them."[12] It was in North Africa that the British witnessed the first large-scale employment of landmines by the Germans. In an effort to augment the outnumbered German tank force at El Alamein, General Field Marshal Erwin Rommel oversaw the laying of two immense minefields. Known as the "devil's garden," Rommel's North African minefields spanned approximately eight kilometres and contained some 500,000 mines.[13]

Prior to the introduction of electronic detectors, British soldiers relied upon a means of mine detection known as prodding. Prodding involved a bayonet or metal rod, which soldiers used to probe the earth in search of mines.[14] Although British troops continued to rely on prodding throughout the Second World War, it had several disadvantages. A prodder risked inadvertently detonating a mine if he exerted too much pressure with the instrument. A British report compiled in 1946 estimated that prodding led to one casualty per 2,000 mines. Moreover, prodding was extremely tedious. On average, soldiers with prodders took around one minute to advance over one and a half metres of ground.[15]

The first electronic mine detector utilised by the British Army became available in 1941. That year, the War Office authorised the production of 250 Polish mine detectors.[16] Mine detection with the Polish detector was contingent on the employment of metallic mines, and as a contemporary report made clear, it was "a slow and deliberate process."[17] Polish detectors could typically detect metallic mines such as the *Tellermine* and the anti-personnel *Schrapnellmine* (S-mine).[18] By 1942, however, the Germans had produced two largely non-metallic mines: the anti-personnel *Schutzenmine* (Schu-mine) and the anti-tank *Holzmine*.[19] As both mines had wooden exteriors, they usually were undetected by electronic detectors and were thus considered "detection-resisting."

10   TNA: WO 232/85, Minefield Clearance, 40A, Further Technical Developments in German Mine Warfare, February 1945 and 43A, Notes on the Problem of Anti-Tank and Anti-Personnel Mines.
11   Croll, *History of Landmines*, p. 35.
12   Quoted in Ibid, p. 36.
13   Ibid, pp. 56, 61.
14   Lt. Col. C.E.E. Sloan, *Mine Warfare on Land* (London: Brassey's, 1986), p. 73.
15   TNA: AVIA 74/15, UHF Mine Detector for Non-Metallic Mines, 99, The Detection of Non-Metallic Mines, Summary of the Problems and of Methods, 1 July 1946.
16   TNA: AVIA 22/862, Mine Detectors: Research and Development, R. Cook, Notes on Mine Detection Development, 1 August 1944.
17   TNA: AVIA 22/861, Mine Detectors: Research and Development, 331B, Detection and Destruction of Anti-Tank Minefields, 20 May 1942.
18   TNA: AVIA 22/862, Mine Dog Training, Appendix 'A' to 21 AGp, 17 January 1945.
19   Croll, *History of Landmines*, p. 43.

Schu-mines and *Holzmines* were not completely devoid of metal, however. The igniters in both mines contained slight traces of metal, and nails were used in the production of *Holzmines*.[20]

The No. 4 Polish detector, introduced in 1943, could detect the slight amount of metal present in non-metallic mines such as Schu-mines and *Holzmines*. The commandant of the Obstacle Assault Centre (OAC) considered the detector "the best available solution" for the location of such mines.[21] Yet, as a post-war report made clear, the detection of Schu-mines remained particularly problematic even after the arrival of the No. 4 detector:

> [The Schu-mine] is not reliably detected by the standard metallic mine detectors due to its small size and low metal content. Due to unreliability of detection men soon lose confidence in their detectors since this mine will almost inevitably blow a man's foot off if trodden on. Prodding is always resorted to for this type.[22]

The employment of the No. 4 detector involved additional limitations. Like earlier Polish detectors, the operation of the No. 4 detector was time-consuming. The detector also reacted to all metallic objects, including shrapnel.[23] Furthermore, electronic detectors, including the No. 4, could not effectively locate mines planted well below the surface.[24] Another version of the Polish detector, the No. 5, was available by late 1943. Although the No. 5 detector enabled human operators to move at a faster pace than other electronic detectors, it was less effective at determining the precise position of mines.[25] Moreover, at over 29 kilograms, the No. 5 detector was especially heavy compared to the No. 4, which weighed just 10 kilograms.[26]

In April 1942, it was predicted that it was "unlikely… that the Germans, in developing a mine that will escape detection will retain in their design even the smallest metallic part."[27] Indeed, in 1944, the Germans unveiled a "non-detectable" mine: the anti-tank *Topfmine*. A War Office report noted that electronic detectors "proved useless" against "the all-important Topfmine" owing to its cardboard construction and

---

20   TNA: AVIA 74/15, 99, Detection of Non-Metallic Mines, 1 July 1946.
21   TNA: DEFE 2/1060, Obstacle Assault Centre: Progress Reports and Summaries, Commandant, Breaching of Obstacles, 4 May 1944. For information on the OAC, see: TNA: DEFE 2/1060, Letter from A. Lambert, 18 March 1943. The OAC was founded in early 1943 to aid the Royal Engineers in "developing an efficient technique for the location and removal of minefields and for surmounting other obstacles, and advising the General Staff on the tactical requirements for the observance of this technique."
22   TNA: AVIA 74/15, 99, Detection of Non-Metallic Mines, 1 July 1946.
23   TNA: WO 232/85, 44A, Minutes of Meeting to Discuss the Mine Problem, 10 February 1945.
24   TNA: DEFE 2/1060, Breaching of Obstacles, 4 May 1944.
25   TNA: WO 203/3126, Report on Trials held at O.A.C, 16 December 1943.
26   TNA: AVIA 22/862, Notes on Mine Detection Development, 1 August 1944.
27   TNA: AVIA 22/861, 330B, Anti-Tank and Chemical Warfare Committee, 18 May 1942.

lack of metal.[28] In northwest Europe, the *Wehrmacht* utilised *Topfmines* along roads, verges and in minefields. The Germans also favoured burying *Topfmines* along with anti-personnel mines such as S-Mines and Schu-mines.[29]

The War Office considered the employment of dogs as mine detectors relatively early in the war. In January 1942, the Imperial General Staff listed dogs among potential mine detection techniques available to the British Army.[30] A May 1942 report submitted by the Director of Staff Duties, War Office indicated that "the possibility of training dogs to locate buried mines… is now being investigated."[31] In his account of the war, Lloyd recalled: "Once the question [of mine detection dogs] was put and a free hand given it was up to the War Dog School to find the answer."[32] He went on to explain that the training of mine detection dogs at the school was influenced by his own work with a detection dog prior to the war.[33] The event to which Lloyd referred was the employment of a Labrador, which in May 1939 identified the source of several leaks in a series of cables at a radio receiving station in southeast England. According to an article in the *Observer*:

> A gas that smelt of cats was introduced into the air pumped into the cable. The dog went along the route and started to dig wherever he detected a smell of the gas. He was successful in detecting fourteen leaks, and thus enabled the cable to be repaired without digging up the two miles of the route.[34]

In preparation for this role, the dog underwent a period of training during which he learned to "associate cats with his food," as Lloyd explained to a journalist in May 1939. Lloyd further described the training process: "Whenever he started digging, we introduced a piece of meat into the hole to reward and encourage him."[35]

On 16 December 1943, a series of mine detection trials involving dogs from the Army's War Dogs Training School took place at the OAC.[36] Opened earlier that year, the OAC served in part to research new methods of mine detection and clearance.[37] Although trainers at the school had conducted prior trials, the exercises on 16 December marked the first mine detection dog demonstration at the OAC. According to a government memorandum, OAC personnel "were incredulous of the

---

28   TNA: WO 232/85, 40A, Further Technical Developments, February 1945.
29   Ibid.
30   TNA: AVIA 22/862, General Staff Policy Statement No. 29, 19 January 1942.
31   TNA: AVIA 22/861, 331B, Detection and Destruction, 20 May 1942.
32   Lloyd, 'Dog in War', p. 188.
33   Ibid.
34   'Dog Performs New Duty', *Observer*, 28 May 1939, p. 15.
35   "'Cats" Thought Rex But it was a Post Office Trick', *Northern Daily Mail*, 27 May 1939, p. 5.
36   TNA: WO 203/3126, Report on Trials, 16 December 1943. See Appendix IV for the complete results of this demonstration.
37   TNA: DEFE 2/1060, Letter from A. Lambert, 18 March 1943.

[mine detection dog] method even after the preliminary tests carried out at the War Dogs training school." Thus, the demonstration "act[ed] as a definite and independent check" to earlier displays at the school.[38]

Five dogs, each with between five to 10 weeks of mine detection training, took part in the trials which aimed to assess the viability of dogs as mine detectors. In the first trial, two dogs were directed to search for mines planted 17 days previously along a 91 metre track. The dogs discovered six of eight mines (75 percent) in just over 22 minutes. A human operator wielding a No. 5 detector completed the exercise at the same speed as the dogs; however, the electronic detector was unable to detect four mines, including two wooden box mines described as "practically non-metallic."[39] The second trial involved the detection of three mines in an area measuring 17 square metres. As in the first trial, the mines were buried 17 days earlier. According to a report submitted by Lieutenant Colonel H.H.C. Withers of the Royal Engineers, the single dog utilised on this exercise "worked well and surely" and "with great eagerness" as he swept the area.[40] The dog finished in 12.5 minutes, during which he discovered all three mines. A human operator, by contrast, needed just 11.5 minutes to locate the mines with a No. 4 detector. Three dogs were utilised in the final trial, which assessed the dogs against a No. 5 detector in the detection of 10 mines on or near a road extending one kilometre. The mines included anti-personnel and anti-tank mines buried 24 hours previously. While the dogs required over 32 minutes to cover the road, the human operator finished in around 22 minutes. Although the detector had the advantage of speed, the dogs discovered nine out of 10 (90 percent) mines. The detector detected just four. Among the mines undetected by the electronic detector were two Schu-mines and two "non-detectable" anti-personnel mines.[41]

As evidenced by the trials, dogs could recognise both metallic and non-metallic mines. In his report, Withers determined that "dogs have a very real possibility for mine clearance" and suggested that "as many dogs as possible be put into [mine detection] training forthwith." Moreover, he noted that canines would be particularly beneficial "should the enemy start the extensive use of the non-detectable mine."[42] The OAC's own report regarded the demonstration as "most encouraging" and proposed the establishment of mine detection dog units.[43] In addition, the aforementioned government memorandum indicated that the "trials carried out under their own control satisfied [OAC personnel] that the [mine detection dog] method gave results."[44]

38   TNA: AVIA 22/862, 487A, S.R.8. Memo, 1 May 1944.
39   TNA: WO 203/3126, Report on Trials, 16 December 1943.
40   Ibid.
41   Ibid.
42   Ibid.
43   TNA: DEFE 2/1060, Obstacle Assault Centre, Report for December 1943.
44   TNA: AVIA 22/862, 487A, S.R.8. Memo, 1 May 1944.

Fifteen dogs participated in another series of trials near Aldershot on 24 March 1944.[45] The first two trials resembled the exercises held in December, as dogs were required to search for mines buried on verges and a cart track. Dogs discovered nine of 12 (75 percent) and 12 of 14 mines (85 percent), respectively. The third exercise involved the location of 12 mines along a road, and dogs were required to work amid gunfire and explosives.[46] Although a report on the trials maintained that the sounds did not have a marked effect on the dogs' performance,[47] the dogs discovered only eight of 12 mines (66 percent). During the following trial, which pitted two dogs against No. 4 detectors, the dogs discovered 14 of 15 mines (93 percent) in 29 minutes. The human operators, by contrast, clocked in at over 32 minutes and discovered only 11 mines (73 percent). In a separate exercise, dogs covered a vehicle park littered with food, petrol and other distracting odours. Although it was mentioned in a separate report that "the foul ground did not impede the dogs," the four dogs in use discovered just two of four *Tellermines*. In the final trial, two dogs detected four of five mines (80 percent). The outcomes of these trials mirrored those from the demonstration at the OAC three months earlier; mine detection dogs, it was shown, could effectively recognise metallic and non-metallic mines.[48] Major R.C. Blyth of the Royal Engineers observed that the employment of mine detection dogs "seems to be a feasible and workable proposition" and noted that canines "appear[ed] to be surer and slightly quicker than detectors."[49]

The successful performance of dogs at these demonstrations led to a decision by the War Office to discuss the official employment of mine detection dogs by the British Army. In April 1944, Army officials authorised the formation of four mine detection dog platoons to operate as part of the Royal Engineers. The first platoon, it was determined, would be raised the following week. At the time of the meeting, however, the Army's War Dogs Training School had thus far turned out relatively few trained mine detection dogs. As the school would require several months to acquire and train enough dogs for the remaining three platoons, it was decided to recruit additional trainers.[50] The platoons consisted of 30 dogs and 10 handlers apiece.[51] Appendix VI shows the entire war establishment of the mine detection dog platoons as of May 1944. They were charged with the location of mines but were not expected to neutralise or

---

45   TNA: WO 203/3126, Report on Mine Detection by War Dogs at Claycart Bottom, 24 March 1944. See Appendix V for the complete results of this demonstration.
46   TNA: WO 203/3126, Programme of Mine Detection by War Dogs at Claycart Bottom, 24 March 1944.
47   TNA: WO 203/3126, Report on Mine Detection, 24 March 1944.
48   TNA: WO 203/3126, Programme of Mine Detection, 24 March 1944.
49   TNA: WO 203/3126, Report on Mine Detection, 24 March 1944.
50   TNA: WO 32/11100, Tradesmen: General: Trade Test for Dog Handlers, 2A, Minutes of a Meeting Held on 24 April 1944 to Consider the Provision of Dog Unit (Mine Detecting) for 21 Army Group, 25 April 1944.
51   TNA: WO 32/11100, 1A, H.F. Hare, 28 April 1944.

remove mines, as this was performed by the engineer units to which the dog platoons were attached while in northwest Europe.[52]

For most dogs at the Army's War Dogs Training School, mine detection training spanned approximately four months, during which dogs were introduced to and began practising with their handlers.[53] Training centred on rewarding dogs for an expected behaviour, namely, the detection of mines. As the War Office training manual *Training of War Dogs* made clear: "The dog is attracted towards a mine by reason of a reward it receives on indicating its presence."[54] This procedure, designated the "reward system" or the "attraction method," differed from the "repulsion system" adopted by American military dog trainers.[55] Under the "reward system," dogs were initially taught to find a small number of mines planted near the surface. Titbits of meat were positioned on mines and served as the dogs' reward upon detection. Over the next several weeks, trainers removed the titbits from the mines, which were planted increasingly lower and in different surroundings.[56]

Throughout the training process, as well as on operations, dogs remained attached to their handlers by a harness and lead. While searching specified areas, which were usually divided into sections measuring nearly two and a half metres in width, dogs learned to signal the existence of mines by sitting.[57] It was then up to the handler to establish a mine's precise position with a prodder.[58] The platoons worked in association with Sappers, who inspected the same ground with prodders or electronic detectors.[59] Thus, canines served as only one means of mine detection available to the British Army and were generally utilised in addition to prodders and electronic detectors.

While most persons who witnessed or worked with mine detection dogs agreed that such canines relied upon scent, they held differing opinions as to precisely which scent(s), or other faculty, led dogs to mines. Lloyd, for example, believed that dogs mostly detected the odour emitted by the explosive material within the mines, rather than the mines themselves. Lloyd explained this line of reasoning in *The Book of the Dog*:

> The freshly buried mine, be it metallic, wooden or glass, could be discovered by the fact that the ground had not been 'weathered' or hermetically sealed, thus

52   TNA: WO 205/1173, 3C, Training Instruction, undated and 42B, Report on Results and Employment of Dogs in Mine Detection, 5 November 1944.
53   NAA: MP742/1, 240/6324, Training of War Dogs, 3 January 1945.
54   War Office, *Training of War Dogs* (1952), p. 54. Although published in April 1952, *Training of War Dogs* detailed the mine detection dog training methods introduced and utilised by trainers at the War Dogs Training School in the Second World War.
55   *Training of War Dogs* (1952), p. 54 and TNA: WO 291/2673, 37B, Outlines of Training, undated.
56   *Training of War Dogs* (1952), pp. 54-56.
57   Ibid.
58   TNA: WO 205/1173, Report on Mine Dogs from 21 Army Group, undated.
59   TNA: WO 205/1173, 42B, Report on Results, 5 November 1944 and 71D, Report on Mine-Detecting, 11-16 February 1945.

A Labrador employed by No. 1 Dog Platoon on operations in France, July 1944. (© Imperial War Museum (B 6501))

Mine detection dogs and handlers employed by No. 1 Dog Platoon in France, July 1944. (© Imperial War Museum (B 6506))

leaving air channels which permitted the scent to ascend. Mines which had been buried for several months appeared to create a chemical reaction on the soil and were equally easily found by the dogs.[60]

The officer commanding, No. 2 Dog Platoon speculated that dogs likely scented mines, as well as the unearthed soil surrounding them.[61] By contrast, the officer commanding, No. 4 Dog Platoon attributed the proficiency of mine detection dogs in part to canine intuitiveness. In a letter to *The Times* in September 1982, he posited: "Although a sense of smell played a part, so too did other senses, and in particular the animal's very highly developed 'sixth' sense."[62] Major Blyth arrived at a similar conclusion after witnessing demonstrations by mine detection dogs in late 1943.[63]

Another prevailing view was that dogs picked up the lingering odours of the persons who had handled the mines.[64] In an effort to understand how dogs located mines, the Military Operational Research Unit, in early 1947, conducted experiments involving mine detection dogs. Four dogs trained in mine detection underwent a surgical procedure resulting in the detachment of their olfactory nerves. Following the procedure, the four dogs exhibited little decline in their ability to locate mines and compared favourably to two mine detection dogs which had not undergone the procedure. A report compiled by the Military Operational Research Unit suggested that, barring complications during the procedures: "Dogs detect mines by either a different sense from that of smell or by a complex group of senses."[65]

Although many of the mine detection dogs employed by the British Army were crossbreeds, trainers and handlers agreed that certain breeds made particularly effective mine detectors. Among these were Alsatians, Collies, and above all, Labradors.[66] While no explanation was provided as to why trainers and handlers were partial to these breeds, size seems to have been a determining factor.[67] Lieutenant James R. Davison, the officer commanding, No. 2 Dog Platoon, found small breeds to be "either intent on game hunting, or are less emenable (sic), sensitive to weather, unable to keep up a sustained effort, and often overawed by the larger dogs."[68] Curiously, another report went so far as to recommend dogs with a particular eye colour. The

60   Lloyd, 'Dog in War', p. 188.
61   Museum of Military Medicine: Box 14, War Diary, No. 2 Dog Platoon, Monthly Reports, Lt. Davison, Supplementary Notes to Report on No. 2 Dog Platoon, 11 January 1945.
62   P. Norbury, 'Using Dogs as Mine Detectors', *The Times*, 13 September 1982, p. 9.
63   TNA: WO 203/3126, Report on Mine Detection, 24 March 1944.
64   TNA: AVIA 74/15, 78, Detection of Non-Metallic Mines, Notes of a Discussion at S.R.D.E., 7 March 1946.
65   TNA: WO 291/1048, Interim Report No. 120, April 1947.
66   TNA: AVIA 22/871, Mine Detection Dogs, undated and TNA: WO 291/1048, Interim Report No. 120, April 1947 and TNA: WO 291/2673, 37B, Outlines of Training, undated.
67   TNA: AVIA 22/871, Mine Detection Dogs, undated. This document, the author of which is unknown, made clear that "the most suitable dog to train appears [to be] a medium sized one."
68   TNA: WO 205/1173, 71D, Report on Mine-Detecting, 11-16 February 1945.

report, whose author was not identified, suggested that whereas dark-eyed canines were "frequently sulky and erratic in their work" and light-eyed dogs "inclined to use their eyes in preference to their nose," a canine with hazel eyes "usually has the firmer character and for this reason should be selected" for mine detection training.[69] As the historian Robert Kirk has shown, such physical indicators were seen by trainers as indicative of positive behavioural traits and thus, potential mine detection ability. Breed, he rightly pointed out, was secondary to temperament and "was only a consideration in terms of practical and economic needs."[70]

While trainers may have sought dogs with certain behavioural traits, it is clear from his writings that Davison did not consider mine detection dogs to possess greater mental capability than other canines. In a report submitted in early 1945, for example, he noted that mine detection dogs were "not particularly intelligent dogs."[71] Moreover, in a separate report, Davison argued against alternating dogs between minefields and tracts of land likely to contain few mines since "the change of duty to this pace and to this degree of concentration necessary [for searching minefields], seems confusing to their 'simplex' minds."[72] Davison's assertions suggest that, in his view, the effective employment of dogs was largely the result of the dog's olfactory ability and the handler's control over his charge rather than canine intelligence.

Anglo-American Co-Operation and Divergence

Even before the American declaration of war against Japan in December 1941, Britain had cultivated a de facto alliance with the United States that involved posting numerous staff in that country to promote British interests and acquire information useful to prosecuting the war. The British Army Staff, as the British contingent in the United States was designated in 1941, expanded to include approximately 1,900 members before hostilities ceased.[73] As the historian Niall Barr has rightly argued, this "infiltration of North America by the British Army Staff was... unheralded" and led to an unparalleled "degree of liaison, collaboration and even integration between the British and American armies."[74] The British Army Staff, therefore, "acted as enablers for an unprecedented level of cooperation" between Britain and the United States.[75]

---

69   TNA: AVIA 22/871, Mine Detection Dogs, undated.
70   Kirk, 'In Dogs We Trust?', pp. 7-8.
71   Museum of Military Medicine: Box 14, War Diary, No. 2 War Dog Platoon, J.R. Davison, Report on the Possibility of Combining in One Dog, the Duties of a Patrol Dog and a Mine Dog, 15 January 1945.
72   TNA: WO 205/1173, 72E, J.R. Davison, Report on Mine Detection by Dogs, undated.
73   Barr, *Yanks and Limeys*, pp. 94-96, 135-136, 342-343.
74   Ibid, p. 342.
75   Ibid, p. 468.

Anglo-American co-operation extended to the training and employment of mine detection dogs. The United States QMC launched a mine detection dog training scheme as early as May 1943.[76] The following November, the United States War Department directed Army Service Forces to raise a mine detection dog unit "for employment in the North African Theater of Operations at the earliest practicable date."[77] The unit, 228th Engineer Mine Detection Company, commenced training in late 1943.[78] While the training of mine detection dogs commenced in both Britain and the United States in 1943, correspondence between members of the British Army Staff suggest that British officials in the United States may have influenced the decision by the QMC to employ mine detection dogs. In the spring of 1943, British Army officer Brigadier Charles Lindemann reached out to Colonel E.M. Daniels of the United States Army Remount Service in an effort to convince the QMC of the need for mine detection dogs.[79] Lindemann may have been influenced by his brother, Lord Cherwell, the Prime Minister's scientific adviser, who expressed enthusiasm for the employment of dogs as mine detectors.[80]

Initial success with mine detection dogs in the United States likely led to the eventual employment of mine detection dogs by the British Army. Lindemann, who was present at multiple American trials in September 1943, urged that a representative of the British Army's War Dogs Training School travel to the United States to attend mine detection dog training exercises.[81] In correspondence with the War Office in late September 1943, the British Army Staff in the United States cited the "great progress" of the American mine detection dog scheme and seconded Lindemann's

76   NARA: Colonel C.S. Hamilton to Director, Military Training Division, Army Service Forces, 24 September 1943 (Hamilton to Military Training Division, 24 September 1943); National Archives Microfilm Publication Roll, 3034 (Roll 3034), Item 3284; Historical Documents of World War II; RG 407; NACP.

77   NARA: Major General Thomas T. Handy, Assistant Chief of Staff to the Commanding General, Army Service Forces, 10 November 1943; 452.1 to 455.2; Security Classified Correspondence, 1942-1946; General Records, G-4; RG 165; NACP. The North African Theater of Operations, which was later renamed the Mediterranean Theater of Operations by the United States military, included Italy in addition to North Africa.

78   NARA: Constitution and Activation of 228th Engineer Mine Detection Company (Dog), 19 November 1943; National Archives Microfilm Publication Roll, 3033, Item 3276; Historical Documents of World War II; RG 407; NACP.

79   NARA: Brigadier General W.A. Wood, Jr. to the Quartermaster General, Military Planning Division, Remount Service, 29 May 1943; Decimal 454.3; Decimal Correspondence Files, 1940-1945; RG 407; NACP.

80   Nuffield College Library, University of Oxford: CSAC 80/4/81, Papers of F.A. Lindemann, Viscount Cherwell of Oxford, Scientific Correspondence, D.71, J.F. Evetts to Lord Cherwell, 15 January 1944.

81   Museum of Military Medicine: Box 14, Reports and Correspondence between UK and USA, Colonel P.A. Clauson to Engineer-in-Chief, War Office, 13 September 1943 and Telegram from British Army Staff, Washington to the War Office, 21 September 1943 and NARA: Hamilton to Director, Military Training Division, 24 September 1943; Roll 3034, Item 3284; Historical Documents; RG 407; NACP.

proposal that a British representative tour the American mine detection dog training facility.[82] Similarly, Colonel C.E.A. Browning of the British Army Staff insisted that mine detection dog training in the United States was "proving to be a really promising development which deserves attention at home."[83] Consequently, the War Office directed the commandant of the British Army's War Dogs Training School to journey to the United States "to obtain all information" concerning the instruction of mine detection dogs by the QMC.[84]

Despite such instances of Anglo-American co-operation, the training of mine detection dogs in the United States differed markedly from that of the British Army's War Dogs Training School. As opposed to British trainers, who utilised food as a training incentive, American trainers adhered to the "repulsion method." Thus, while British trainers encouraged dogs to actively search for mines, dogs instructed by the QMC were conditioned to fear, and consequently, eschew mines.[85] In a technical bulletin published in August 1944, the United States War Department detailed the first stage of American mine detection dog training, which entailed the laying of steel traps in lieu of mines:

> [The handler] carefully maneuvers (sic) his dog so that he will become ensnared in one of the traps. When the teeth of the trap close on the dog's foot, the dog howls or whines from the shock and surprise… The handler waits 8 to 10 seconds, until he thinks that the dog is sufficiently impressed by the pain and the shock, and then hurriedly removes the trap from the dog's foot. During this operation, the handler again assumes a role: he simulates fear and horror when touching the trap, hurling it away as soon as it is removed. The handler's ability as an actor in impressing his own fear and horror of these metallic objects upon the dog's consciousness is an important factor in creating and building up the dog's fear of them.[86]

Moreover, the instructions advised that handlers with "under-sensitive" canines could apply electricity to the traps to ensure the dogs felt physical discomfort. As the dogs began to effectively uncover the traps, handlers replaced them with practice mines.[87]

82   Museum of Military Medicine: Box 14, Reports and Correspondence between UK and USA, British Army Staff, Washington to the War Office, 21 September 1943.
83   Museum of Military Medicine: Box 14, Reports and Correspondence between UK and USA, Colonel C.E.A. Browning, British Army Staff to Chief Engineer, British Army Staff, 24 September 1943.
84   Museum of Military Medicine: Box 14, Reports and Correspondence between UK and USA, Telegram from the War Office to British Army Staff Washington, 7 October 1943.
85   NARA: Captain John B. Fetzer, Jr., Engineer Intelligence Report No. 19, Visit to the War Dogs Training School, 21 August 1944 (Engineer Intelligence Report No. 19), pp. 1-2; National Archives Microfilm Publication, Roll 3032 (Roll 3032), Item 3268; Historical Documents of World War II; RG 407; NACP.
86   TNA: WO 203/3126, War Department Technical Bulletin TB 10-396-1, Mine Detection Dog (M-Dog), 4 August 1944.
87   Ibid.

For a time, American trainers employed both techniques prior to settling on the "repulsion method." Likewise, trainers at the British Army's War Dogs Training School explored the possibility of utilising the "repulsion method."[88] After the war, Lloyd acknowledged that, although British trainers briefly considered the "repulsion method," it became clear that the American technique was less effective. Compared to the "attraction method," he pointed out, the "repulsion method" produced overcautious dogs which failed to pinpoint the location of mines.[89] Upon attending a mine detection trial at the British Army's War Dogs Training School, a member of the British Army Staff observed that canines trained at the British facility more accurately identified the position of mines compared to American mine detection dogs.[90]

The contrast in training styles is significant given that the British Army Staff may have assisted in the development of the American mine detection dog scheme. Yet as Niall Barr has shown, even with the extensive material passed between Britain and the United States on various aspects of the war, both nations occasionally opted to proceed in different directions. That the British and American military dog schemes differed regarding the instruction of mine detection dogs even after the British Army Staff considered the methods of each country should not be seen as an aberration but as one of the many instances in which the Allies diverged during the war.[91]

British Mine Detection Dogs in Northwest Europe

The first British canine mine detection unit, No. 1 Dog Platoon, deployed to Normandy in late June 1944 just weeks after the initial Allied landings.[92] Almost immediately, the platoon experienced a number of setbacks in France. While taking part in a trial with 1 Corps Troops (RE) in mid-July, the platoon's officer commanding was severely wounded after stepping on an anti-personnel mine which the dogs had missed. Human operators with electronic detectors subsequently located an additional nine mines in the area over which the dogs had worked.[93]

Although the dogs' performance improved during training exercises the following week, the success was short-lived. The platoon's next assignment, the clearance of Carpiquet Airfield outside Caen, required that the dogs work in more difficult surroundings than they were accustomed to in prior training. The platoon's new officer commanding, Lieutenant F.J.S. Morgan, described the area surrounding the airfield:

88 NARA: Engineer Intelligence Report No. 19, pp. 1-2, 5, 8; Roll 3032, Item 3268; Historical Documents of World War II; RG 407; NACP.
89 Lloyd, 'Dog in War', p. 191.
90 TNA: WO 205/1173, Note on Visit to British War Dog Training Centre on 13 March 1945.
91 Barr, *Yanks and Limeys*, pp. 302-305, 344-347.
92 Museum of Military Medicine: Box 14, War Diary of DAVRS, June 1944.
93 TNA: WO 205/1173, 7A, CE, 1 Corps to CE, Second Army, 17 July 1944.

Here the ground was far rougher, grass tough and long, ground pitted with shell craters, littered with shrapnel and with an average of 10 bomb or shell craters every 100 y[ar]d run. There were apparently no mines present in the ground, but much buried shrapnel, shells, bit of t[an]k metal and cartridge cases. There was much gun fire near at hand and a strong smell of dead bodies.[94]

Following its recapture by Canadian forces in early July, Carpiquet Airfield was thought to contain few, if any, mines. To ensure this was the case, the platoon was directed to search the site alongside 24 Airfield Construction Group. The use of electronic detectors was especially arduous considering the airfield was a scene of battle less than two weeks earlier and thus contained a substantial amount of shrapnel. Mechanical rollers were employed over some sections of the airfield but were ineffective for covering the uneven surfaces near the hangars.[95] Between 22 and 24 July, the dogs worked over 67,720 square metres, but as Lieutenant Morgan noted: "The dogs were becoming tired easily and could be seen to be not working on many occasions."[96] To counter the effects of fatigue, the platoon recommenced training. Once again, the dogs' performance improved; they located nearly every mine during training. When the platoon returned to Carpiquet Airfield the following day, however, the dogs seemed increasingly distracted and apathetic as no mines were discovered. In an effort to keep the dogs engaged, handlers began laying mines for the dogs. According to a report submitted by Lieutenant Morgan, the laying of mines succeeded for a time, but poor weather in early August led to further difficulties. After 12 dogs balked at continuing in intense heat and dust, the platoon was again obliged to resume training.[97]

Problems were also noted by No. 2 Dog Platoon, which landed in Normandy on 1 September 1944. Upon arrival in France, the dogs and their handlers resumed training exercises at Bretteville-sur-Laize near Caen. In the platoon's war diary, Lieutenant Davison noted that a number of dogs were "off work" during their first weeks in France. Moreover, he observed that members of 25th Bomb Disposal Company (RE), the unit to which the platoon was initially attached, appeared "sceptical about safety" following a demonstration by the dogs. Although Davison indicated that their apprehension was "mainly due to the carelessness of handlers," he noted the tendency of dogs to paw at mines upon discovery was also of concern.[98] For his part, the officer commanding, 25th Bomb Disposal Company surmised:

94   TNA: WO 205/1173, 22C, Report on Employment of No 1 Dog Pl RE between 15 July and 11 August 1944, 11 August 1944.
95   TNA: WO 205/1173, 16B, Report on the Employment of No. 1 Dog Pl, RE at Carpiquet Airfield, 31 July 1944.
96   TNA: WO 205/1173, 22C, Report on Employment, 11 August 1944.
97   Ibid.
98   TNA: WO 171/1824, 2 Platoon, War Diary of No. 2 Dog Platoon, September 1944. Davison did not provide further details as to what he meant by "carelessness."

A mine detection dog and men equipped with a prodder and electronic detector search Carpiquet Airfield in France, July 1944. (© Imperial War Museum (CH 20417))

If total clearance is to be the aim of deliberate work in L[ines] of C[ommunications] areas and also as far as possible, freedom from casualties then it would seem that dogs are unsuitable for the task because they cannot achieve such a high percentage of clearance as men with prodders and [electronic] Mark IV detectors.[99]

While working with 240th Bomb Disposal Company (RE) on 19 September, half of the dogs proved unable or unwilling to locate several anti-tank mines, some of which were clearly visible. Davison attributed the poor results to a combination of reasons, including the sodden ground and the amount of time the mines had been buried. On a separate occasion, during which the dogs were directed to search a minefield, the presence of vermin led several dogs astray. Davison recorded in the war diary: "Not encouraging work… many dogs 'off' work."[100]

As illustrated by these accounts, the first months in France for No. 1 and No. 2 Dog Platoons were fraught with difficulties. Wet and battle-scarred terrain, inclement weather and distracting odours frustrated some dogs. Furthermore, the dogs' training in Britain had focused on the detection of mines *within* minefields. Since trainers at the Army's War Dogs Training School had planted numerous mines in each mine-field, dogs had become accustomed to frequently encountering mines during training

99   Museum of Military Medicine: Box 14, War Diary, No. 2 War Dog Platoon, Monthly Reports, Major A.G. Bainbridge to CRE, 10 L of C Tps Engrs, 28 September 1944.
100 TNA: WO 171/1824, War Diary, September 1944.

exercises.[101] In France, however, No. 1 and No. 2 Platoons came across relatively few mines, which led to apathy on the part of some canines. In the view of Lieutenant Morgan, the dogs were not solely to blame for his platoon's mediocre performance in Normandy. Like Davison, he commented on the importance of the handlers' actions on operations: "Handlers are far too kind and trusting. The dog appears almost always to slack off if he is fed and treated too well. On the job they must be handled very strictly. They do stop working without appearing to... and the handler must be alert to watch this."[102]Although he emphasised that further training was necessary, Morgan expressed confidence in the platoon:

> The dogs are doing excellent work, each sec[tion] doing the work of an RE pl[atoon] in the same time... I take the view that the dogs are highly satisfactory, but fresh pl[atoon]s could be a lot more so with some slight alterations in their basic tr[ainin]g and equip[ment].[103]

Similarly, a report submitted by 24 Airfield Construction Group in late July described the dogs of No. 1 Platoon as "invaluable." The report emphasised the advantage of utilising dogs over electronic detectors at sites containing numerous metal fragments.[104]

In November 1944, No. 2 Platoon moved to the Netherlands, where it remained through March 1945. Between 22 November 1944 and 5 January 1945, the platoon searched areas on or near Walcheren, including railway lines, dykes and the causeway linking the island to the Dutch mainland. In November alone, the platoon covered nearly 188,130 square metres. Walcheren, as the platoon learned, contained few mines. During two days in late November, for example, the dogs covered some 83,600 square metres only to discover two mines.[105] While searching near railway lines on 30 November, the dogs located nine mines and two grenades buried 15 centimetres beneath the surface and missed by electronic detectors. In the platoon's war diary, Lieutenant Davison described the operation as an "ideal job for dogs," considering the unreliability of electronic detectors which picked up the metal tracks and quartz ballast.[106]

Although less information is available concerning No. 1 Platoon after its first months in northwest Europe, it is known that the platoon was also utilised in the Netherlands in late 1944. While searching railway and road verges with 246 Field Company (RE), the platoon discovered some 600 mines in just over a week in late November and early

101 TNA: WO 205/1173, 22B, Lt. Col. T.I. Lloyd, HQ 7 Army Troops Engineers to 10 AGRE, undated.
102 TNA: WO 205/1173, 22C, Report on Employment, 11 August 1944.
103 Ibid.
104 TNA: WO 205/1173, 16B, Report on the Employment, 31 July 1944.
105 TNA: WO 171/1824, War Diary, November-December 1944 and TNA: WO 171/5377, 2 Platoon, War Diary of No. 2 Dog Platoon, January-March 1945.
106 TNA: WO 171/1824, War Diary, November 1944.

December. On one occasion, the remains of animals in the vicinity frustrated some dogs, and human operators with electronic detectors completed the assignment. A report detailing the platoon's performance in late 1944 noted that loud sounds negatively impacted the effectiveness of dogs and they required rest after 30 minutes on the job. Nonetheless, the same report determined that, apart from working over particularly wet terrain or crops, "dogs can be relied on to find all types of mines on all types of ground."[107]

No. 1 and No. 2 Platoons were joined in northwest Europe by No. 3 and No. 4 Platoons, both of which had arrived by November 1944.[108] After sustaining a casualty shortly after commencing operations in the Netherlands, No. 3 Platoon was charged with searching the verges along a canal. On 19 December, just two days after beginning the assignment, the platoon sustained another casualty when its officer commanding was injured after detonating a Schu-mine. A report by 12 Corps Troops (RE) stressed that the officer was to blame for the incident:

> It is felt that this accident should not be allowed to throw discredit on the conception and training of the dog platoon. The cause appears to have been a human error on the part of the individual, and in no way attributable to a faulty performance or technique on the part of the dog or handler.[109]

No. 3 Platoon did experience some success during its first months in the Netherlands, however. In correspondence with the owner of Ricky, a mine detection dog employed by the platoon, the dog's handler expounded on the significance of the dog's actions:

> [Ricky] was one of the best mine dogs I have ever seen or worked with. We have had many escapades together both funny and serious, and he has a queer way of coming out on top. The nearest escape we had was in Holland… We were actually within three feet of the mine [which detonated] and in the middle of a minefield. I am confident that he was as steady as the Rock of Gibraltar and I think it was his coolness that brought us out of a sticky patch safely.[110]

In addition to expressing confidence in Ricky, his handler's statement reflects a sense of camaraderie towards his canine charge.[111]

When asked to provide feedback concerning the use of mine detection dogs in northwest Europe, the Chief Engineer, Second Army surmised: "The dog pl[atoon] does justify its existence" and pointed out that dogs "provide the quickest method of

107 TNA: WO 205/1173, 42B, Report on Results, 5 November 1944.
108 TNA: WO 171/1825, 4 Platoon, War Diary of No. 4 Dog Platoon, November 1944 and TNA: WO 205/1173, 61B, CE 12 Corps to RE 12 Corps Troops, 17 January 1945.
109 TNA: WO 205/1173, 61B, R.E. 12 Corps Tps to C.E. 12 Corps, 17 January 1945.
110 Quoted in St. Hill Bourne, *They Also Serve*, pp. 184-185.
111 The relationship between handlers and trained dogs is discussed in more detail in Chapter 6.

locating minefields and subsequently defining their limits."[112] The officers commanding of No. 1, No. 2 and No. 4 Platoons expressed similar opinions. Following an informal meeting in February 1945, the officers commanding of No. 1 and No. 4 Platoons agreed that, in addition to searching areas likely to contain mines, "the most practical and valuable work that dogs can at present perform" was the detection of minefield edges.[113] That same month, Lieutenant Davison observed that dogs were "most usefully employed" when working over vast tracts of land.[114] Consequently, much of the work carried out by the platoons in the final year of the war involved searching large tracts of land, as well as along roads and railway lines.[115] During six days in February 1945, for example, No. 2 Platoon covered more than nine kilometres of railway lines in the central Netherlands. Working in association with 240 Field Company (RE) and the Dutch Army, the platoon discovered 11 minefields as well as 68 mines buried an estimated four months before. Although vermin in close proximity diverted the attention of some dogs, the platoon missed just four mines, all of which were discovered by electronic detectors or prodders.[116] Moreover, during an 11 day period in March, the platoon covered approximately 225,750 square metres near the Dutch-German border; the platoon's employment resulted in the discovery of nearly 550 mines and 36 grenades.[117]

Although No. 2 Platoon experienced more success in the Netherlands than in France, the platoon nonetheless encountered difficulties in the final year of the war. While attached to 19th Field Company (RE), the dogs of No. 2 Platoon detected less than half of the mines located during a three day period in late February. On the final day of the operation, the dogs accounted for just 112 of 545 picric pots, while handlers and Sappers located 100 and 333 mines, respectively. As the officer commanding of 19th Field Company pointed out, humans had a significant advantage over the dogs; by recognising the minelaying pattern, they could locate mines within minefields more efficiently than dogs.[118] Similarly, Lieutenant Davison observed that "only

112 TNA: WO 205/1173, 49A, Chief Engineer, Second Army to Chief Engineer, 21 Army Group, 16 December 1944.
113 TNA: WO 171/5376, 1 Platoon, War Diary of No. 1 Dog Platoon, February 1945. Although the officer commanding, No. 3 Platoon was unavailable at the time, the platoon was represented by another officer.
114 TNA: WO 205/1173, 71D, Report on Mine-Detecting, 11-16 February 1945.
115 TNA: WO 171/5377, War Diary, February-October 1945 and TNA: WO 171/5378, 4 Platoon, War Diary of No. 4 Dog Platoon, February-May 1945. Excepting the February 1945 war diary for No. 1 Dog Platoon, the war diaries for No. 1 and No. 3 Dog Platoons for 1945 could not be located. However, considering that officers from each of these platoons were present at the February 1945 meeting, it is likely that they were employed on similar operations as the other platoons.
116 TNA: WO 205/1173, 71D, Report on Mine-Detecting, 11-16 February 1945.
117 TNA: WO 171/5377, War Diary, March 1945.
118 TNA: WO 205/1173, 71C, Summary of Comparisons Made during 26, 27, 28 Feb 45 of Sappers Working with No. 2 Dog Pl, 28 February 1945.

signs, visible mines and knowledge of pattern saved the handlers from treading on the mines."[119] He attributed the poor performance to the platoon's lack of experience with picric pots, as training at the Army's War Dogs Training School did not incorporate such mines.[120]

In March 1945, No. 4 Platoon was utilised in the Reichswald Forest near the German-Dutch border in preparation for the arrival of the British Prime Minister later that month.[121] Bruce, a Labrador described as "one of the most reliable dogs on mine detection," was decorated by the RSPCA for his role in the Reichswald Forest. According to the citation submitted to the RSPCA:

> On one occasion [Bruce] worked for three hours on a task of checking an approach to the Reichswald Forest under the most trying conditions. A strip of railway line was cleared in record time so enabling vitally important supplies to be got through.[122]

Rex, another canine member of No. 4 Platoon, was also praised for his efforts in the Reichswald Forest:

> He worked under the worst of undergrowth and climatic conditions... with complete disregard to the very heavy shelling. He helped to clear a path-way through a thickly sown anti-personnel minefield, so enabling forward troops to proceed without the casualties that would most certainly have occurred but for his devotion to duty.[123]

On 24 March 1945, one section of No. 4 Platoon participated in Operation Plunder, the crossing of the Rhine near Rees, Germany by Allied forces. Fourteen dogs were transported by storm boat across the river. They discovered two S-Mines on the operation, during which the platoon was subjected to artillery fire. Although no dogs were killed, a veterinary sergeant was injured. As indicated in the platoon's war diary, the dogs appeared "very nervous under [the] heavy barrage" prior to the crossing and "very shaken" upon their return.[124] Texas, a Labrador which participated in Operation Plunder, was lauded for his composed demeanor during the operation. According to the citation submitted to the RSPCA, the dog:

---

119 TNA: WO 205/1173, 71B, Lt. J.R. Davison to OC 19 Fd Coy RE, 22 February 1945.
120 Ibid. Davison also pointed out that although 10 dogs were employed, a single dog was responsible for locating 95% of mines detected by dogs.
121 TNA: WO 171/5378, War Diary, March 1945.
122 TNA: WO 32/14999, 17A, Bennison to Moss, 2 October 1945.
123 Ibid.
124 TNA: WO 171/5378, War Diary, March 1945.

Worked under continuous gunfire on the Rhine Crossing, detecting mines with complete disregard to the shelling and mortar fire. Through his devotion to duty he contributed largely to the successful conclusion of the task set, that of clearing the approaches for the bridging of the Rhine on both banks.[125]

The surrender of Germany in May 1945 did not spell an end to the employment of mine detection dogs in northwest Europe. No. 2 and No. 4 Platoons continued to search railway lines, roads, verges and other sites likely to contain mines in Germany and the Netherlands.[126] Between May and November 1945, No. 2 Platoon searched some 64,400 square metres, as well as nearly 320 kilometres along railway and power lines, in the Netherlands.[127]

Particularly in the final year of the war, canines offered a number of advantages over other means of mine detection. First, dogs could search vast tracts of land likely to contain few mines in less time than humans with prodders, and in some cases, electronic detectors.[128] The dog platoons typically covered around 14 metres per minute. A report compiled by 21st Army Group noted: "Generally speaking the rate of work [by dogs] is about the same as with [electronic] mine detectors, rather faster if conditions are ideal."[129] The speed at which mine detection dogs worked was recognised soon after No. 1 Platoon commenced operations in 1944. Although the platoon experienced several difficulties while in Normandy, an officer of the unit to which the platoon was attached in July 1944 noted that at Carpiquet Airfield, the dogs were "much quicker than a mine detector party" owing to the substantial amount of shrapnel.[130]

The advantage of speed became increasingly clear following the realisation in late 1944 and early 1945 that the platoons were better suited to detecting minefield edges and searching vast tracts of land. According to a report by the Chief Engineer, Second Army, some dogs could detect minefields from a distance of some 90 metres.[131] Following the employment of No. 2 Platoon near the Dutch-Belgian border in February 1945, Lieutenant Davison observed:

Dogs are most usefully employed... [when] checking and declaring free, large areas of ground, tracks, etc thus utilising their speed. In a small known Schuminefield, an expert with a prodder is quicker and safer... If 100% success is

125 TNA: WO 32/14999, 17A, Bennison to Moss, 2 October 1945.
126 TNA: WO 171/ 5377, War Diary, May-October 1945 and TNA: WO 171/5378, War Diary, May 1945.
127 TNA: WO 205/1186, Mine Clearance in the Netherlands, Confidential Report on Mine Clearance in the Netherlands, 7 May 1945-1 November 1945.
128 TNA: WO 205/1173, 71D, Report on Mine-Detecting, 11-16 February 1945 and TNA: WO 205/1173, Report on Mine Dogs, undated.
129 TNA: WO 205/1173, Report on Mine Dogs, undated.
130 TNA: WO 205/1173, 16B, Report on the Employment, 31 July 1944.
131 TNA: WO 205/1173, 49A, Second Army to 21 Army Group, 16 December 1944.

not essential, and time a vital factor, then the dog can be used to clear the ground even more quickly than a man with a prodder.[132]

Lieutenant T.L. Reid of the Royal Canadian Engineers (RCE) offered a similar opinion. After working with No. 2 Platoon in March 1945, he asserted: "The dogs are fast and can check an area many times quicker than by standard detector methods. Areas that are only suspected and in which it eventually turns out that there are no mines are rapidly checked by this method."[133]

Second, mine detection dogs were especially advantageous when working along railway lines. While the metallic tracks and quartz precluded the effective employment of electronic detectors, dogs were without this limitation. While searching along a railway line on Walcheren in November 1944, for example, the dogs of No. 2 Platoon discovered nine *Tellermines* and two grenades, all of which were unidentified by human operators with electronic detectors. The following month, the platoon located another five *Tellermines* along railway lines which were undetected by electronic detectors.[134] The same was true of sites which contained substantial amounts of shrapnel. No. 1 Platoon was useful at Carpiquet Airfield as electronic detectors could not distinguish between mines and the numerous metal fragments.[135]

Lastly, unlike electronic detectors, canines regularly located non-metallic mines, as well as mines planted well below the surface. Experience in northwest Europe indicated that dogs could typically find metallic or non-metallic mines planted in 20 centimetres or less of soil.[136] However, exceptional canine detectors could recognise objects buried multiple metres below the surface. While at Carpiquet Airfield, the dogs of No. 1 Platoon located two shells and two unexploded bombs buried between two and three metres.[137] By contrast, human operators with electronic detectors struggled to locate mines planted well below the surface. According to the commandant of the OAC, the No. 4 detector could detect Schu-mines buried in 10 to 13 centimetres of soil. Although he did not specify a depth at which electronic detectors could effectively detect mines, he made clear that the No. 4 detector had difficulty in locating "deeply buried mines." Moreover, he pointed to the advantage of dogs over electronic detectors in locating non-metallic mines. In fact, he referred to dogs as "the ONLY proved detectors of non-metallic mines."[138]

Despite the overall improved performance of mine detection dogs in late 1944 and 1945, the scheme was not devoid of problems in the final year of the war. Difficult

132 TNA: WO 205/1173, 71D, Report on Mine-Detecting, 11-16 February 1945.
133 Museum of Military Medicine: Box 14, War Diary, No. 2 Dog Platoon, Monthly Reports, Lt. T.L. Reid, Mine Clearance Using Dogs as Detectors, 3 April 1945.
134 TNA: WO 171/1824, War Diary, November-December 1944.
135 TNA: WO 205/1173, 16B, Report on the Employment, 31 July 1944.
136 TNA: WO 205/1173, Report on Mine Dogs, undated.
137 TNA: WO 205/1173, 17B, HQ 7 Army Troops Engineers to 10 AGRE, undated.
138 TNA: DEFE 2/1060, Breaching of Obstacles, 4 May 1944.

terrain and inclement weather often negatively impacted the performance of mine detection dogs. Experience in northwest Europe indicated that dogs generally performed better when employed over short grass. Their performance tended to suffer when operating over sand, tall grass or particularly dense or sodden ground.[139] Rain and especially high temperatures also limited the effectiveness of dogs.[140] Lieutenant Davison believed that precipitation rendered mine detection more difficult for dogs because especially sodden ground "reduc[ed], or seal[ed] in, the scent."[141] While it is clear that the effective employment of mine detection dogs was dependent on environmental factors, it is likely that such factors also impacted the performance of humans. At Carpiquet Airfield, for example, the officer commanding, No. 1 Platoon noted that the rising temperatures in early August 1944 "were appalling even for men."[142]

The effectiveness of mine detection dogs was also dependent on the amount of time between the planting and detection of mines. The employment of the platoons in northwest Europe revealed that although canines could locate mines planted three to six months earlier, they were more likely to discover those buried for less than a month.[143] Lieutenant Davison maintained: "The length of time the mines have been lying undisturbed is a most important factor, affecting the dogs efficiency... and has been the theme of almost every report on dogs failing to find mines" in northwest Europe.[144] While working over mines planted some four months before in the central Netherlands, some dogs exhibited what Davison believed were signs of uncertainty:

> After the recent bad weather, the mines which had been lying undisturbed for 4 months, were detected by the dogs, but none seemed to draw the dog... and many a dog sniffed very close to the mine, deliberated for a moment, and then pointed, not too decided as to whether he was right or not.[145]

Furthermore, although dogs in training at the Army's War Dogs Training School were described by one witness as "extraordinarily unsusceptible" to shellfire and other sounds,[146] reports on the use of mine detection dogs in late 1944 and 1945 indicate

---

139 TNA: WO 205/1173, 54B, Mine Dog Training, undated and 49A, Second Army to 21 Army Group, 16 December 1944 and 72E, Report on Mine Detection by Dogs, undated.
140 Museum of Military Medicine: Box 14, War Diary, No. 2 War Dog Platoon, Monthly Reports, Report on Mine Detection Carried Out by No. 2 Dog Pl, Report 16, 18-31 July 1945.
141 Museum of Military Medicine: Box 14, War Diary, No. 2 War Dog Platoon, Monthly Reports, J.R. Davison, Report on No. 2 Dog Platoon, 11 January 1945.
142 TNA: WO 205/1173, 22C, Report on Employment, 11 August 1944.
143 TNA: WO 205/1173, 72E, Report on Mine Detection by Dogs, undated and 49A, Second Army to 21 Army Group, 16 December 1944.
144 TNA: WO 205/1173, 72E, Report on Mine Detection by Dogs, undated.
145 TNA: WO 205/1173, 71D, Report on Mine-Detecting, 11-16 February 1945.
146 TNA: AVIA 22/862, Weapon Development Committee, Note on Visit to War Dogs Training School by D.G.S.R.D., 17 May 1944.

that this was not the case for several dogs in northwest Europe. While the distressed behaviour exhibited by the dogs of No. 4 Platoon during Operation Plunder provides an extreme example, other correspondence and reports indicate similar responses by some dogs when subjected to such sounds. In correspondence with 21st Army Group in December 1944, for example, the Chief Engineer, Second Army asserted that the platoons were less effective in forward areas, as dogs seemed troubled by shellfire.[147] Similarly, in a report related to the employment of No. 2 Platoon in March 1945, Lieutenant Davison noted:

> Battle noises from mortars, M[achine] G[uns] and rifles nearby disturbed some dogs... Many V1 bombs and A[nti-] A[ircraft] fire combined during the week to un-nerve the dogs, and on hearing rifle fire seemed to cringe in anticipation of the big explosion. Though distracted only momentarily, they continued work but with limited concentration. Their sense of frustration at being denied an opportunity of coursing a hare which negotiated the schuminefield successfully was apparent for many minutes.[148]

As evidenced by Davison's account, the numerous vermin in northwest Europe and their impact on canine behaviour also continued to plague the mine detection scheme throughout the war.

Another difficulty confronting the platoons throughout the Second World War was that dogs continued to become apathetic when few mines were detected. No. 1 and No. 2 Platoons attempted to rectify this problem in 1944 by having dogs search for practice mines, as well as providing them with extra rest.[149] While such measures led to fewer incidents of apathetic behaviour,[150] reports on the use of the platoons in the Netherlands indicate that the problem persisted throughout the duration of the mine detection dog scheme.[151] However, a report on No. 2 Platoon in the Netherlands shifted some of the blame to the handlers:

---

147 TNA: WO 205/1173, 49A, Second Army to 21 Army Group, 16 December 1944.
148 TNA: WO 205/1173, 72E, Report on Mine Detection by Dogs, undated.
149 TNA: WO 205/1173, 22C, Report on Employment, 11 August 1944 and TNA: WO 205/1173, Report on Use of Dog Platoons RE, undated.
150 Museum of Military Medicine: Box 14, War Diary, No. 2 Dog Platoon, Monthly Reports, Davison, Report on No. 2 Dog Platoon, 11 January 1945. Davison reported that these measures proved "quite successful" in the Netherlands. He provided the example of a dog which discovered multiple mines after having covered nearly half a kilometre without locating a single mine.
151 TNA: WO 205/1173, 49A, Second Army to 21 Army Group, 16 December 1944 and Museum of Military Medicine: Box 14, War Diary, No. 2 Dog Platoon, Monthly Reports, Reid, Mine Clearance Using Dogs as Detectors, 3 April 1945 and TNA: WO 205/1186, Confidential Report, 7 May 1945-1 November 1945.

The main difficulty has been to maintain interest of dog handlers and dogs in checking ground day after day without encountering 'operational mines'. Rest-days and exercise on purpose laid mines were necessary... A number of the handlers in No. 2 Dog Pl[atoon] RE have failed to appreciate the degree of care and patience required with the dogs when the 'prey' is unnatural. It is essential that the men selected for this work should have not only a knowledge of and an interest in dogs, but also considerable enthusiasm for the work.[152]

Thus, as was the case with all roles in which dogs were employed during the Second World War, the effectiveness of mine detection dogs depended in part on the humans involved. Instructions related to the use of mine detection dogs referred to the handler's role on operations. The handler, the instructions made clear, "ensures that [dogs] actually cover the ground."[153] Lieutenant Davison noted that some handlers appeared increasingly apathetic while training in France; they did not correct a dog for pawing at a mine, for example, or neglected to notice when dogs were no longer working.[154] While some handlers had worked with dogs before the war, Davison considered that self-discipline and dedication on the part of handlers were more important than having previous knowledge of canines.[155] Writing several years after the war, Davison once again highlighted the importance of the handler's role:

The dogs vary between individuals as to speed and endurance, as well as to accuracy, so that each handler must know the idiosyncrasies and mannerisms of each of his three dogs, 'reading' these signs as if it were a delicate instrument not an animal... Patience and understanding of the canine mind are the handler's essential qualities and a real love for working his four-legged comrade. The dog is wrong sometimes. More frequently one can trace a dog's error to a mistake on the part of the handler. It is the teamwork which counts.[156]

As Robert Kirk has rightly pointed out, mine detection dogs were perceived not as "interchangeable technology" but as "individual[s]" and counterparts to their human handlers. Thus, "a successful minedog... relied on the maintenance of a positive

152 TNA: WO 205/1186, Confidential Report, 7 May 1945-1 November 1945.
153 TNA: WO 205/1173, 3C, Training Instruction, undated.
154 Museum of Military Medicine: Box 14, File of Captain James Rankin Davison, Progress Report, J.R. Davison to Commandant, War Dogs Training School, 7 October 1944. It is likely that this is what Davison meant when he referred to "the carelessness of handlers" in the platoon's war diary of September 1944.
155 Museum of Military Medicine: Box 14, File of Captain James Rankin Davison, Welfare, J.R. Davison to Commandant, War Dogs Training School, 7 October 1944.
156 J.R. Davison, 'History and Records of No. 2 Dog Platoon Royal Engineers', in IWM: 94/1219, Hunt, 'A Brief Look', Book 2.

intersubjective bond between handler and dog."[157] Although Davison likened the mine detection dog to an "instrument," his remarks on dogs as "individuals" and "teamwork" clearly indicate the perception to which Kirk referred.

The effective employment of mine detection dogs was also contingent on the actions of other humans involved with the scheme. Apart from handlers, persons who came into contact with mine detection dogs were prohibited from petting them. As was the case with messenger dogs in the First World War, it was thought that mine detection dogs would be "ruined" if soldiers regarded them as pets.[158] Moreover, like dogs in other military roles, it was recognised that mine detection dogs could have a positive effect on human morale. Following a period during which his company worked with No. 2 Platoon, Lieutenant Reid (RCE) remarked: "The dog handlers… appear to have the utmost confidence in the ability of their dogs which in turn gives great confidence to the sappers."[159] This emphasis on human-animal co-operation was not unique to the mine detection dog scheme. Several handlers, trainers and other servicemen who worked with other military dogs referenced the influence of humans on operations involving trained dogs, as well as the impact dogs had on human thinking and behaviour.

While the employment of mine detection dogs by the British Army in the Second World War was limited to continental northwest Europe, the available records reveal that military officials did contemplate extending the scheme to other theatres of war. In August 1944, dogs took part in a trial which required that they search for mines planted along the shoreline at Southend-On-Sea in southeast England.[160] Presumably, the aim of this trial was to assess the possibility of utilising dogs to detect British mines laid earlier in the war in preparation for an expected German invasion. In *The Book of the Dog*, Lloyd highlighted the difficulty involved in such work: "As it was impossible to *prove* to the dog he was correct at the time (some of the mines, due to the shifting sands, being buried as deep as 10 f[ee]t) it seemed a very chancy business and was discontinued."[161]

A number of British military officials and civilian advisers in South East Asia Command also contemplated the employment of mine detection dogs in that theatre of war. The Commander-in-Chief, 11th Army Group, for example, showed interest in the use of mine detection dogs.[162] Although the War Office deliberated on the potential employment of dogs in South East Asia Command, their use was ultimately

157 Kirk, 'In Dogs We Trust?', p. 8.
158 TNA: WO 205/1173, 3C, Training Instruction, undated.
159 Museum of Military Medicine: Box 14, War Diary, No. 2 War Dog Platoon, Monthly Reports, Reid, Mine Clearance Using Dogs as Detectors, 3 April 1945.
160 TNA: AVIA/871, 19B, Detection of Mine by Dogs, 6 August 1944. This document referred only to the date and location of the upcoming trial rather than its results.
161 Lloyd, 'Dog in War', pp. 190-191.
162 TNA: WO 203/3126, S.H. Persse to T.W.J. Taylor, 5 August 1944.

rejected in September 1944.[163] This outcome was largely determined by concerns of maintaining the health of dogs in the tropical climate of South East Asia.[164]

The British mine detection dog platoons certainly experienced greater success than their American counterparts. Following a period of training in early 1944,[165] United States 228th Engineer Mine Detection Company deployed to Italy, where it was to be employed alongside the Fifth Army. Prior to the company's employment on operations, however, canine performance declined markedly. During a trial in Italy in September 1944, the dogs missed 70 percent of practice mines. Captain Howard White, an officer in 228th Engineer Mine Detection Company, attributed the disappointing performance to a lack of foresight on the part of the humans involved in the American mine detection dog scheme. In contrast to training conditions in the United States, White pointed out, the war-torn landscape of Italy featured various unfamiliar odours which hampered the dogs. An intelligence report based on White's observations noted that he considered the American mine detection dog scheme "doomed to failure from the start."[166] Following the trial, the company was employed alongside Seventh Army. However, as the same report noted, "again [the dogs] failed to work out."[167]

As pointed out by Brigadier General Garrison H. Davidson, an officer in Seventh Army, the dogs of 228th Engineer Mine Detection Company were prevented from taking part in training exercises while *en route* to Italy. In an interview conducted in early 1945, Davidson surmised that this interruption in training likely resulted in the dogs "not perform[ing] up to expectations" in Italy.[168] Eventually, 228th Engineer Mine Detection Company was disbanded, and the QMC suspended mine detection dog training for the duration of the war.[169]

163 TNA: WO 203/3126, Anti-Tank Committee Minutes for the following dates: 14 July 1944, 21 July 1944, 4 August 1944, 15 September 1944.
164 TNA: WO 203/3126, B.W. Pain to T.W.J. Taylor, 22 July 1944 and T.W.J. Taylor to W.H. Stephens, 20 October 1944. See also the above minutes of the Anti-Tank Committee.
165 Museum of Military Medicine: Box 14, Reports and Correspondence between UK and USA, Extract from Royal Engineers, British Army Staff Liaison Letter, March 1944.
166 NARA: HRPE Report No. 1128, Performance of War Dogs, 31 January 1945; Roll 3032, Item 3259; Historical Documents of World War II; RG 407; NACP.
167 Ibid.
168 NARA: Interview with Brigadier General Garrison H. Davidson, Army Service Forces, Office of the Commanding General, Technical Intelligence Report, 12 January 1945, 5; Roll 3032, Item 3262; Historical Documents of World War II; RG 407; NACP. Davidson also noted: "The mines [the company] practiced on had been subjected to weather over a period of time." It is unclear whether he was referring to the mines utilised during training exercises in the United States or in Italy.
169 NARA: Report #4248, *Dogs and National Defense*, p. 32; 4243-4370; DRB Reference Collection; RG 407; NACP. The 228th Engineer Mine Detection Company was one of two American mine detection dog companies formed, and subsequently disbanded, during the Second World War.

In *War Dogs: A History of Loyalty and Heroism*, Michael G. Lemish convincingly argued that the American employment of mine detection dogs in the Second World War was an "experimental failure" weakened by a combination of factors, including those mentioned by White and Davidson, as well as drawbacks associated with the chosen training method. While acknowledging the American adherence to the "repulsion method" was partly to blame, Lemish concluded:

> The failure of this ambitious program should not be placed on the handlers or their dogs—it was doomed even before the first dog started training… Like other crash programs instituted during the war the [mine detection dog] program was hastily conceived without sufficient background knowledge to implement the program… Unfortunately, the [mine detection dog] program had little information to work with and not enough time and thus was unable to succeed.[170]

Although Lemish was right to consider the American mine detection dog scheme a failure for the aforementioned reasons, his argument seemed to imply that the use of dogs was not a practical form of mine detection in the Second World War. He largely ignored that the British Army experienced significant progress with mine detection dogs despite similar time constraints. As mentioned by Lemish, the decision by American trainers to utilise the "repulsion method" placed American mine detection dogs at a distinct disadvantage. It is likely that this decision contributed, at least in part, to the vastly different outcomes experienced by the British and American Armies in the employment of mine detection dogs.

The United States Army also seems to have been less willing to retain its mine detection dogs. Although the British mine detection dog platoons encountered a number of setbacks, particularly in 1944, the scheme remained intact throughout the Second World War. Thus, while the American mine detection dog companies were never utilised operationally, British mine detection dogs and their handlers not only gained significant experience but discovered several thousand mines during the last two years of the war. By contrast, the QMC allowed fewer missteps following the deployment of mine detection dogs before disbandment. Thus, it is likely that the performance of American mine detection dogs may have also improved over time if given the chance to remain in Italy.

As one post-war report rightly pointed out, the British Army's mine detection dogs were "not a satisfactory or complete answer to the problem" of non-metallic mines. Yet, as the same report made clear, prodding and electronic detectors also had certain limitations; consequently, it concluded that "there is at present no real answer."[171] An Australian report, citing the performance of British mine detection dog platoons in northwest Europe, noted: "The general opinion of RE personnel in 21[st] A[rmy]

---

170 Lemish, *War Dogs*, pp. 94-97.
171 TNA: AVIA 74/15, 99, Detection of Non-Metallic Mines, 1 July 1946.

G[roup] is that Dog Pl[atoon]s, whilst not capable of replacing mechanical detection devices, are a valuable subsidiary weapon in mine clearance" and "the best means of combatting non-metallic mines... encountered in Europe" as of early 1945.[172] As highlighted by the aforementioned reports, canines served as just one means of mine detection, all of which had disadvantages. Thus, the limitations of the British mine detection dog scheme should in no way negate the contributions made by mine detection dogs in northwest Europe in 1944 and 1945. Dogs covered substantial distances in France, Germany and the Netherlands, and in doing so, discovered several thousand mines. Furthermore, as Davison rightly noted, much of what the platoons accomplished in northwest Europe could not be quantitatively measured:

> The value of the mine-detecting dog cannot be assessed by the number of mines located with his aid. Even if it was, the many thousands of mines detected by dogs would justify his presence in the Army. His real value however was in the saving of time and of labour, and in the saving of lives of both soldiers and civilians.[173]

After the Second World War, the mine detection dog scheme was not cast aside as a curious measure adopted in wartime. On the contrary, representatives from the Department of Chief Scientific Officer determined at a May 1946 meeting that the employment of mine detection dogs "should proceed under high priority."[174]

172 NAA: MP742/1, 240/6/324, Capt. H.O. Bamford, Training of War Dogs in Australia, 3 April 1945.
173 Quoted in Lloyd, 'Dog in War', p. 190.
174 TNA: AVIA 22/862, Research into Clearance and Detection of Land Mines, Minutes of Meeting, 27 May 1946.

5

The Employment of Rescue Dogs in the London Civil Defence Region

On 10 June 1945, King George VI attended a parade in London to recognise the Britons employed in Civil Defence roles during the Second World War. Included in the procession were two dogs which had been utilised by rescue teams in the London Civil Defence Region.[1] Irma, an Alsatian, discovered 21 live persons and 170 fatal casualties during her time as a rescue dog in the capital. Along with Peter, the other rescue dog in attendance, Irma earned the Dickin Medal for her role in the war.[2] Irma and Peter were two of at least 18 canines employed by the London Civil Defence Region during a five month period in 1944 and 1945.[3]

Civil Defence in London and Untrained Dogs as Rescuers

The progress made in aircraft design during the interwar period represented, as the historian Richard Overy put it, "a quantum leap in technology."[4] Bombing, therefore, emerged as "the most obvious instrument of total war."[5] In the years leading up to the Second World War, British politicians and civilians alike envisaged widespread bombing on an extraordinary scale. Contemporaries also recognised that the devastation wrought by enemy bombing would no doubt influence civilian morale.[6] Sir John

---

1 'Civil Defence Farewell', *The Times*, 11 June 1945, p. 2.
2 St. Hill Bourne, *They Also Serve*, pp. 166-167 and Le Chêne, *Silent Heroes*, p. 100.
3 London Metropolitan Archives (LMA): LCC/CL/CD/03/022, London Civil Defence Region-Operations Circulars, London Civil Defence Region Operations Circular 158, 24 February 1945. As the employment of rescue dogs in the London Civil Defence Region continued for nearly five weeks after the date of this circular, the total number of dogs ultimately employed in and around the capital may have been slightly higher.
4 Overy, *The Bombing War*, p. 40.
5 Ibid, pp. xxiii.
6 Ibid, pp. 3-55.

Anderson, who in 1939 became Home Secretary, correctly predicted prior to the war: "The distinction between combatants and non-combatants would largely disappear."[7]

Plans to protect British civilians in the Second World War were devised as early as the 1920s, when the Committee for Imperial Defence established an Air Raid Precautions (ARP) subcommittee. Further arrangements were made in the 1930s as war with Germany became increasingly likely. In 1935, the Home Office created an ARP Department. Three years later, as the Munich Crisis cast an ominous shadow over Europe, local authorities began to formulate more concrete policies for civil defence.[8] The object of ARP, or Civil Defence as the numerous services were designated after 1941, extended beyond preparing civilians in advance of enemy bombing. Civil Defence also entailed the employment of gas decontamination experts, rescue workers and fire and ambulance teams, all of which were required in the aftermath of air raids.[9] When Britain entered the war in September 1939, Civil Defence already boasted some 1,500,000 personnel.[10]

From April 1939, the London Civil Defence Region encompassed the entire Metropolitan Police District.[11] The London Region, therefore, extended beyond central London and included parts of Essex, such as Chigwell, Walthamstow, Wanstead and Woodford.[12] Regions were further divided into groups, of which the London Region had nine. Local authorities maintained report centres, so when an air raid took place in the vicinity, workers at the report centre were notified of the location and any relevant details. Such information was then communicated to controllers, who requested the rescue workers and other personnel required at the scene. Depending on the severity of the raid, light or heavy rescue parties were called upon to locate live and fatal casualties.[13]

The Blitz, the series of air raids which spanned some eight months in late 1940 and early 1941, resulted in more than 41,000 fatalities. During September alone, nearly 7,000 British civilians were killed by German bombs. The culmination of the Blitz in the spring of 1941 marked the beginning of a three year period during which London was, for the most part, subjected to less frequent raids. It was not until the "Baby Blitz" of early 1944 that casualties began to mount again in and around the capital. Even so, relatively few bombs hit London during the "Baby Blitz," which lasted until May 1944.[14]

7   Quoted in Ibid, p. 35.
8   Mike Brown, *Put that Light Out!: Britain's Civil Defence Services at War 1939-1945* (Stroud: Sutton, pp. 1-4.
9   Doyle, *ARP and Civil Defence in the Second World War* (Oxford: Shire, 2010), pp. 17-26.
10 Calder, *The People's War*, p. 68,
11 O'Brien, *Civil Defence*, p. 178.
12 Stanley Tiquet, *It Happened Here: The Story of Civil Defence in Wanstead and Woodford 1939-1945* (Borough Council of Wanstead & Woodford), p. 5.
13 Brown, *Put that Light Out!*, pp. 29-33, 74-76.
14 Overy, *The Bombing War*, pp. 73, 116-121, 145, 186-187, 191.

At the time of the Blitz, Civil Defence was less equipped to handle air raids compared to its position in the latter part of the Second World War. Having counted on a conflict involving extensive gas warfare on the Home Front, Civil Defence had perceived poison gas to be the primary danger and planned accordingly. As Overy has argued, the focus on poison gas diverted attention from other areas of Civil Defence. As a result, Civil Defence confronted "the shock of heavy explosive and incendiary raids" of the Blitz "without sufficient forethought or experience."[15] Civil Defence also increased in size as the war continued; by late 1943, some 1,860,000 Britons were engaged in Civil Defence. Whereas the London Civil Defence Region relied upon just 350 rescue squads in 1941, it employed nearly 1,370 by the end of the following year. Although this figure started to dip in 1944, Civil Defence remained primed for further air raids in the years following the Blitz.[16]

In the early hours of 13 June 1944, an explosion took place in Kent, followed by a similar blast in east London. From northern France, the Germans had discharged several pilotless aircraft known as *Vergeltungswaffen*, or V1s, towards London. This initial attack was followed by a further onslaught a few days later, when 73 V1s struck the London area.[17] For two weeks in June and July 1944, London was subjected to a steady barrage of V1s, which resulted in some 1,600 fatalities and several thousand injuries.[18] Designated "flying bombs" by the War Cabinet, V1s produced a powerful droning sound until their engines failed, at which point the vessels plummeted and detonated upon impact.[19] In June 1944, Chief of the Imperial General Staff Sir Alan Brooke remarked: "Flying bombs have again put us in the front line."[20] That same month, Prime Minister Winston Churchill described the V1 raid as "of a trying character, a worrisome character," particularly as bombing continued after dark.[21] New public shelters were erected in London, and around 1,000,000 women, children and the elderly evacuated the capital.[22] Between 13 June 1944 and 28 March 1945, more than 2,400 V1s hit the London Region, resulting in the deaths of some 5,370 persons.[23]

A large proportion of flying bombs which reached the London Region landed in south and east London. The residents of West Ham, for example, endured 57 V1 attacks, while East Ham and Ilford each reported 36 flying bombs. Lewisham suffered 117 V1 attacks.[24] Since the commencement of the Blitz in September 1940,

15   Ibid, pp. 36, 134, 149, 185 186.
16   Ibid, p. 186-188.
17   Philip Ziegler, *London at War 1939-1945* (London: Pimlico, 2002), pp. 282, 287-289.
18   O'Brien, *Civil Defence*, p. 653.
19   Calder, *The People's War*, pp. 559-560.
20   Quoted in Juliet Gardiner, *Wartime Britain 1939-1945* (London: Review, 2004), p. 639.
21   Hansard: HC Deb 6 July 1944 vol 401 c1326.
22   Gardiner, *Wartime Britain*, pp. 647-648.
23   TNA: HO 186/2955, Regional Organisation: History of Civil Defence, No. 5 London Civil Defence Region, 28.
24   Basil Collier, *The Defence of the United Kingdom* (London: Her Majesty's Stationery Office, 1957), p. 525.

the Ministry of Information had devoted especial attention to civilian morale in east London, where residents were said to harbour "ill-feeling" upon having endured so many air raids.[25] The MP Harold Nicolson noted in mid-September 1940: "Everybody is worried about the feeling in the East End," where "there is much bitterness."[26]

Although Allied forces recaptured northern France in August 1944, the *Luftwaffe* began dropping V1s from aircraft. Furthermore, in early September, the Germans introduced a second *Vergeltungswaffen* known as the V2. At 14 tons apiece, V2 rockets caused considerable devastation upon impact. Unlike the V1, the V2 produced no sound ahead of detonation, thus allowing no opportunity for civilians to seek cover prior to an attack. Following the first V2 raid, which occurred in west London on 8 September 1944, more than 500 V2s descended upon London.[27] The capital suffered the most attacks; residents of the London Region accounted for approximately 90 percent of V2 casualties during the war.[28] Although the material damage inflicted by each V2 was less widespread compared to that of the V1, V2s formed craters of up to three metres beneath the surface and could result in scores of fatalities in an instant.[29] A London resident recalled the harrowing experience of a V2 attack near his home in Islington:

> I thought the end of the world had come. The earth trembled, the very air seemed to vibrate, my ears seemed to be deafened and a buzzing sound was passing through them... Goodness knows where the houses that had been struck had disappeared to. It looked as though a huge bulldozer had lifted them from the earth and there was quite an open space. Never have I seen buildings so cleanly swept away.[30]

By March 1945, more than 1,000,000 homes in and around London had suffered at least slight damage as a result of V1 or V2 raids.[31] Once again, east London bore the brunt of the onslaught; 35 V2s descended upon Ilford, for example.[32] A Ministry of Information employee observed:

> We had to stop the knowledge of their arrival being circulated, first so as not to inform the Germans that they had landed in any particular area, but more important, there was the question of morale of the civilian population, because

25   Quoted in McLaine, *Ministry of Morale*, pp. 92, 109-110.
26   Quoted in Calder, *The People's War*, p. 164.
27   Ibid, pp. 561-562.
28   Collier, *Defence of the United Kingdom*, p. 528.
29   Norman Longmate, *How We Lived Then: A History of Everyday Life during the Second World War* (London: Arrow, 1977), p. 494 and Gardiner, *Wartime Britain*, pp. 653-655.
30   Quoted in Ziegler, *London at War*, p. 297.
31   Hansard: HC Deb 15 June 1945 vol 411 c1900W.
32   Ziegler, *London at War*, p. 298.

they were devastating in their effect. One rocket could demolish a whole street in a working-class area. There was no defence against them. And there was no warning that they were on their way.[33]

A survey carried out by Mass Observation in summer 1944 found in London "on the whole people were very very (sic) depressed" following the commencement of the V1 attacks. While acknowledging the multitude of differing responses from civilians regarding the V1 raids, the survey shed light on the ways in which flying bombs influenced civilian morale in the capital. One London resident described the V1 as "worse than anything yet," while another lamented the raids were "not like the old blitz, [and] people are just getting down and disheartened."[34] Hitler, like many political and military leaders of the time, foresaw bombing as a means to instil trepidation in the British populace. Yet while earlier air raids against Britain had also sought to erode morale on the Home Front, the V1 and V2 raids of 1944-1945 marked the commencement of, as Overy put it, "the entirely indiscriminate assault of British targets."[35]

As the V1 and V2 attacks continued into the autumn of 1944, trainers at the MAP Guard Dog Training School began training canines for employment on rescue operations.[36] According to Baldwin, the commandant of the school, the scheme was the result of his initiative. In an interview with the *Gloucestershire Echo*, Baldwin explained that the use of rescue dogs was a natural extension of teaching canines to hunt animals, as both activities required that dogs utilise their excellent sense of smell.[37]

Yet while the use of dogs to locate air raid victims was novel, dogs had been employed in similar roles prior to the Second World War. Although Bloodhounds were not utilised on rescue operations, they were employed as trackers in England by the 15th century.[38] In the late 19th century, police forces in Britain increasingly relied upon Bloodhounds to seek out fugitives. Among the breeders whose dogs were employed by British police forces prior to the First World War was E.H. Richardson. One of Richardson's Bloodhounds led police on a search for a killer near Manchester in 1909.[39] By the First World War, a number of foreign militaries relied upon canines known as ambulance or Red Cross dogs to alert medical personnel to live casualties.[40] Richardson had trained a number of ambulance dogs in the years leading up to the First World War. Upon the outbreak of war in 1914, he had supplied dogs to Belgian

33 Quoted in Gardiner, *Wartime Britain*, p. 653.
34 MOA: File Report 2121, A Survey on the Pilotless Planes, 18 April 1945, pp. 2, 11.
35 Overy, *The Bombing War*, pp. 3, 9-11, 60, 80, 85-86, 106, 113.
36 TNA: HO 186/2572, Rescue Services: Electric Detector Apparatus and Dogs for Locating Trapped Air Raid Casualties, Notes of a Conference held at Regional Headquarters, 2 October 1944.
37 'Rescue Dogs', *Gloucestershire Echo*, 9 October 1944, p. 3.
38 Sloane, 'Dogs in War', p. 388.
39 Neil Pemberton, 'The Bloodhound's Nose Knows? Dogs and Detection in Anglo-American Culture', *Endeavour*, 37:4 (2013), p. 196.
40 Phayre, 'War Duties for the Dog', *Windsor Magazine*, June-November 1916, pp. 69-74.

and French units on the Western Front.[41] Towards the end of the First World War, the British Army also utilised a few Bloodhounds provided by Richardson to seek out fugitive POWs in France.[42]

The Second World War also provided opportunities for dogs to perform search and rescue work. Following the onset of the Blitz in 1940, a number of pet dogs proved able to detect live casualties in the aftermath of air raids. The press periodically published accounts of pet dogs which led to the recovery of casualties. In December 1940, the *Daily Mirror* featured a photograph of an Airedale Terrier which had rescued a woman whose house was demolished during an air raid. According to the accompanying article, civilian Marjorie French was saved after the canine "went on scratching, and when he had made an opening large enough, seized Mrs. French's clothing and dragged her out."[43] Similarly, in early 1941, the *Daily Express* ran a front-page story which described how a dog alerted personnel to the presence of a live casualty amid the ruins of a house struck by a German bomb five days previously.[44]

Such accounts abounded in the wartime press. While they were likely true to an extent, they also served as propaganda to galvanise Britons on the Home Front. As the historian Hilda Kean has pointed out, these portrayals of canines "were constructed to complement the myths of resistance."[45] Such thinking was also encouraged by Maria Dickin, who as editor of *PDSA News*, spoke of canine pets "who have refused to leave their injured owners in bombed buildings," and in doing so, "reach[ed] the heights of human chivalry and self-sacrifice."[46] Dogs on the British Home Front were also celebrated for being "cheerful" in spite of the dangers of war. In summer 1939, the Secretary of the Canine Defence League was, according to the *Dogs' Bulletin*, imploring dog owners to "imitate your dogs" as "they are unfailingly cheerful, optimistic, unruffled, and unconcerned."[47] Similarly, during a radio broadcast which aired in late 1940, a veterinary surgeon maintained that dogs and other animals did not tend to "show any great fear during a raid" and had proven themselves "splendid example[s] to all of us [people] of the virtue of keeping cool under difficult conditions."[48] Whether true or not, reports of dogs disregarding their own safety to ensure that of their owners during the Blitz fed into the broader contemporary perception that Britons were "self-sacrificing, relentlessly cheerful" and "heroically withst[anding] the Blitz,"

41   'The Emergencies of the Battlefield', *First Aid*, August 1914, p. 30.
42   IWM: 69/75/1, Waley, Messenger Dog Service, Appendix B, p. 121 and Richardson, *Forty Years*, p. 268.
43   'Medal for Dog', *Daily Mirror*, 30 December 1940, p. 1.
44   'Girl of 3 Five Days in Debris', *Daily Express*, 19 February 1941, p. 1.
45   Kean, *Animal Rights*, p. 196.
46   M.E. Dickin, Letter to Associates, *P.D.S.A. News*, February 1941, p. 6.
47   'Dogs and International Crises', *Dogs' Bulletin*, June-July 1939, p. 7.
48   'Dogs in Air Raids', *Leicester Mercury*, 20 September 1940, p. 3.

representations which, as the historian Sonya O. Rose has shown, were propagated by both the British government and the wartime media.[49]

A small number of untrained canines were utilised in unofficial rescue roles by the Civil Defence and the PDSA during the early years of the Second World War. In Poplar, a dog called Rip began working with members of an ARP post after being taken in by a warden in late 1940. Despite no prior training, the mongrel assisted rescue workers in the search for casualties in east London.[50] According to Rip's owner, E. King:

> He was very valuable in helping us to locate persons trapped in the debris. During the alerts, heavy gunfire, and incendiary raids Rip was always out on duty—never in the way, but always eager to do his bit... Rip's training was gained the hard way. When I came across Rip sniffing around on the job, I always knew that there was someone trapped in the ruins.[51]

The PDSA, which before the war had operated a fleet of mobile dispensaries and ambulances, repurposed the vehicles for use by their newly-established Rescue Squads, whose purpose was to locate and render treatment to pets in the aftermath of air raids.[52] The Blitz afforded ample opportunities for the 14 PDSA Rescue Squads in operation across Britain. By early 1942, they had recovered some 82,000 animals.[53] A PDSA Rescue Squad mascot called Beauty regularly joined her owner and other PDSA personnel at the scene of air raids, where they sought to find and tend to lost or wounded animals. Following an incident in 1940, Beauty alerted rescue workers to the presence of a live cat buried in the rubble. Thereafter, the untrained terrier assisted rescue workers in the detection of animal casualties. During her tenure with the Rescue Squad, Beauty accounted for the recovery of 63 animals.[54] Although a useful addition to the Rescue Squad, Beauty undoubtedly served as a means of propaganda much like the untrained pets which alerted their owners during air raids. The *Evening News* extoled the canine's "self-imposed duty"[55] and she was photographed and covered by the press on multiple occasions.[56]

49   Rose, *Which People's War?*, p. 2.
50   St. Hill Bourne, *They Also Serve*, pp. 156-158.
51   Quoted in Ibid, p. 158.
52   Dickin, *Cry of the Animal*, pp. 73, 82.
53   'Lord Mayor Inspects P.D.S.A. Rescue Squads', *P.D.S.A. News*, February 1942, p. 11.
54   St. Hill Bourne, *They Also Serve*, pp. 156-157.
55   Quoted in 'Lord Mayor Inspects P.D.S.A. Rescue Squad', *P.D.S.A. News*, February 1942, p. 11.
56   'Lord Mayor Inspects P.D.S.A. Rescue Squad', *P.D.S.A. News*, February 1942, p. 11 and Front Cover, *P.D.S.A. News*, January 1942 and 'This Dog Saves Others', *P.D.S.A. News*, April 1941, pp. 2-3 and Front Cover, *P.D.S.A. News*, May 1941.

Rip, an untrained rescue dog utilised by the ARP in East London. (PDSA)

Beauty, an untrained rescue dog utilised by the PDSA Animal Rescue Squad in London. (PDSA)

Beauty at the scene of an air raid. (PDSA)

Rescue Dogs for the Capital

At a meeting with officials from the London Civil Defence Region in early October 1944, MAP representative Lieutenant Colonel William Dove proposed the employment of dogs in and around London to assist in the recovery of human casualties. Dove made clear that the scheme would proceed "on an experimental basis" and that the dogs required further training prior to commencing operations in London.[57] On 7 October 1944, four dogs took part in a trial in Birmingham. The Home Secretary Herbert Morrison and rescue officers from the London Region were in attendance.[58] As the trial took place in an area of the city previously wrecked by a German bomb, it required that the dogs work over a substantial amount of rubble.[59] The dogs successfully discovered four "victims" concealed in the wreckage, to which small fires had been added to further replicate a real incident. An ARP official who witnessed the trial described the way in which the dogs and their trainers worked:

57   TNA: HO 186/2572, Notes of a Conference, 2 October 1944.
58   TNA: HO 186/2572, E.G. Bax to Col. Sir Edward Warner, 13 October 1944.
59   'Rescue Dogs', *Gloucestershire Echo*, 9 October 1944, p. 3.

Four rescue workers were literally buried in rubble, and we placed burning rags on top of the 'bomb damage'. The dogs were released from 30 yards away and given the command 'Find'. In less than two minutes each dog had fought its way through the flames, and had discovered its man.[60]

Major E.G. Bax of the London Regional Headquarters acknowledged that although the dogs required training at real incidents, the display in Birmingham "proved that it would be an advantage to the London Region to accept the offer made by the M.A.P."[61] Consequently, the MAP proceeded with its plans to deploy a trained rescue dog to the London Region with four dogs at the ready provided the scheme was successful.[62]

Prior to serving on operations, rescue dogs completed a period of training lasting between six and eight weeks at the MAP Guard Dog Training School.[63] Upon posting to London, the dogs resumed training for a time during which their trainers were advised to "learn the ropes" by observing the employment of trained rescue dogs.[64] Many rescue dogs had undergone prior training at the MAP Guard Dog Training School and served as guards before their employment in the London Civil Defence Region.[65] Two dogs, Irma and Storm, had previously worked in Civil Defence, albeit in a different capacity. The Alsatians delivered dispatches for an ARP unit in Surrey. When telephonic communication was unavailable, Irma and Storm served as a form of communication between a warden's post and the local report centre. Storm was also briefly employed during the war as a tracker by police in Somerset. With Storm's assistance, the police located a fugitive who had been on the run for several hours.[66]

Like most dogs at the MAP Guard Dog Training School,[67] the canines employed by the London Civil Defence Region were supplied by civilians. Liverpool resident Hilda Babcock Cleaver provided a litter of Alsatian puppies, one of which grew up to be the first canine employed in an official capacity by the London Civil Defence Region.[68] The aforementioned Peter was also donated by a civilian with whom he was reunited after the V1 and V2 attacks ceased in 1945.[69] Yet the Civil Defence dog scheme differed from wider military dog training at the Army and the MAP training centres in that many of the rescue dogs were provided by and employed during the war

60   TNA: HO 186/2671, Rescue Services: Dogs Used by Rescue Parties to Locate Buried Casualties, Extract from *Star*, 11 October 1944.
61   TNA: HO 186/2572, Bax to Warner, 13 October 1944.
62   Ibid.
63   'Rescue Dogs', *Manchester Guardian*, 18 December 1944, p. 4.
64   TNA: HO 186/2671, London Civil Defence Region M.A.P. Rescue Dogs, 29 November 1944. Once in London, dogs likely endured another two to three weeks of training.
65   'Rescue Dogs', *Manchester Guardian*, 18 December 1944, p. 4.
66   St. Hill Bourne, *They Also Serve*, p. 163.
67   'Dogs for War Service', *The Times*, 14 January 1944.
68   Brown, *Jet of Iada*, pp. 3, 13-15.
69   St. Hill Bourne, *They Also Serve*, pp. 171-172.

by their dog fancier owners. Cleaver herself was an Alsatian breeder, and her dog Jet was related to Baldwin's own Alsatians.[70] Several of the dogs utilised on rescue operations in London were Alsatians bred or owned by dog fancier and trainer Margaret Griffin.[71] Through her attendance at dog shows before and during the Second World War, Griffin became a prominent figure among dog fanciers.[72] Along with fellow Alsatian enthusiasts L.W. Charles and Dorothy and Marjorie Homan, Griffin trained guard dogs at the MAP Guard Dog Training School prior to serving with the London Civil Defence Region.[73] Like Griffin, Charles and the Homans provided and trained their own dogs for rescue operations.[74] Thus, in contrast to the military dog scheme, which involved the training and use of pets and strays previously unknown to their servicemen handlers, the employment of rescue dogs was a small-scale undertaking largely composed of civilian dog fanciers and their personal dogs.

Jet, the first dog utilised by the London Civil Defence Region, joined Chelsea Light Rescue in Group 1 in October 1944.[75] That month, Jet was requested following a V1 attack in north London. According to an officer of the Edmonton Civil Defence Rescue Service, the Alsatian was overly distracted by onlookers at the scene, and as a result, "did not have a favourable try-out."[76] Jet's performance improved over the next few days, however. Following a V1 raid in Purley, three deceased victims were extricated thanks to the Alsatian. Having hitherto solely indicated the presence of live persons, Jet's actions in Purley marked a positive step in the employment of canines in Civil Defence.[77]

Also in October, two dogs were posted to Group 7 in Essex, where they were attached to Chigwell Light Rescue.[78] Thorn, an Alsatian whose civilian owner acted as his trainer while in London, joined Jet in Group 1 in early November.[79] By mid-December 1944, Jet and Thorn had located some 30 air raid victims.[80] In early November, the Director of Regional Organisation for the MAP acknowledged that although "the operational conditions proved far more difficult" in London as

70   Brown, *Jet of Iada*, pp. 13-14.
71   St. Hill Bourne, *They Also Serve*, pp. 162, 172. At least five of the Alsatians employed by the London Civil Defence Region were of the "Crumstone" pedigree bred by Griffin.
72   'Kettering Dog Show', *Northampton Mercury*, 21 July 1939, p. 18 and 'Gloucester Dog Show a Big Success', *Citizen*, 24 July 1944, p. 7.
73   'Notes & News of the Breeds', *Our Dogs*, 26 December 1941, p. 1283.
74   'Notes & News of the Breeds', *Our Dogs*, 22 June 1945, p. 714.
75   LMA: LCC/CL/CD/03/022, London Civil Defence Region Operations Circular No. 151, 17 October 1944.
76   TNA: HO 186/2572, Report on Work of Rescue Dog at Fly Bomb Incident, 27 October 1944.
77   TNA: HO 186/2572, Leslie C. Price to Ernest C. King, 7 November 1944.
78   Essex Record Office, Chelmsford (ERO): C/W 2/10, Use of Dogs, Rescue Service Group 7, Frank Foster to A.R.P. Sub-Controllers, 25 October 1944.
79   TNA: HO 186/2572, Notes of an Interview with Mr S. Hudson, 8 November 1944 and Charles F. Prudames, 'War-time Relief Column', *Our Dogs*, March 1945, p. 360.
80   'Alsatian Rescue Dogs Take a Bow', *Sunday Express*, 17 December 1944, p. 7.

compared to the display in Birmingham, "the results have been very encouraging."[81] The MAP, therefore, assigned eight more dogs to the London Region.[82]

Eventually, four groups within the London Civil Defence Region employed canines, so that by February 1945, a total of 18 rescue dogs were based in and around the capital.[83]

Table 3 Rescue Dogs in the London Civil Defence Region, February 1945[84]

Group and Location	Number of Dogs
Group 1 (Chelsea)	4
Group 4 (Lewisham)	4
Group 6 (Hendon)	4
Group 7 (Chigwell)	6
Total, London Civil Defence Region	18

While it is not entirely clear why the dogs were assigned to Groups 1, 4, 6 and 7, the decision seems to have been largely based on ensuring that several groups had access to dogs. Representatives from the MAP and the London Civil Defence Region proposed the aforementioned groups in January 1945, as it was recognised that "to prevent a time lag in getting dogs to incidents they should be deployed over the Region sooner than to concentrate them in one area."[85] Similarly, a circular issued in February 1945 acknowledged that "the dogs are widely distributed to secure rapid attendance at incidents."[86] Thus, the dogs were likely designated to Groups 1, 4, 6 and 7 to allow them to be in close proximity to as many other groups as possible. Had the rescue dog scheme commenced earlier, it is likely the use of dogs would have expanded beyond the London Region. Civil Defence officials from Cambridge and Luton enquired about rescue dogs in early 1945, but as the London Region had relatively few dogs and the scheme had only been in operation a few months, the MAP was reluctant to provide dogs to other regions.[87]

A circular issued by the London Civil Defence Region advised local authorities to "immediately... call for dogs for every incident at which trapped casualties are reported," as the effectiveness of rescue dogs "depends to a considerable extent on their

81   TNA: HO 186/2671, J.F. Smith to H.A. Strutt, 2 November 1944.
82   Ibid.
83   LMA: LCC/CL/CD/03/022, London Civil Defence Region Operations Circular No. 158.
84   Ibid.
85   TNA: HO 186/2572, Notes of a Conference held at R.H.Q., 17 January 1945.
86   LMA: LCC/CL/CD/03/022, London Civil Defence Region Operations Circular No. 158.
87   TNA: HO 186/2572, J.W. Oatley to K.P. Wood, 18 January 1945 and TNA: HO 186/2671, R. Alderson to Col. Baldwin, 21 February 1945 and W. Dove to R. Alderson, 28 February 1945.

A rescue dog employed by the London Civil Defence Region at the scene of a V1 attack, January 1945. (© Imperial War Museum (PL 6445F))

early arrival at the incident."[88] The dogs were billeted in local authority depots and referred to incidents anywhere within the London Region. Working alongside light rescue parties, a team of two dogs was accompanied to incidents by their trainer, who conferred with the incident officer and senior rescue officer at the scene. As a 1945 Ministry of Home Security circular made clear, dogs were intended "as a valuable aid" to casualty detection and recovery rather than "a substitute for reconnaissance."[89] Thus, dogs were brought to the scene of attacks after initial rescue operations had commenced and visible casualties had been cleared.[90]

Such a policy also meant that rescue dogs were utilised in addition to other means and instruments for casualty detection and recovery. Following a V1 attack in January 1945, for example, the *Derby Daily Telegraph* reported that "searchlights, cranes, dogs

---

88   LMA: LCC/CL/CD/03/022, London Civil Defence Region Operations Circular No. 158.
89   TNA: HO 186/2671, Circular from W.B. Brown, 9 January 1945.
90   Ibid.

and sound location units" were made available to rescue personnel at the scene.[91] An incident officer's description of the scene of a V2 attack in south London later that month also highlighted the significant number of personnel and machinery involved in casualty detection and recovery:

> At 16.30 hrs Column Officer J., N[ational] F[ire] S[ervice], reported with two pumps and two salvage tenders. He was requested, owing to the absence of large fires, to use his personnel in rescue and reconnaissance duties... At approximately 16.55 hrs I was contacted by the Town Clerk, who offered me additional services, but as the approaches to the incident were somewhat congested with vehicles of H[eavy] R[escue] and L[ight] R[escue] parties, who were doing a most excellent job, I declined more of these but accepted the offer of a mobile crane. At about this time... the rescue dogs and sound location apparatus were sent for and arrived quickly... At dusk refreshment vans were in attendance and rescue parties continued work at the incident floodlit with army searchlights.[92]

Clearly, rescue dogs were not used in isolation but were viewed as one option to be used along with other means.

Although the ways in which dogs signalled trapped persons varied, most alerted trainers to a specific location through pointing or clawing.[93] Some dogs could seemingly distinguish between human remains and bodies still intact. Following a V2 attack in November 1944, Group 1 trainer Malcolm Russell observed: "Although dogs will mark scraps of human flesh, they do not show any tendency to mark on them too strongly."[94] Such differentiation allowed rescue workers to focus their efforts on seeking out live casualties.[95] Another trainer referenced the ability of dogs to distinguish live persons: "If the dogs find a dead person, there is a most tragic look on their faces. But if the person they locate is alive they get very excited."[96] Similarly, in her journal, Margaret Griffin noted that following a raid in West Ham, her dog Irma "was so keen [that] I felt sure the victim must be alive."[97] Consequently, rescue personnel were able to free two persons previously concealed in the wreckage.[98]

In contrast to the use of dogs in military roles, the employment of rescue dogs was restricted to a small number of canines. Moreover, the scheme was a somewhat haphazard

91   'Children Killed by V-Bomb While Visiting Library', *Derby Daily Telegraph*, 5 January 1945, p. 8.

92   Quoted in Norman Longmate, *Hitler's Rockets: The Story of the V-2s* (Barnsley: Frontline Books, 2009), p. 334.

93   TNA: HO 186/2671, Circular from Brown, 9 January 1945.

94   TNA: HO 186/2572, Hazelhurst Road Incident, 19 November 1944.

95   Ibid.

96   Quoted in 'V-Deaths are Tragedy for Alsatians', *Citizen*, 7 March 1945, p. 4.

97   Quoted in Le Chêne , *Silent Heroes*, p. 97.

98   Le Chêne, *Silent Heroes*, p. 97.

and experimental venture. Lieutenant Colonel Dove admitted as much as late as February 1945.[99] Similarly, less than two weeks before the last incident attended by rescue dogs, Deputy Inspector General C.H. Kitchin of the Home Office acknowledged: "The use of [rescue] dogs at all is very much in the experimental stage." He went on to emphasise the improvised nature of the scheme: "Nobody knew until we gained recent experience just how they were wanted to function or how they should be trained."[100]

Rescue dogs were similar to dogs in military roles in that their effectiveness was largely dependent on environmental factors beyond the control of the dogs and their trainers. The performance of dogs employed by the London Region also varied among dogs, as well as by incidents. While some canines worked effectively despite distractions, such as fires or the use of floodlights, such conditions interfered with the successful employment of others. The ability of some dogs to perform in difficult surroundings was recognised by London Civil Defence Senior Regional Officer Edward Warner. Floodlighting and odours, he pointed out in November 1944, had thus far "not seriously affected" the performance of rescue dogs, while machinery such as cranes "does not seem to worry them to any extent."[101] Margaret Griffin also noted the ability of one of Group 7's dogs to work effectively in difficult surroundings following a V2 attack in Walthamstow:

> Searching a house, things were made no easier by water pipes burst in all directions and a bad gas leak under the debris. A smashed meter was pouring gas into the rubble. Worked Irma. In spite of the stench of gas, she indicated distinctly at a point at the back of the debris. From front of building, she and I went right under the floors crawling on our stomachs in the water.[102]

Irma's indication allowed for rescue personnel to remove three casualties shortly thereafter.[103] At a separate incident, one of Group 1's dogs refused to advance towards a row of burning houses. The other dog in use, however, persisted in his search. According to the Rescue Officer in charge:

> Whilst 'Jet' would not go into the smoke, 'Thorn' went slowly, step by step through the thickest smoke. He repeatedly flinched but was encouraged forward until eventually he reached a spot approximately over the seat of the fire and gave positive indication there. In my opinion the work of 'Thorn' at this spot was the best I have yet seen from any Rescue dog for I found it impossible to see when in this smoke and had to be helped down to where the air was cleaner.[104]

99   TNA: HO 186/2671, Dove to Alderson, 28 February 1945.
100 TNA: HO 186/2671, C.H. Kitchin to R. Alderson, 15 March 1945.
101 TNA: HO 186/2671, M.A.P. Rescue Dogs, 29 November 1944.
102 Quoted in Le Chêne, *Silent Heroes*, pp. 94-95.
103 Le Chêne, *Silent Heroes*, p. 95.
104 TNA: HO 186/2572, E. Warner to PDSA, 20 February 1945.

Several dogs from Groups 1 and 6 were deployed to Heston, where a V2 had struck a factory, causing multiple fires. Upon reporting to the scene on 21 March 1945, dogs Rex and Silva alerted their trainer to five buried casualties even as they had "to clamber over steelwork and twisted girders which were still hot from the effects of the fire."[105] According to the Group Rescue Staff Officer:

> The dog [Rex] was withdrawn when the burning roof started to fall, pieces having dropped on to the dog. In this connection the dog was unwilling to leave and I have no doubt but that he had at this moment caught some scent which would have resulted in his giving then an indication which he did, in fact, give later in the day... At 14.00. hours the dogs were again set to work, the fire being largely under control although the sections not actually burning were still very hot and fire hoses were continuously played on the debris, being shut down from time to time as the dogs worked over the various parts of the site. Despite the heat Rex and Silva made their way across the debris in many places and gave indication of five casualties within the first four minutes.[106]

By contrast, fires at an incident in Potters Bar in January 1945 thwarted the efforts of two dogs from Group 6. Although Rex and Duke signalled that persons were buried in the wreckage, smoke prevented the dogs from accurately identifying their location. As noted by the Group Rescue Staff Officer, the detection of casualties was made more difficult by fresh snow:

> The weather at this time was extremely cold and snow had commenced to fall. Two of the demolished properties were on fire and dense smoke tended to handicap Rescue operations... On being taken to the other end of the site the dogs gave clear indication that they could detect the presence of bodies but seemed unable to point out any particular spot. No doubt the snow, together with the fires burning here, would have some bearing on this.[107]

Certainly, as these examples illustrate, obstacles such as fires, flooding and poor weather impacted the performance of humans as well as dogs.

Dust also proved problematic for some dogs, as evidenced by a report concerning the work of Group 1's Thorn in November 1944. In addition to substantial damage resulting from the blast, dust slowed the Alsatian's search. Nonetheless, Thorn found two fatal casualties.[108] Margaret Griffin reported a similar experience involving the

---

105 TNA: HO 186/2572, Reports on Work of Rescue Dogs at Heston 21-24 March 1945.
106 Ibid.
107 TNA: HO 186/2572, Reports on Operations of Rescue Dogs at Southgate Road, Potters Bar, 20 January 1945.
108 TNA: HO 186/2572, Incident, 22 November 1944.

dogs of Group 7 at an incident in southeast London. "The dust… was the worst I had encountered," she noted in her journal, "and made the dogs constantly sneeze."[109]

Furthermore, attacks resulting in numerous casualties sometimes impacted the performance of dogs, as they detected the lingering scents of persons recovered during earlier rescue operations. When a V2 landed in Enfield in January 1945, for example, the scent left behind by seven casualties discovered by rescue personnel earlier in the day frustrated two dogs employed by Group 6. According to the controller in charge, the dogs provided only vague indications as to where the victims were buried.[110]

In addition to the aforementioned difficulties, the rescue dog scheme met with other obstacles. As dogs relied on scent to find victims, incidents marked by powerful wind and thick or solid debris were likely to negatively impact their performance. The incident report concerning a V2 attack on a school in Islington, for example, noted: "Great difficulty was experienced… as the debris was large and heavy."[111] As a result, the dogs and trainers of Group 7 were prevented from fully accessing the scene of the blast while workers cleared the rubble. The wind further frustrated the dogs' efforts. Odour emanating from another casualty in the area led to an erroneous indication by one dog, which owing to the wind, could not accurately determine the origin of the scent.[112] A similar experience was reported in December 1944 concerning two of Group 1's dogs. Jet and Thorn were brought to a site in Bexley, where a fatal casualty remained trapped after a V2 attack. Although the dogs assisted rescue personnel in locating the victim, the dense rubble negatively impacted their performance. Group 8 Deputy Group Controller Brian Clapham noted as much in his report on the dogs:

> The body was recovered from that section at a point about 2 feet from where the dogs had shown only very slight indication. The dogs appeared handicapped by the tight mass of debris, particularly the concrete floor. What slight indications they did give were in the right direction, but were not marked.[113]

Just as the effective employment of military dogs was dependent on their handlers and the servicemen with whom they worked, the successful performance of rescue dogs was contingent on the actions of the humans involved. The importance of the trainer's role in the rescue dog scheme was recognised by Group 7 Deputy Group Rescue Officer John Potter, who noted that "a good portion of the success was due as

---

109 Quoted in Le Chêne, *Silent Heroes*, p. 93.
110 TNA: HO 186/2572, Reports on Work of Rescue Dogs at Enfield, 25 January 1945.
111 TNA: HO 186/2572, Use of Trained Dogs at Incident, No. 9, 16 November 1944.
112 Ibid.
113 TNA: HO 186/2572, B. Clapham to E. Warner, 21 December 1944. The lacklustre performance by dogs on this occasion did not seem to dissuade Clapham from utilising rescue dogs in the future. He acknowledged that: "While the dogs were able to give only a little help on this incident, I would not hesitate to ask for them again in similar circumstances."

much to the interpretation placed on the dogs actions by the trainer as by the actions of the dog."[114] In addition to the need for capable trainers, the effective employment of dogs was dependent on the behaviours and actions of Civil Defence officers and rescue personnel. For dogs to be utilised, controllers had to first seek their employment from the groups to which the dogs were attached. Even when controllers asked for dogs, the actual employment of dogs at incidents was subject to the approval of the incident officers and senior rescue officers at the scene.[115]

Apprehension on the part of rescue personnel as to the usefulness of dogs occasionally prevented their effective employment. Following an incident in West Ham in October 1944, the Rescue Staff Officer was initially hesitant to employ dogs, and according to an account of the incident, "decided to carry on in the usual way."[116] On a separate occasion in November 1944, rescue personnel were reluctant to search a location indicated by Group 1's Thorn. A trainer at the scene appealed to the incident officer, who directed workers to inspect the specified area. According to trainer Malcolm Russell: "It was obvious, from the efforts of the working party, that they were not convinced, and consequently, were not thorough in the search. Owing to the definite lack of cooperation, dogs were recalled."[117] Russell reported a similar experience just four days later. Despite indications from both Jet and Thorn, rescue personnel in Wandsworth refused to commence operations. Nonetheless, Russell remained optimistic. "By the time the dogs are withdrawn," he noted in a report, "[Civil Defence personnel] are usually most apologetic and very grateful for assistance given them."[118] Margaret Griffin also referred to insufficient co-operation between trainers and Civil Defence personnel following a raid in January 1945. Along with a fellow trainer and four dogs, Griffin attended an incident in West Ham, where the presence of numerous rescue workers led to disagreement over the employment of dogs. Griffin recalled:

> I was shown a piece of ground and asked to work the dogs over this... The Officer could not get the personnel sufficiently in hand either to stop the chatter nor to keep 20 or 30 men from standing in the wind, as well as crowding close about the dogs... I got a very fleeting run over the central part of this site and I believe got indications from both Irma and Bruce... but it was terribly difficult to read the dogs under these conditions... Going across to the other site, I again got what I believe to have been an indication from Irma, also [from] Bruce but just as

114 ERO: C/W 2/10, Meeting with Maj. Bax, 14 December 1944.
115 TNA: HO 186/2572, Notes of a Conference held at Ministry of Aircraft Production, 8 November 1944.
116 ERO: C/W 2/10, Incident 12.30 Hrs, Hamfrith Rd. Bridge/Earlham Grove, West Ham, 30 October 1944. The report pointed out, however, that the dogs were brought back to the site the following day.
117 TNA: HO 186/2572, Incident at Kilgour Road, 15 November 1944.
118 TNA: HO 186/2572, Hazelhurst Road Incident, 19 November 1944.

the latter dog was getting down to his job, the sound location van backed right on to the site, and... a party of men... over ran (sic) the site... one man actually fell over Bruce and almost got bitten in the leg, some wires were thrown on the ground in such a manner as to foul the dogs legs, and when I asked a Leader near me if these gentlemen could not be persuaded to wait until the dogs had worked this spot as we had been told to go there, he replied that these men could not be interferred (sic) with... Realizing that on this incident at least, more reliance was being placed on the machine than the dogs, I told [fellow dog trainer] Mr. Brett I would withdraw.[119]

Even the point at which dogs should be brought to incidents was up for discussion. In a report submitted in November 1944, Senior Regional Officer Edward Warner outlined the reasons for the disagreement among Civil Defence officers:

Opinions differ as to how soon the dogs should arrive. On the one hand the sooner they arrive the better chance of success they have; on the other it is not desirable that they should be set to work until surface and other obvious casualties have been removed and preliminary reconnaissance been carried out... I consider that they will not be of such value until 30 minutes to one hour has elapsed.[120]

A controller in Wandsworth came to a similar conclusion. Following an incident at which dogs were utilised three hours after a V2 attack, Controller R.H. Jerman concluded that dogs should be employed "at a much earlier hour before the ground becomes trampled."[121]

Despite its limitations, the rescue dog scheme offered a number of advantages. At many incidents dogs signalled that victims were concealed in the wreckage shortly after reaching the scene. Following a V2 attack in Bexley in November 1944, a dog was brought to the scene where 12 homes lay in ruins. According to the incident report: "The dog made a quick and very accurate pointing, and... two bodies were recovered within a short time."[122] Similarly, at an incident in West Ham, two of Group 7's dogs detected two victims in less than three minutes.[123] Reports compiled by rescue dog trainers and Civil Defence personnel reveal that such examples were not isolated events. Shortly after being put to work at an incident in Ilford, Irma of Group 7 detected a fatal casualty concealed by one metre of wreckage despite nearly two hours having elapsed since the attack. The Alsatian's performance was particularly remarkable considering that it was the first incident at which she was

119 ERO: C/W/ 2/10, Practice at Hermitage and Incident at West Ham, 3-4 January 1945.
120 TNA: HO 186/2671, M.A.P. Rescue Dogs, 29 November 1944.
121 TNA: HO 186/2572, R.H. Jerman to Col. Trench, 6 December 1944.
122 TNA: HO 186/2572, Use of Trained Dogs at Incident, No. 11, 18 November 1944.
123 TNA: HO 186/2572, Warner to PDSA, 20 February 1945.

employed.[124] According to the incident report related to a V2 attack in Woolwich, dogs provided "immediate indication of casualties... and two women were extricated from 8 feet of cover."[125]

As also indicated in the above reports, dogs were able to detect casualties concealed multiple metres below the surface. The aforementioned incident in Ilford at which Irma was employed involved substantial damage to a group of houses. The incident report for the V2 attack revealed the extent of destruction: "Missile fell directly upon houses; penetrated in ground and exploded; forming crater 20 f[ee]t across and 10 f[ee]t. deep. Three houses each side of crater totally collapsed. Houses opposite side of Courtland Avenue demolished – only flank walls standing."[126] The significant amount of destruction did not prevent Irma from detecting an additional three casualties, which were unearthed from some four metres of wreckage.[127] Following a V2 attack in Walthamstow which left 21 homes and several shops in ruins, the employment of dogs led to the recovery of two fatal casualties hidden in more than three metres of rubble.[128] Similarly, in December 1944, Bruce of Group 7 discovered a victim concealed by nearly two metres of wreckage. At the same incident, Irma and Psyche located a victim buried six metres under the surface. Consequently, the Group Rescue Staff Officer at the scene concluded: "It is better to rely upon the indications given by Rescue dogs than on information given by persons who are believed to have been aware of the spot at which any missing person may have been at the time an incident occurred."[129]

Rescue dogs also proved able to find victims several hours after an attack, as well as at locations rescue personnel believed were free of casualties. In November 1944, for example, dogs were used to search for victims at an incident in East Ham, where some 100 casualties had already been recorded. The dogs discovered five casualties, including a victim who was brought out alive six hours after the attack.[130] That same month, a similar occurrence took place involving the dogs of Group 1. Jet and Thorn signalled the presence of a live casualty almost 12 hours after a raid.[131] In March 1945, Group 1's dogs were brought to the scene of a V2 raid in Stepney. Although the attack

124 ERO: C/W/ 2/10, Use of Trained Dogs at Incident, No. 1, 26 October 1944 and Le Chêne, *Silent Heroes*, p. 87.
125 TNA: HO 186/2572, Use of Trained Dogs at Incident, No. 7, 11 November 1944.
126 ERO: C/W 2/10, Use of Trained Dogs at Incident, No. 1, 26 October 1944.
127 Le Chêne, *Silent Heroes*, p. 87.
128 TNA: HO 186/2572, Use of Trained Dogs at Incident, No. 14, 1 December 1944.
129 TNA: HO 186/2572, London Civil Defence Region M.A.P. Rescue Dogs, Extracts from Reports, December 1944.
130 TNA: HO 186/2572, Use of Trained Dogs at Incident, No. 12, 20 November 1944 and Report on Reconnaissance Dogs, 21 November 1944.
131 TNA: HO 186/2671, London Civil Defence Region, Extracts from Reports 1-25 November 1944.

An incident in Stepney attended by rescue dogs, March 1945.
(© Imperial War Museum (HU 88803))

had taken place the previous evening and over 19 hours had elapsed, Peter discovered three casualties.[132]

Similarly, in December 1944, the dogs of Group 7 detected a live victim following a V2 attack in Southgate. According to the incident report:

> Irma suddenly became excited and began scratching at the debris. Investigations proceeded, and it was determined by her actions that there was a casualty in close proximity. A call for silence on the site was sufficient for the Rescue Officer to hear a woman saying that she was in a Morrison shelter… The woman was rescued apparently unhurt after being buried for nearly four hours… This woman definitely owes her life to the dogs.[133]

On a separate occasion, Irma was again responsible for detecting a live casualty despite several hours having elapsed since the attack. Margaret Griffin described the performance of Irma, as well as the Alsatian Psyche, in her journal:

---

132 A. Knight, Commercial Road Report, 29 March 1945 in IWM: 07/45/1, Private Papers of
     A. Knight, *Peter VC 1941-1952*, p. 18.
133 TNA: HO 186/2572, Use of Trained Dogs at Incident, No. 16, 14 December 1944.

Irma and Psyche *together* suddenly ran to a point in the debris. Beneath this rubble we found a collapsed floor. A woman was trapped there between two floors. She had been there over nine hours and was still conscious... This was a wonderful find, as the position of the floors was quite hidden by a mound of rubble and the woman's presence was quite unsuspected. The rescue and other workers were walking about over the very spot where this unfortunate woman was sandwiched with her small son dead beneath her feet.[134]

When a V2 struck an area of Walthamstow in December 1944, Irma was brought to the scene where nearly 150 casualties had already been reported. The Alsatian located a fatal casualty, which according to the incident report, "must have been passed by numerous rescue workers" in the time since the attack.[135] Irma was not alone in detecting casualties at locations considered free of casualties by rescue personnel. At an incident in early 1945, another Alsatian discovered blood unnoticed by rescue personnel at the scene. Believing no further casualties to be in that particular location, rescue workers were sceptical until excavations revealed a bed. Consequently, multiple casualties were recovered from the scene.[136]

Like dogs employed in military roles, rescue dogs offered advantages over electronic technology utilised by human personnel. In addition to dogs, rescue workers in the London Civil Defence Region could call upon sound location units to detect casualties concealed by debris. The first sound location set was utilised in the London Region in late 1940. By early 1945, the London Region possessed three sets, and sound location personnel were directed to attend every incident involving missing persons.[137] In contrast to dogs, sound location sets were only effective if the victim generated noise. Thus, rescue personnel wielding sound location sets could not identify the position of dead or unconscious victims.[138] As Major Bax pointed out in a March 1945 meeting, sound location units were advantageous in a minority of situations. In January 1945, for example, sound location units were called to 32 incidents yet were utilised at just eight. Even then, their use led to the recovery of just one person.[139] Furthermore, as sound location sets required silence to function, rescue personnel tended to prefer the employment of dogs since their use did not similarly impede rescue efforts. An account of the London Civil Defence Region produced by the Cabinet Office in 1945 concluded that while the use of sound location sets was still

---

134 Quoted in St. Hill Bourne, *They Also Serve*, pp. 163-164.
135 TNA: HO 186/2572, Use of Trained Dogs at Incident, No. 14, 1 December 1944.
136 St. Hill Bourne, *They Also Serve*, p. 173.
137 TNA: HO 186/2955, History of Civil Defence, p. 37.
138 TNA: HO 207/166, Region No. 5 (London): Equipment and Stores and Rescue Services: Rescue Parties: Provision of Sound Detecting Apparatus, Electrical Apparatus for the Detection of Buried Casualties-Description and Notes on its Employment, February 1943.
139 TNA: HO 207/166, Meeting held in Mr O.C. Allen's Room, 8 March 1945.

relatively novel, the "present indication appears unlikely to prove that the sets have much value in present conditions."[140]

It was believed at the time that the employment of dogs by the London Region had a positive impact on morale. Following the onset of the V1 raids in June 1944, Herbert Morrison remarked to the Cabinet: "The people have had nearly five years of war strain – they will resent this new trouble increasingly and want to know what we are going to do about it."[141] Indeed, morale on the Home Front seems to have suffered following the arrival of the V1. A civilian observed: "There is not one man I know who's getting used to it; if anything, it is getting everybody down."[142] Similarly, a "long-suffering Londoner" commented: "We have had to face up to horrible things for nearly five years, [so] I suppose we shall continue to do so, but, God, how tired we are of it!"[143] The psychological impact of the raids was not lost on the Prime Minister, who in an address to the House of Commons in November 1944 described the V2 as "another attempt by the enemy to attack the morale of our civil population."[144]

The employment of rescue dogs in London, and the impact their presence had on morale, was recognised by several people involved with the scheme. A report concerning an incident at which dogs were employed in October 1944 emphasised: "The psychological effect of the dogs on the populace is great in that people become impressed with the fact that everything humanly possible is being done to expedite extrication of casualties, thereby increasing the preservation of life."[145] The press drew attention to the scheme, as national and provincial newspapers alike frequently reported on the use of dogs in and around London.[146] Moreover, in December 1944, Londoners had the opportunity to attend a demonstration during which Jet and Thorn simulated the rescue of a person concealed by debris.[147] Following the employment of an inexperienced dog at an incident in January 1945, Deputy Group Controller Clapham recommended that rescue personnel proceed without dogs if experienced canines were unavailable, as "the performance put up by a partly trained animal leaves in the minds of those present on the incident a poor impression as to the value of the use of dogs in rescue operations."[148] Colonel Dove exhibited a similar mindset when

140 TNA: HO 186/2955, History of Civil Defence, p. 37.
141 Quoted in Ziegler, *London at War*, p. 294.
142 Quoted in Ibid, p. 293.
143 Quoted in Gardiner, *Wartime Britain*, p. 642.
144 Hansard: HC Deb 10 November 1944 vol 404 c1653-4.
145 ERO: C/W 2/10, Incident Hamfrith Rd., 30 October 1944.
146 'V-Bomb Raids on Allied Armies', *Derby Evening Telegraph*, 17 November 1944, p. 1 and 'Saved by Rescue Dogs', *Northern Daily Mail*, 14 December 1944, p. 8 and 'Many Casualties from V-Bombs', *The Times*, 29 January 1945, p. 2 and 'Home Ruined and Two Children Dead', *The Times*, 3 February 1945, p. 2 and 'Dogs Locate V-Bomb Victims', *Dundee Evening Telegraph*, 7 March 1945, p. 4.
147 'Rescue Dogs', *Manchester Guardian*, 18 December 1944, p. 4.
148 TNA: HO 186/2572, Brian Clapham to Chief Administration Officer, 8 January 1945.

he argued against the employment of canines outside the London Region. He pointed out that the effective use of rescue dogs was dependent on their being led by capable trainers. As the few people familiar with the training of rescue dogs were currently serving in and around London, the extension of the scheme beyond the capital would require that untrained persons take part. To accept this risk, Dove warned, would threaten the reputation of rescue dogs in the eyes of the public.[149]

As the war in Europe reached its end, so too did the V1 and V2 raids, which finally ceased in late March 1945.[150] In fact, rescue dogs from all four groups were utilised at a number of incidents during the final week of V2 raids on London.[151] That multiple canines were employed at these incidents and trainers "were continually receiving calls from [rescue] parties" at the scene of one of the raids is indicative of the progress experienced by the rescue dog scheme.[152] Civil Defence, including the employment of rescue dogs, concluded in the spring of 1945 shortly before Victory in Europe Day (V-E Day) was celebrated on 8 May.[153] Almost 9,000 Britons had perished as a result of Hitler's *Vergeltungswaffen*.[154]

As the Civil Defence dog scheme spanned just six months, rescue dogs constituted only a small percentage of the canines trained at the MAP Guard Dog Training School. Yet the rescue dog scheme should not be viewed as a mere side project to the training of dogs for the British Armed Forces. Moreover, the improvised nature of the rescue dog scheme was not unique to that aspect of Civil Defence; as O'Brien's official history put it: "Improvisation was the order of the day."[155] Despite the difficulties encountered by the scheme, rescue dogs constituted a valuable adjunct to Civil Defence. Rescue dogs aided Civil Defence personnel by detecting several hundred casualties. Group 7's dogs alone discovered 221 casualties, including 21 live persons.[156] The dogs of Group 1 led to the recovery of more than 100 casualties,[157] while Storm

149 TNA: HO 186/2671, Dove to Alderson, 28 February 1945.
150 Calder, *The People's War*, p. 565.
151 TNA: HO 186/2572, Heston Report, 21-24 March 1945 and ERO: C/W 2/10, London Civil Defence Region, Group 7, Rescue by Dogs, undated and TNA: HO 186/2572, D. Sheppard to Group Officer, 28 March 1945. See also: A. Knight, Hughes Mansions Report, 29 March 1945 and A. Knight, Commercial Road Report, 29 March 1945 and A. Knight, Whitfield Street Report, 29 March 1945 in IWM: 07/45/1, Knight, *Peter VC*, pp. 18-20.
152 Knight, Hughes Mansions Report, 29 March 1945 in IWM: 07/45/1, Knight, *Peter VC*, p. 19.
153 Robin Woolven, '1945 Stand-Down', in Tim Essex-Lopresti (ed.), *A Brief History of Civil Defence* (Matlock: Civil Defence Association, 2005), p. 32 and TNA: HO 186/2572, E.G. Bax to William Dove, 20 April 1945.
154 Gardiner, *Wartime Britain*, p. 653.
155 O'Brien, *Civil Defence*, p. 578.
156 ERO: C/W 2/10, London Civil Defence Region, Group 7, Rescue by Dogs, undated.
157 Charles F. Prudames, 'War-time Relief Column', *Our Dogs*, March 1945, p. 360. It is unclear if this number refers to the total casualties detected by dogs Thorn and Jet or the total number of casualties discovered by Group 1's dogs.

and Drift of Group 4 accounted for a similar number.[158] In a letter to Sir Stafford Cripps, London Civil Defence Regional Commissioner Sir Ernest Gowers rightly acknowledged that the use of rescue dogs "ha[d] undoubtedly been the means of saving the lives of trapped persons on a number of occasions and has also saved the Rescue Services many hours of work."[159]

158 'Notes & News of the Breeds', *Our Dogs*, 22 June 1945, p. 714. Complete figures for all groups with canines are unavailable.
159 TNA: HO 207/186, Region No. 5 (London): Rescue Services: Miscellaneous Papers, Ernest Gowers to Stafford Cripps, 27 April 1945.

6

Working Animals or Pets?: The Perception and Demobilisation of British Military Dogs and Pets

On 18 February 1946, the *Hull Daily Mail* featured a photograph of a smiling young-ster playing with his pet Alsatian. The accompanying article, entitled "Wolf Has Been Demobbed," told how after being donated to the Army's War Dogs Training School earlier in the war, Wolf the Alsatian had devoted "three and a half years' honourable service with H[is] M[ajesty's] Forces." "His name," the article continued, "will... go down in the illustrious roll of those who have served their King and Country in times of mortal peril."[1] Wolf, like many dogs employed by the British Armed Forces in the Second World War, spent his early life not as a trained military or police dog but as a family pet. Just as human servicemen were expected to readjust to life as civilians, many military dogs resumed their peacetime roles as pets after the war. The demobili-sation of military dogs, therefore, exemplified and accentuated the blurred distinction between working animal and pet. Similarly, anecdotal evidence suggests that many military dog handlers and other servicemen who interacted with trained dogs saw them as pets, a perception which could influence canine performance. Dogs donated by their owners to the British Armed Forces thus retained their status as pets of their owners while also assuming the dual role of working animal and companion to their military handlers. Even canine mascots and pets, dogs which never passed through the Army's War Dogs Training School or the MAP Guard Dog Training School, were viewed by some servicemen as both companions and untrained working animals. The perception of such dogs, some of which were utilised as unofficial guard dogs, further highlighted the vague distinction between working animal and pet.

---

1   'Wolf Has Been Demobbed', *Hull Daily Mail*, 18 February 1946, p. 3.

The (Incomplete) Transformation from Pet to Working Animal

That military dogs had begun life as pets was often evident upon their entering the Army's War Dogs Training School. In an article for *Animal World*, the former DAVRS Brigadier Murray described the sometimes uneasy transition from pet to military dog which occurred during the dogs' initial weeks at the school:

> Owing to the variations in feeding by owners it has been found that a large percentage [of dogs] refuse food for several days after arrival. This is due to fretting in new surroundings, or to the unaccustomed time of feeding, or nature of the food, or probably a combination of these... Generally speaking the dogs which join, can be correctly described as 'house dogs' rather than kennel dogs, and to a large extent it is this factor which leads to a good deal of the sickness that crops up in a kennel of this nature.[2]

Although Murray admitted that "fretting" was usually temporary,[3] the use of pets also resulted in longer-term problems for the British military dog scheme. The War Office publication *Training of War Dogs* acknowledged the disadvantages involved in the canine recruitment process adopted in the Second World War: "Although many first class dogs were thus obtained, it entailed endless correspondence as owners desired to be regularly informed of their pets welfare. Again, with the coming of peace these dogs had to be returned to their owners and their services lost to the Army."[4] As per the policy of the AVRS, the units to which military dogs were attached were not expected to communicate with owners during the course of the war. If owners contacted the Army's War Dogs Training School, they were duly contacted by the AVRS, which was also responsible for advising owners in the event of their pets becoming casualties.[5] Nonetheless, it seems that staff at the school felt obliged to correspond with owners whose dogs were in training.[6] The difficulties involved with employing pets became increasingly apparent when a dog disappeared from the school in May 1943. According to the war diary of the DAVRS, the dog's owner had "continue[d] to infer that culperable (sic) negligence has occurred."[7] The RAF also endeavoured to remain in contact with at least some owners of RAF police dogs employed overseas during the war. Per the instructions of the Provost Marshal, Mediterranean Allied Air Forces

---

2   Murray, 'War Dogs', *Animal World*, September 1944, p. 69.
3   Ibid.
4   War Office, *Training of War Dogs* (1952), p. 32.
5   TNA: AIR 23/6002, 73A, Provost Marshal, Air Ministry to O.C. Provost and Security Unit, RAF (CMF), 20 October 1944. This policy was applicable to military dogs employed outside the United Kingdom. It is unclear how the Army's War Dogs Training School handled communication from owners of military dogs employed on the Home Front.
6   'Training Dogs for the Army', *Manchester Guardian*, 3 June 1943, p. 3.
7   Museum of Military Medicine: War Diary of DAVRS, May 1943.

(MAAF), RAF personnel were "to keep the owners informed as to the health of their dogs."[8]

Earlier in the war, owners who supplied dogs to the Army's War Dogs Training School had received a letter which outlined the terms of the agreement. It stipulated that each dog was "enlisted for the duration of the present emergency or as long as his services are needed."[9] The language used in the contract entered into by military dog owners led to some confusion after the cessation of hostilities. A few weeks after Japan surrendered to the Allies in September 1945, a civilian whose dog was employed by the British Armed Forces questioned why her dog had yet to be demobilised. "I loaned my dog... till the end of the War," she insisted in correspondence with the Assistant Secretary of the RSPCA.[10] She was not alone. According to Major H.A. Clay of the AVRS, the cessation of hostilities in September 1945 prompted several owners to demand the release of their pets.[11] That month, the British Army was obliged to release a small number of dogs from employment in northwest Europe as a result of their "owners... agitating for their early return."[12] Even before the war in the Pacific was brought to an end, the AVRS resolved that the Army would no longer accept canines offered on a temporary basis.[13] In fact, shortly after the war, a number of Britons permanently sold their dogs to the Army. Upon purchase, the canines were designated "W[ar] D[epartment] property" and could be resold or euthanised following employment.[14]

That military dogs could be seen as pets by their handlers or other servicemen was recognised in contemporary training instructions and regulations. Instructions related to the employment of mine detection dogs made clear that: "The dogs will be completely ruined if all and sundry try to make friends with them. They must not be petted or even spoken to except by trained handlers."[15] *Tactical Employment of War Dogs*, a training manual developed in 1942 for units with military canines, emphasised:

> All troops located near any [trained military] dogs must be warned that in no circumstances are they to attempt to contact the animals or interfere with them

---

8   TNA: AIR 23/6002, 64A, Provost and Security Unit, RAF, CMF to Provost Marshal, Air Ministry, 20 September 1944.

9   NAA: MP742/1, 240/6/324, Training of Dogs for Use in War, Appendix B, Instructions and Conditions for Loaning Dogs for War Purposes, undated. See Appendix VII for a copy of the letter provided to military dog owners.

10   Quoted in TNA: WO 32/10800, Assistant Secretary, RSPCA to H.A. Clay, 1 October 1945.

11   TNA: WO 32/10800, H.A. Clay to A.W. Moss, 3 October 1945.

12   Museum of Military Medicine: War Diary of DAVRS, September 1945.

13   Museum of Military Medicine: War Diary of DAVRS, July 1945.

14   Ibid, November 1945.

15   TNA: WO 205/1173, 3C, Training Instruction, undated. The instructions further noted: "Any attempt to do so should be treated as a serious military offence."

in any way. The dogs must not be fed by anyone except the handler nor must they be treated as pets by the troops.[16]

It also urged servicemen to refrain from "mak[ing] friends with or pet[ting] any of these dogs."[17] Similarly, commanding officers who oversaw the use of dogs at RAF stations were supplied with guidelines from the Army's War Dogs Training School, in which it was emphasised that, apart from handlers, "under no circumstances should anyone be allowed to contact or pat" trained dogs for "the dog's usefulness [will be] negligible."[18] The perception of military dogs as pets may have contributed to the British Army's short-lived use of patrol dogs during the war. Noting that at the Army's War Dogs Training School "the training and general management [was] excellent," the DAVRS suggested in June 1943 that an absence of such oversight among units with patrol and messenger dogs contributed to the dogs' lack of success. Consequently, the dogs tended to "develop into regimental pets and become cowardly, noisy and useless."[19] In commenting on the lacklustre performance of patrol and messenger dogs in North Africa, the General Staff Policy Committee on Weapons and Equipment went so far as to proclaim that "nothing will teach the normal British unit not to make a pet out of a dog."[20]

In a 2001 interview, James Baty, a veteran of 9th Parachute Battalion, spoke of the dual role of trained military dog and pet occupied by Glen, the Alsatian attached to the battalion:

> Everybody loved him... Naturally he was the pet of the battalion, but nobody was allowed to pet him... You weren't allowed to feed him or pet him... You didn't want him to lose his potential... He'd get too soft or too friendly. Well actually he was a war dog, wasn't he really.[21]

As illustrated by Baty's comments, some trainers and handlers not only viewed trained dogs as working animals but also as companions. While serving as a trainer at the MAP Guard Dog Training School, Margaret Griffin referred to "the interest and affection felt by trainers and patrols alike for the pupils first and the pals in the latter

16   TNA: WO 199/416, 89A, Draft of Tactical Employment, 13 August 1942.
17   Ibid.
18   TNA: AIR 2/8734, 28A, Advice by the Head Trainer and Veterinary Officer for Commanding Officers Upon Completion of Dog Handlers' Course Held at the War Dogs Training School.
19   Museum of Military Medicine: War Diary of DAVRS, DAVRS Report for the First Period, 3 June 1943.
20   TNA: WO 163/183, General Staff Policy Committee on Weapons and Equipment, Paper No. 'BZ', Employment and Training of Dogs for War Purposes, undated.
21   IWM: 21192, Interview with James Baty, Reel 3.

half of their education which these dogs are to their human companions."[22] Corporal A. McLellan, a dog handler in the RAF, described his canine charge as "a faithful and devoted companion." In addition to praising the guard dog's performance on operations, McLellan expressed grief over the Alsatian's career-ending injury and subsequent departure from the RAF:

> I struggled for months to save the life of my devoted dog... The anxiety was very trying for me. I still struggled to save him, never forgetting what he meant to me. He could no longer accompany me on duty and I dreaded the day when his services would end. Soon the day came when we took farewell of each other. I had to accompany him to his owner. On leaving him at home he told me in his own way he wanted to come with me. Any dog lover will agree that was a very trying moment for us both.[23]

Similarly, in correspondence with the Allied Forces Mascot Club, Leading Aircraftman H.C. Shimmins emphasised the companionship he shared with Rex, a trained guard dog:

> Rex is a splendid pal... I have handled him for nearly two years and I almost dread the day coming when he must go back to his owner for I am going to miss him very much... Even returning from leave is a pleasure, for you have what I consider one of the greatest delights—your dog's welcome.[24]

Indeed, for some handlers, the end of hostilities led to an emotional separation from dogs they had befriended in the war. In correspondence with the Allied Forces Mascot Club, a rescue dog trainer wrote of his canine: "Do I miss him? Every day I think of him. He was a pal any man could be proud of."[25] Another handler expounded on his relationship with military dog Rex and their separation after the war:

> I did my best to get possession of [Rex] from his owner but he would not part with him. The parting was very hard as I had grown to love him as my own. He received all my attention at all times. I nursed him when sick and stitched his wounds when he was badly torn on barbed wire. I still think of him and wonder how he is. To have him with me would have made me very happy, and I'm sure he would be too. Three years together takes some forgetting after sleeping, working and playing together.[26]

---

22   Letter from Margaret Griffin in 'Notes & News of the Breeds', *Our Dogs*, 26 December 1941, p. 1283.
23   Quoted in St. Hill Bourne, *They Also Serve*, p. 178.
24   Quoted in Ibid, p. 180.
25   Quoted in Ibid, p. 175.
26   Quoted in Ibid, pp. 182-183.

In addition to viewing military dogs as pets, several servicemen spoke of trained dogs as if they were fellow servicemen. Peter Downward of 13th Parachute Battalion, for example, referred to patrol dog Bing as a "member of the platoon."[27] Similarly, a paratrooper in 9th Parachute Battalion described an Alsatian employed by the unit as "more or less one of us."[28] After working with the mine detection dogs of No. 2 Dog Platoon, Lieutenant T.L. Reid of the Royal Canadian Engineers (RCE) noted that dogs sought positive reinforcement as they worked. For Reid, this served as "an indication that 'war dogs' are also soldiers."[29] Furthermore, just as many dog owners believed their pets were "doing their bit" as military dogs, a number of handlers expressed similar opinions. In a letter to the Allied Forces Mascot Club, McLellan commented on the "gallant and faithful dogs" which "laid down their lives for their country."[30] Similarly, the trainer of a Civil Defence rescue dog felt that the canine was "always ready to help mankind" while employed in the London Civil Defence Region.[31]

Just as several servicemen perceived of trained military dogs as occupying a dual role as working animal and pet, a number of canine mascots and pets were seen by their servicemen owners as both pets and untrained working animals. Canine pets were prevalent among British servicemen during the Second World War. The Allied Forces Mascot Club consisted of some 3,000 animals by 1947.[32] In North Africa and the Middle East, feral dogs known as pyards were popular pets among British servicemen. A soldier commented on the widespread presence of pyards in the *Daily Mirror*: "Wherever you go, you'll find him… up in the desert, back in the bases… And he's sure to be in close proximity to an Army camp."[33] The Eighth Army accumulated so many dogs in North Africa that following the Allied victory at El Alamein, Montgomery forbade each unit from possessing more than four animals.[34]

To be sure, stray dogs were not always appreciated or accepted by British servicemen or civilians. In a 2001 interview with the Imperial War Museum, Hugh Weldon of the RAF Regiment described the numerous "wild dogs" which roamed RAF Cuttack in India as "a nuisance." To eliminate the presence of strays from the airfield, Weldon and other servicemen used their weapons to "have a shooting day," during which they killed a number of the feral animals.[35] Similarly, in a letter to the *Western Morning News*, a

27 Quoted in Woolhouse, *13–Lucky for Some*, p. 534.
28 Quoted in Goldstraw, 'The Paratrooper and His Dog', p. 33.
29 Museum of Military Medicine: War Diary, No. 2 Dog Platoon, Monthly Reports, Reid, Mine Clearance Using Dogs as Detectors, 3 April 1945.
30 Quoted in St. Hill Bourne, *They Also Serve*, p. 178.
31 Quoted in Ibid, p. 175.
32 St. Hill Bourne, *They Also Serve*, pp. vii, 1-4.
33 'The Pyard is Desert Army's Pet', *Daily Mirror*, 17 April 1943, p. 3.
34 Montague, *Let the Good Work Go On*, p. 98.
35 IWM: 22087, Interview with Hugh 'Enoch' Weldon, 3 August 2001, Reel 3.

civilian expressed contempt for the "hordes of dogs at every soldiers' camp." "These mongrel dogs, who have no owners," he wrote, "are taken from camp to camp."[36]

The Army Council, in early 1940, emphasised "the danger involved in allowing stray dogs or cats to attach themselves" to servicemen and stipulated that all strays were to be dealt with by the Military Police.[37] In an effort to alleviate the severity of the problem, the RSPCA, in late 1941, began working with the Army to euthanise dogs prior to the withdrawal of servicemen from camps in Britain.[38] The prevalence of stray dogs among Allied servicemen in Britain also prompted Supreme Allied Commander General Dwight Eisenhower to address the subject in 1944. Shortly before D-Day, Eisenhower announced:

> Upon the final departure of troops from a camp, post or station, the commanding officer concerned will not permit domestic pet animals to be abandoned, but will cause them to be placed in the custody of the local representative of the Royal Society for the Prevention of Cruelty to Animals.[39]

That year, the RSPCA handled nearly 650 dogs and cats discovered at camps in Britain.[40] In total, the animal welfare organisation handled more than 2,500 camp animals between 1939 and 1945.[41] In the months following the end of the war, British Army units in the Middle East were directed by the AVRS to euthanise all "surplus camp dogs," as recommended by the RSPCA.[42]

Although untrained as guards, anecdotal evidence indicates that a number of canine pets provided protection for servicemen and helped secure military equipment and supplies. In the Middle East, for example, British servicemen employed indigenous dogs to protect military installations, such as ammunition stores.[43] A dog attached to 193 Railway Operating Company also operated as an unofficial guard in the Middle East. According to a member of the unit:

> The lads used to take him with them for days at a time. When they slept he used to watch over them, and no one dared come near them. We have a number of

36   'Dogs at Camps', *Western Morning News*, 25 July 1942, p. 5.
37   *Army Council Instructions*, Issue 931 (14 February 1940), No. 109, Importation of Dogs and Cats into the United Kingdom.
38   'Abandoned Animals at Army Camps', *Animal World*, November 1941, p. 83 and *Army Council Instructions*, Issue 1090 (11 October 1941), No. 1979, Stray Dogs and Cats in Military Camps.
39   'Stray Dogs at Army Camps', *Animal World*, June 1944, p. 45.
40   'The Work Ahead', *Animal World*, June 1945, p. 41.
41   Moss and Kirby, *Animals Were There*, p. 113.
42   Museum of Military Medicine: War Diary of DAVRS, January 1946.
43   'The Pyard is Desert Army's Pet', *Daily Mirror*, 17 April 1943, p. 3.

Egyptian labourers, who are renowned for stealing. I am afraid [the dog] gives them a rough time—none dare come near our tent.[44]

Similarly, the canine mascot of 13th Field Sanitation Section provided protection for the unit during the Italian campaign. The dog "was an asset on guard duty," veteran Eric Griffin recalled in correspondence with the National Army Museum.[45] According to Army veteran Malcolm Leonard Connolly, a dog attached to the 3rd Carabiniers displayed an intense dislike for Japanese soldiers. The dog, Connolly explained in an interview with the Imperial War Museum, was in critical situations "on guard and... could actually tell if there was a Jap[anese] in the vicinity... before we did."[46]

Perhaps the most well-known canine pet to double as a guard dog was a Pointer called Judy. Reflecting on his experience with Judy, Royal Navy veteran Leonard Walter Williams described the naval mascot and pet as "a saviour" which served as an unofficial guard dog for Williams and several other British seamen in a Japanese POW camp during the war. In an interview with the Imperial War Museum, Williams insisted: "A lot of people owe their lives to Judy."[47] He recalled that for nearly four years Judy "was all the time a prisoner of war with [the British POWs]" and explained how Judy would "warn [them] with her growl... when the Japanese were approaching."[48] In May 1946, Judy became the twelfth canine to earn the Dickin Medal as a result of work carried out during the Second World War.[49] The decision by the PDSA to confer the Dickin Medal on Judy, an untrained pet, is thus reflective of the blurred distinction between military dogs and pets during the war.

Judy, a Royal Navy mascot and Dickin Medal recipient.
(PDSA)

44   Quoted in St. Hill Bourne, *They Also Serve*, p. 59.
45   National Army Museum, London (NAM): 2005-05-53, Eric Griffin to Alastair Massie, 5 July 2000.
46   IWM: 19049, Interview with Malcolm Leonard Connolly, 7 June 1999, Reel 4.
47   IWM: 11542, Interview with Leonard Walter Williams, 21 September 1990, Reel 3.
48   Ibid.
49   'PDSA Dickin Medal', online <https://www.pdsa.org.uk/what-we-do/animal-awards-programme/pdsa-dickin-medal> (accessed 29 January 2018)

The Challenges of Demobilising Military Dogs

The AVRS had expressed doubt over the military dog demobilisation process shortly after taking over the recruitment of canines in early 1942. In correspondence with the Quartermaster General to the Forces (QMGF), it was admitted by the DAVRS:

> It is exceedingly difficult to devise now any precise machinery to be adopted for restoring dogs to their owners at the end of the war, complicated as the situation may be, by questions of repatriation and quarantine. We agree that we cannot go further than promise the public that if the dogs are still in the Army when they are no longer required and if their owners can be traced, they will be sent back to them.[50]

It seems that neither the War Office nor the Army's War Dogs Training School produced detailed records concerning individual dogs prior to the involvement of the RAVC in March 1942.[51] Yet even after the RAVC introduced a more organised system of documentation, not all units maintained efficient records. This was especially clear when the War Office, in early 1944, attempted to locate a contingent of military dogs deployed to North Africa in late 1942 as part of 78th Division.[52] Similar problems were encountered in August 1944 after multiple British Army units deployed to northwest Europe with military dogs. Just days after the units' arrival in France, the war diary of the AVRS noted: "The location of War Dogs is proving very difficult, owing to the number of moves the units are making."[53] After the war, the AVRS in West Germany attempted to rectify the situation by conducting a military dog census. However, it was admitted towards the end of 1946 that "very great difficulties have been experienced in tracing War Dogs which were originally posted to units of 21st Army Group, and which, through the lack of complete records were subsequently lost sight of."[54]

The demobilisation of military dogs commenced in early 1945 when a number of canines employed on the British Home Front were discharged from duty. Between

---

50   TNA: WO 32/10800, Minutes, Veterinary and Remount Services to QMGF, 18 March 1942.

51   'Danby, 'A War Dogs' Training School', *Journal of the RAVC*, p. 42. According to Danby, it was only in March 1942 that "the keeping of records relating to the health of the dogs was commenced."

52   TNA: WO 204/7732, 48A, Deputy Chief Administrative Officer to 8 Army, 6 January 1944 and 73A, 78th Division to Rear 13 Corps HQ, 31 January 1944. Records concerning these canines, which had been employed by a total of seven infantry battalions in North Africa, were virtually non-existent. In correspondence with the War Office, 78th Division revealed that the dogs had become casualties or were unofficially transferred to other units.

53   TNA: WO 171/191B, War Diary of Veterinary and Remount Services, August 1944.

54   TNA: WO 267/587, British Army of the Rhine: Quarterly Historical Reports, Veterinary and Remount Services, Quarterly Historical Report, 30 September 1946.

January and September 1945, some 200 military dogs were reunited with their owners.[55] Several more utilised as guards at POW camps throughout Britain were demobilised in late 1945.[56] Major H.A. Clay of the AVRS acknowledged that while the demobilisation of military dogs on the Home Front was "comparatively simple," quarantine laws and the continued employment of canines outside the United Kingdom rendered the complete demobilisation of military dogs impractical.[57] Allied Forces Headquarters (AFHQ), for example, indicated in July 1945 that every one of the 169 military dogs employed in the Mediterranean theatre was still needed. Similarly, 21st Army Group proposed to discharge just 23 of its 423 dogs.[58]

In April 1945, the Army's War Dogs Training School relocated to Zellik, Belgium with some 90 dogs. The MAP Guard Dog Training School was thus charged with the subsequent instruction of guard dogs requested by the British Army for employment on the Home Front.[59] The Army's War Dogs Training School was based in Belgium until November 1945, when it relocated to the British Army of the Rhine (BAOR) Training Centre in Sennelager, West Germany. In addition to the dogs from Northaw, the Army's War Dogs Training School received trained dogs previously employed by the British Army in northwest Europe. Moreover, it acquired several canines, including former German Army police dogs, in Belgium and Germany.[60] In this way, the AVRS sought to phase out the use of dogs owned by civilians, of which more than 400 were still employed by the British Army in northwest Europe in July 1945.[61]

The MAP Guard Dog Training School also underwent significant changes in the months following the Second World War. In late 1945, the school was acquired by the Air Ministry and designated the RAF Police Dog Training School.[62] The RAF Provost Department appeared opposed to the widespread demobilisation of dogs considering that, as of March 1946, the RAF Police employed an estimated 750 canines. Rather than reduce the number of dogs in its employ, the RAF Police requested additional animals.[63] In addition to seeking permission from owners to retain their trained dogs, staff at the RAF Police Dog Training School also embarked on a breeding programme after the war.[64] In the late 1940s, Baldwin and his staff endeavoured to multiply the number of Alsatians through breeding. Purebred Alsatians, including some owned by Baldwin and Margaret Griffin, were used in the hopes of boosting the school's

55   Randolph, 'Demobbing the War Dogs', *Dundee Evening Telegraph*, 4 September 1945, p. 2.
56   Museum of Military Medicine: War Diary of DAVRS, October 1945.
57   TNA: WO 32/10800, Clay to Moss, 3 October 1945.
58   Museum of Military Medicine: War Diary of DAVRS, July 1945.
59   Ibid, January-April 1945.
60   TNA: WO 171/3937, War Diary of Veterinary and Remount Services, April-May 1945 and October-November 1945.
61   Museum of Military Medicine: War Diary of DAVRS, July 1945.
62   Ibid, December 1945 and Davies, *RAF Police Dogs on Patrol*, p. 6.
63   'Dogs to Speed Demob', *Dundee Evening Telegraph*, 7 March 1946.
64   'R.A.F. Police Dogs', *Gloucestershire Echo*, 15 March 1946, p. 3.

canine population to some 550 dogs.[65] The breeding policy adopted at the RAF Police Dog Training School was short-lived, however. Considering that staff were required to care for and feed the puppies for several months before training commenced, the programme necessitated a substantial commitment of time and money. Furthermore, it was found that some of the Alsatians lacked the physical or behavioural characteristics required of RAF Police dogs.[66]

In the summer of 1945, the AVRS corresponded with owners of military canines employed outside the United Kingdom to determine if they sought the immediate return of their pets. Roughly half of those who responded prior to November 1945 expressed interest in allowing their dogs to remain in the military.[67] The family of Eileen Cox Woods, whose dog was donated to the Army's War Dogs Training School during the war, opted for the Labrador to remain in the Army in peacetime. "Food was still rationed for us," Woods later explained, "so it was kinder to let him stay in the Army."[68] For the owners of military dog Flick, concerns over how the Alsatian would transition from RAF Police dog to docile pet were enough to convince them to allow Flick to remain a part of the military.[69]

In early 1946, a journalist for the British Army publication *Soldier* found that some 400 canines were currently undergoing "de-training" at the Army's War Dogs Training School in West Germany. "De-training" was overseen by RAVC personnel, and according to the article, involved "relaxing the aggressive training and eventually giving the dog only sufficient 'peaceful' exercise to keep it in good health and spirits."[70] An instructor at the school further observed:

> To understand dog psychology is just as important in 'de-training' as it is in teaching a dog to trace mines or attack an enemy soldier. Once you get to know a dog you can do almost anything with it. Only a few people have the art, which involves a great deal of patience, a sense of fair play, and a strict demand for obedience.[71]

According to the commandant of the school, canines were "given no training, but [were] handled and exercised as much as possible together, in order to make them

65   Hennessey, *Story of the Royal Air Force Police*, p. 74 and Cecil Russell Acton, *Dogs, their Care and Training* (London: Witherby, 1949), p. 129.
66   Stephen R. Davies, *Fiat Justitia: A History of the Royal Air Force Police* (London: Minerva, 1997), p. 109.
67   Museum of Military Medicine: War Diary of DAVRS, June and October 1945. Some owners sought payments of up to £200, an amount substantially higher than the £25 approved by the Army.
68   IWM: 06/26/1, Cox, 'An Evacuee Remembers Speldhurst'.
69   Davies, *RAF Police Dogs on Patrol*, p. 13.
70   Captain E.J. Grove, 'Taking the Bite Out!', *Soldier*, 2 March 1946, p. 7.
71   Quoted in Ibid, p. 7.

more amenable as pets."[72] In addition, the *Dundee Evening Telegraph* described the "detraining process" for British Army dogs as "detrain[ing] by endless repetition of correction."[73]

Although little information is available regarding precisely how military dogs were "de-trained," the articles in *Soldier*, the *Journal of the RAVC* and the *Dundee Evening Telegraph* suggest the process centred on leisurely play and exercise to ensure the mental and physical well-being of canines. Thus, while it is likely that dogs were no longer subjected to regimented drills as part of "de-training," the process was similar to wartime training in that patience among human instructors was considered integral to successfully altering the behaviour of canines.

Guard dogs, in particular, were assessed in regards to their behaviour and ability to readjust to life outside the military. The AVRS allowed dogs designated "Class C" to be reunited with their owners, but "Class A" and "Class B" dogs were considered "too savage" and "uncertain in temperament," respectively. Although "Class B" dogs could be released to civilians, owners were advised of any behavioural issues and required to sign documentation acknowledging the potential consequences of their decision.[74] The war diary of the DAVRS indicated that, owing to their work during the war, a number of British Army canines were considered "dangerous with persons other than their own handlers," and as a result, were not restored to their owners.[75] While the fate of these particular dogs is unknown, according to former military dog handler Les Coates, several canines deemed "unsuitable for repatriation" were euthanised at the Army's War Dogs Training School in West Germany.[76] Moreover, the DAVRS investigated a claim from a British Army dog handler in Italy that multiple canines employed by the Central Mediterranean Force were, as the war diary of the DAVRS put it, "not humanely destroyed."[77]

According to the *Cheltenham Chronicle*, canines employed by the RAF Police underwent a "demobilisation course" at the RAF Police Dog Training School prior to their release.[78] While Baldwin acknowledged that dogs employed by the RAF experienced some alteration in their behaviour, he was convinced that those reunited with

---

72   Major G.D. Young, 'War Dogs Training School', *Journal of the RAVC*, 18:1 (1946), p. 20. Young did not elaborate on the school's demobilisation procedure.
73   'Training in Reverse', *Dundee Evening Telegraph*, 1 June 1946, p. 4. It is unclear if the author of this article had first-hand knowledge of or had visited the Army's War Dogs Training School.
74   Museum of Military Medicine: War Diary of DAVRS, July 1945.
75   Ibid, February 1946.
76   IWM: 94/1219, Hunt, 'A Brief Look', Book 2, p. 81.
77   Museum of Military Medicine: War Diary of DAVRS, January 1946. The canines to which the handler referred were likely military police dogs, as the Deputy Director, Veterinary and Remount Services, Central Mediterranean Force had recently indicated that some 100 CMP dogs in Italy were "surplus." The outcome of the investigation is unknown.
78   'Dog Demob', *Cheltenham Chronicle*, 28 June 1947, p. 4.

their owners could successfully readjust to living as pets outside the military. In a letter to an owner whose dog was scheduled to be demobilised in a few weeks' time, he admitted the canine's "temperament has undergone some change during his absence from home" as a result of his role in the RAF. Nonetheless, Baldwin was adamant that the dog would "readily adapt himself to home life again."[79] Indeed, the dog to which Baldwin referred seemed to thrive in his role as pet while retaining some of the skills learnt in wartime. Just two weeks after leaving the RAF Police Dog Training School, the Collie had, according to his owner, "become a good housedog and 'watcher'."[80] Ultimately, however, the dog's owner donated him to the Metropolitan Police.[81] In a letter reminiscent of those sent during the war, she explained her decision:

> I don't think I can keep Robber here [at home] now… I don't think the dog would be properly looked after here. I thought, therefore, of offering him to your service, because as he is so well trained, he might be of use to you, and I would like to think that his special talents were being properly used.[82]

It is unclear how many former British military dogs were ultimately reunited with their owners after the war, nor is it clear to what extent they suffered behavioural consequences for having been trained and utilised by the military. At least one former British military dog was thought to be unable to readjust to life in peacetime. In June 1946, the *Dundee Evening Telegraph* reported that a dog previously employed by the British Army had attacked a man near Leeds. The author of the article assumed the dog's aggressive behaviour was the result of wartime training and noted that the Alsatian was to be euthanised accordingly.[83] A similar incident occurred in the United States, where a child was mauled by a former guard dog. The *New York Times* quoted a New Jersey health officer, who believed the Belgian Shepherd had attacked the child on account of his khaki clothing, the colour of which resembled POW uniforms.[84] Such incidents involving former military dogs were seemingly rare in the United States, where some 3,000 Army canines donated by civilians were reunited with their owners after the war.[85]

79   TNA: MEPO 2/6208, Introduction and Development of Police Dog Scheme, Lt. Col. J.F. Baldwin to M.L. Spring-Rice, 11 January 1946.
80   TNA: MEPO 2/ 6208, 149B, Margery L. Spring-Rice to Sir Maurice Drummond, 2 February 1946.
81   TNA: MEPO 2/6208, 146B, Margery L. Spring-Rice to the Chief Constable, East Suffolk County Police, 15 January 1946 and 152A, M. Drummond to Margery L. Spring-Rice, 6 February 1946.
82   TNA: MEPO 2/6208, 146B, Spring-Rice to East Suffolk County Police, 15 January 1946.
83   'Training in Reverse', *Dundee Evening Telegraph*, 1 June 1946, p. 4.
84   'K-9 Mistakes Boy for Foe', *New York Times*, 3 August 1946, p. 13. It is not known if the dog was euthanised following the attack. The article only noted that the canine was "be[ing] kept under observation."
85   NARA: Report #4248, *Dogs and National Defense*, p. 49; 4243-4270; DRB Reference Collection; RG 407; NACP. According to Waller, "all borrowed dogs" were demobilised

While a similarly precise figure regarding British military dogs is not available, records compiled by the AVRS in the late 1940s shed some light on the lives of British military dogs after the Second World War. The records indicate that several canines held by the British Army in West Germany were destroyed in the immediate post-war period. Between July 1946 and March 1950, the dates for which relevant records are available, 245 military dogs in BAOR were put down or died, 58 were sold and 25 went missing. By contrast, 100 military dogs were reunited with their owners throughout the same period.[86] See Appendix VIII for a complete breakdown of the number of military dogs released from service or otherwise no longer utilised by the British Army in West Germany between July 1946 and March 1950. It should be noted that these figures are for military dogs in BAOR only and most likely included dogs acquired in Belgium and West Germany in the months and years following the end of the Second World War.

The movement and quarantine of military dogs and pets from outside the United Kingdom was a complicated logistical process which involved military and civilian personnel on both sides of the English Channel. Owing in part to the institution of muzzling laws throughout much of Britain in the latter part of the 19th century, rabies was no longer present in the United Kingdom by the early 20th century.[87] However, the illegal transport of dogs after the First World War resulted in the re-emergence of rabies in Britain. A rabid dog was discovered in 1918, and by 1922, some 320 occurrences, several of which were attributed to the pets of British servicemen, had been recorded in England and Wales.[88] According to the *Observer*, the Board of Agriculture largely blamed RAF personnel for "flagrantly disregarding orders, and… smuggling dogs into this country from France and Belgium."[89] Although the Parliamentary Secretary to the Board of Agriculture, in June 1919, denied that servicemen had used aircraft to circumvent the quarantine regulations in the preceding year, he did confirm

as of early 1947. See Lemish, *War Dogs*, pp. 142-146 for a detailed description of the demobilisation of United States Army and United States Marine Corps canines in the months following the Second World War.

86   TNA: WO 267/587, Veterinary and Remount Services Quarterly Historical Reports, 30 September 1946 and 31 December 1946 and TNA: WO 267/588, British Army of the Rhine: Quarterly Historical Reports, Veterinary and Remount Services, Quarterly Historical Reports, 31 March 1947, 30 June 1947, 30 September 1947 and 31 December 1947 and TNA: WO 267/589, British Army of the Rhine: Quarterly Historical Reports, Veterinary and Remount Services, Quarterly Historical Reports, 31 March 1948, 30 June 1948, 30 September 1948 and 31 December 1948 and TNA: WO 267/590, British Army of the Rhine: Quarterly Historical Reports, Veterinary and Remount Services, Quarterly Historical Reports, 31 March 1949, 30 June 1949, 30 September 1949 and 31 December 1949 and TNA: WO 267/591, British Army of the Rhine: Quarterly Historical Reports, Veterinary and Remount Services, Quarterly Historical Report, 31 March 1950.

87   John K. Walton, 'Mad Dogs and Englishmen: The Conflict over Rabies in Late Victorian England', *Journal of Social History*, 13:2 (1979), pp. 229-230.

88   *Army Council Instructions*, Issue 931 (14 February 1940), No. 109.

89   'Rabies Order Defied', *Observer*, 1 June 1919, p. 12.

that at least 30 canines had been illegally transported by Army and Navy personnel within the same period.[90] The re-establishment of muzzling laws and other stipulations, including canine curfews, led to fewer occurrences of the disease; by 1923, rabies had again vanished in the United Kingdom.[91]

To discourage a similar situation during the Second World War, the Army Council, in February 1940, stipulated that officers outside the United Kingdom were to "absolutely prohibit and take all possible steps to prevent dogs and cats being embarked by military passengers on ships proceeding to the United Kingdom."[92] Similarly, in late 1945, the Army Council drew attention to rabies by warning soldiers that although the disease had been wiped out in the United Kingdom, rabies was "prevalent in the majority of countries abroad" and "nobody coming from a country where rabies exists can be sure that his dog or cat has not been infected."[93] In addition to the rules imposed by the military, the Diseases of Animals Acts prevented the entry of dogs into Britain barring permission from the Ministry of Agriculture and Fisheries (MAF). Quarantine laws also remained in effect.[94]

Upon completion of "de-training" in West Germany, Army canines were held at the RAVC Dog Holding Section in Belgium before being transported to the United Kingdom to undergo quarantine.[95] As the Director of Sea Transport restricted the movement of canines by troopship,[96] tank landing ships (LSTs) or motor tankers conveyed dogs across the English Channel.[97] In the United Kingdom, RAVC personnel manned No. 1 Dog Holding Section, a temporary establishment in Northaw primarily intended as a sort of clearinghouse for military dogs following their release from units on the Home Front. To this end, the holding section managed around 65 kennels, which were inhabited by dogs prior to their discharge from the military.[98] By September 1945, the kennels were operating at capacity.[99] Although most of the kennels at No. 1 Holding Section were earmarked for military dogs employed on the Home Front, 10 were designated for "emergency quarantine" of military dogs discharged from

90   Hansard: HC Deb 2 June 1919 vol 116 cc1724-5W.
91   Neil Pemberton and Michael Worboys, *Mad Dogs and Englishmen: Rabies in Britain, 1830-2000* (Basingstoke: Palgrave Macmillan, 2007), pp. 165-171.
92   *Army Council Instructions*, Issue 931 (14 February 1940), No. 109.
93   *Army Council Instructions*, Issue 1505 (3 October 1945), No. 1148, Animals—Importation of Animals into Great Britain—Quarantine Scheme for Dog Pets.
94   Ibid.
95   Grove, 'Taking the Bite Out!', *Soldier*, p. 7.
96   Museum of Military Medicine: War Diary of DAVRS, March 1945.
97   TNA: WO 171/3937, War Diary of Veterinary and Remount Services, November 1945 and Museum of Military Medicine: War Diary of DAVRS, November 1945. In November 1945, the Dog Holding Section relocated from Ostend to Antwerp.
98   Museum of Military Medicine: War Diary of DAVRS, January-March 1945 and TNA: WO 32/10800, 39A, D.E. Ling to the War Office, 22 April 1945.
99   Museum of Military Medicine: War Diary of DAVRS, September 1945.

units in other theatres of war.[100] Spratt's, the dog food company, also offered the use of its kennels near Croydon for military dogs released from units outside the United Kingdom.[101] Beginning in October 1945, British military dogs re-entering the United Kingdom from abroad were assigned to the newly-built RAVC facility, No. 1 Military Quarantine Station, in Hampshire.[102] Kennel space was determined by theatre of war, so that a certain number of kennels were designated for canines from each overseas British Army Group or Command. Interestingly, it seems that no distinction was made between trained military dogs and pets when determining the number of dogs allowed from each theatre of war. In December 1945, canine pets outnumbered trained military dogs at No. 1 Military Quarantine Station 58 to 37.[103]

The War Office, in late 1945, instituted a scheme to allow British servicemen to enter the United Kingdom with their canine pets. Although no longer required to gain permission from the MAF, servicemen had to request approval from RAVC officers stationed in the relevant theatre of war. As before, the scheme demanded that all dogs remain quarantined for six months. However, the Special Services Scheme made the entire process more affordable; the shipping and quarantine expenses owed by servicemen ranged between £5 and £20 depending on rank. The scheme, as the related Army Council Instruction made clear, stipulated that all dogs must be "genuine pet[s] which [have] not been recently acquired."[104] By March 1946, No. 1 Military Quarantine Station was home to some 370 canine pets.[105] This number constituted only a percentage of dogs whose servicemen owners desired to bring them to the United Kingdom, however. In April 1946, the Secretary of State for War informed the House of Commons that while nearly 2,400 servicemen had enquired about returning to the United Kingdom with their canine pets, insufficient kennel space meant that the majority of applications had to be turned down.[106] The Special Services Scheme came to an end in September 1947 following the disbandment of the No. 1 Military Quarantine Station.[107]

---

100 TNA: WO 32/10800, 20A, J.C. Bennison to DSD, 29 January 1945.
101 Museum of Military Medicine: War Diary of DAVRS, August-September 1945.
102 'No. 1 Military Quarantine Station', *Journal of the RAVC*, 18:1 (1946), p. 37 and TNA: WO 171/3937, War Diary of Veterinary and Remount Services, October 1945.
103 Museum of Military Medicine: War Diary of DAVRS, December 1945-January 1946. That fewer military dogs were in quarantine was perhaps due to their continued use overseas following the end of hostilities.
104 *Army Council Instructions*, Issue 1505 (3 October 1945), No. 1148. The application form called for servicemen to include the length of time they had owned their pets.
105 'No Bones for 28 Days', *Dundee Courier*, 19 March 1946, p. 2.
106 Hansard: HC Deb 9 April 1946 vol 421 c293W.
107 TNA: ADM 1/20854, Quarantine (82): Importation of Dogs into Great Britain, Draft Admiralty Fleet Order, Termination of Special Services Scheme for Quarantine of Dog Pets, September 1947. Scheduled shipments of dogs were allowed to proceed as part of the scheme. However, after September 1947, servicemen had to request a licence from the MAF as had been necessary prior to the implementation of the scheme.

The "figurative mobilization" of dogs during the Second World War referred to in Chapter 2 also occurred upon the demobilisation of military dogs at the end of the war. Military dogs were lauded as heroes upon their return to Britain. In this way, it may be argued that military dogs were figuratively *de*mobilised in the British press. Towards the end of the Second World War, a family in Surrey was contacted by an officer in 6th Battalion, Cameronians (Scottish Rifles). He informed them that Khan, the Alsatian they had donated to the Army's War Dogs Training School earlier in the war, was now a holder of the Dickin Medal. The officer explained:

> For this gallant, loyal and faithful action, Khan was awarded the Dickin Medal, which was presented to him at a full battalion parade by the Commanding Officer. I would like to express to you on behalf of the battalion our grateful thanks for the loan of Khan, who stood firmly by us through all our battles.[108]

The Alsatian was lauded as a "hero" in the *Sunday Post*, which in early 1945 ran an article describing his performance in northwest Europe.[109] The *Aberdeen Journal* also reported on the Alsatian, noting that the Dickin Medal would soon be conferred on the "canine hero."[110]

Britons tuning in to the BBC "Victory Day" radio broadcast on 8 June 1946 were greeted by barks from the Royal Navy mascot Judy. In addition to receiving the Dickin Medal, Judy was designated a former POW by the Returned British Prisoners of War Association.[111] Also involved in the festivities in London for "Victory Day" were two Civil Defence rescue dogs and a trainer from the MAP Guard Dog Training School.[112] Moreover, a number of military and Civil Defence dogs were exhibited at dog shows or similar contests after the war. In July 1946, for example, former Civil Defence dogs Jet, Irma and Storm participated in a show organised by the Alsatian League and Club of Great Britain, of which Baldwin served as Vice Chairman. In its coverage of the event, the *Gloucestershire Echo* referred to the canines as "V.C.s of the dog world."[113] Similarly, an advertisement for the Star Dog Tournament in July 1947 announced the inclusion of "dog heroes of the blitz and the battle front" at the upcoming contest in Wembley.[114] Among the dogs featured at the tournament was former Civil Defence dog Rex, whose owner capitalised on his pet's newfound fame to raise money for the PDSA and other charities in the years following the Second World War.[115]

---

108 Quoted in St. Hill Bourne, *They Also Serve*, p. 19.
109 'No Medal for this Hero!', *Sunday Post*, 14 January 1945, p. 2.
110 'Canine Hero', *Aberdeen Press and Journal*, 30 March 1945, p. 2.
111 St. Hill Bourne, *They Also Serve*, pp. 6, 12.
112 'Trainer for Victory March with V.C. Dog', *Aberdeen Press and Journal*, 27 May 1946, p. 4.
113 'Dogs V.C.s Show their Paces', *Gloucestershire Echo*, 8 July 1946, p. 5.
114 'Dog V.C.'s in Wembley Show, *Whitstable Times and Tankerton Press*, 5 July 1947, p. 8.
115 IWM: Misc 289 (3861), Papers Relating to the Second World War Rescue Dog, 'Rex', S.P. Ramshaw to J.Y. Baldwin, 10 January 1950.

In the months and years following the war, the British press and the military continued to anthropomorphise military dogs by emphasising their status as veterans similar to human servicemen. In his report on the Army's War Dogs Training School in West Germany, the author of the aforementioned *Soldier* article described the military dogs at the training facility as "veterans" and referred to those slated for demobilisation as "turn[ing] their backs on war and look[ing] forward to that armchair and cushion in civvy street."[116] The press frequently likened former military and Civil Defence dogs to human servicemen by referring to canines as "veteran[s]" or "war hero[es]."[117] In March 1946, the *Sunday Post* featured on its children's page an article on Rob, the aforementioned Collie employed by the SAS. Young readers were told the "brave dog" from Perthshire was "a credit to Scotland."[118] The *Northern Daily Mail* also heaped praise on British military dogs and mascots, proclaiming in early 1947: "No more faithful and tireless service was rendered than that given by the 'dogs in uniform'."[119] Similarly, the War Office, in a letter to the owner of a deceased military dog, recognised the "brave dog [which] served our country well."[120] The Air Ministry used similar language in certificates issued to former RAF Police dogs. Entitled "For Loyal and Faithful Service" and addressed to the dogs rather than their owners, the certificates recognised the "tireless effort and constant devotion to duty willingly rendered to Britain and all the free peoples of the World in time of War."[121] British Army and RAF Police canines were not the only military dogs to be anthropomorphised in this way. In the United States, the QMC produced a "Certificate of Faithful Service and Honorable Discharge" for military dogs.[122] Such accolades, and the anthropomorphic language therein, comprised, as Steven Johnston put it, the "projecti[on] onto animals what [humans] take to be our best patriotic qualities."[123]

After the war, Britons who had provided dogs to the Army's War Dogs Training School were given a "War Dog Certificate of Service" for their pets from the DAVRS. While the certificate noted the "most valuable service" carried out by the dog to which it was addressed, the accompanying letter also emphasised the "patriotic gesture" made

116 Grove, 'Taking the Bite Out', *Soldier*, p. 7.
117 See for example: 'Dog Gains Award for War Patrol Work', *Aberdeen Press and Journal*, 30 July 1946, p. 4 and 'Dog V.C.s Show their Paces', *Gloucestershire Echo*, 8 July 1946, p. 5 and 'Canine V.C.'s Cemetery', *Western Morning News*, 28 June 1948, p. 2 and 'War Dogs' Day', *Dundee Evening Telegraph*, 26 June 1947, p. 3.
118 'Famous Scottish Mascots', *Sunday Post*, 3 March 1946, p. 14.
119 'Our Canine Friends: 5,000 "Enlisted" for War Service', *Northern Daily Mail*, 13 January 1947, p. 5.
120 IWM: Misc 162 (2490), Letter Reporting Dog Has Been Killed in Action, Major H.A. Clay to J.E. Sullivan, 14 April 1945.
121 IWM: Misc 164 (2529), Certificate Recording the Service of an RAF Patrol Dog, Second World War, August 1947.
122 NARA: Report #4248, *Dogs and National Defense*, p. 45; 4243-4270; DRB Reference Collection; RG 407; NACP.
123 Johnston, 'Animals in War', p. 369.

by the owner.[124] Hilda Kean has examined the purpose of memorialising military animals, suggesting that physical memorials to dogs and other animals constructed in the decades following the Second World War, particularly the London-based Animals in War Memorial, tended to emphasise their service to humans while disregarding the animals' individuality. Such memorials, she further alleged, downplay or overlook completely the ethical concerns associated with the employment of animals in the past and at present. Thus, while commemorative structures such as the Animals in War Memorial seemingly honour military animals, they are anthropocentric in that they "implicitly reinforce a hierarchy in which human interests are always put before those of animals."[125]

In some ways, accolades conferred on military and Civil Defence dogs in the press during and shortly after the Second World War were similar to post-war memorials in that they focused disproportionately on the contributions of the human owners and the ways in which canines benefited humans rather than the dogs themselves. While awards such as the Dickin Medal drew attention to the actions of individual dogs, the press coverage surrounding the employment of specific canines often prominently featured the owners.[126]

As Clare and Christy Campbell have pointed out, the canine recipients of the Dickin Medal belonged to individual owners who requested their return at the end of the war. Neither the War Office nor the PDSA were inclined to confer medals on former strays or pets permanently relinquished to the military by their owners. The Dickin Medal, Campbell and Campbell rightly argued, served in part to maximise publicity for the animal welfare organisation. The medal, as well as similar accolades and celebrations, allowed the War Office and the animal welfare organisations involved in the wartime assemblage of military dogs to depict "a happy-seeming end to the war-dog story" of the Second World War.[127]

Animal welfare organisations also "figuratively mobilized" dogs in an effort to transform British society. Throughout the Second World War, many Britons viewed the conflict, and the social upheaval it brought, as a springboard for comprehensive

---

124 NAM: 1987-06-23, War Dog Certificate Awarded to 'Binks' and Letter from Director, AVRS to Mrs Theobald, 1 August 1946.

125 Hilda Kean, 'Commemorating Animals: Glorifying Humans?: Remembering and Forgetting Animals in War Memorials', in Maggie Andrews, Charles Bagot Jewitt and Nigel Hunt (eds.), *Lest We Forget: Remembrance and Commemoration* (Stroud: The History Press, 2011), pp. 60-69. See also: Johnston, 'Animals in War', pp. 359-371. Johnston also reflected on the increasing number of "animal memorials" and their purpose in what he termed "the patriotic memorial complex." (p. 360) As for the Animals in War memorial specifically, he argued the structure "projects patriotic meaning into the deeds [animals] perform in war." (p. 369)

126 For examples, see: Randolph, 'Demobbing the War Dogs', *Dundee Evening Telegraph*, 4 September 1945, p. 2 and 'Toby From the R.A.F.', *Dundee Evening Telegraph*, 28 February 1946, p. 3 and 'Wolf Has Been Demobbed', *Daily Mail*, 18 February 1946, p. 3

127 Campbell and Campbell, *Dogs of Courage*, pp. 291-307.

Animals in War Memorial in
London, 2011. (Author)

Brian, a patrol dog employed by 13th Parachute Battalion, is presented with the Dickin Medal, 1947. (Airborne Assault Museum, Duxford)

Rob, a patrol dog attached to the SAS, receives his Dickin Medal. (PDSA)

reforms within British society.[128] As the historian Angus Calder put it, during the war "post-war planning… became a kind of universal craze with institutions great and small."[129] Unsurprisingly, animal welfare organisations saw an opportunity to promote a more animal-friendly society in peacetime. The *Tail-Wagger Magazine*, for example, included in its March 1945 volume an article which made clear the organisation was "determined to have a hand in the shaping of the brave new world" and "secure a better deal for dogs" in post-war Britain.[130] Similarly, Maria Dickin, the editor of *PDSA News*, called for "a radical change in [man's] attitude to the animals." Writing in early 1942, Dickin opined:

> We should do well to look ahead to the time when the terrible warfare now raging throughout the world is over and we begin to lay the foundation for a better world… If a new world is to be built on a solid and lasting foundation, the greatest change of all must take place in the attitude of man to his fellow men… And this change of attitude between man and man must go further. If man is to progress there must also be a radical change in his attitude to the animals… And so in the year that lies before us we must see that in all the planning for a new world of which we hear so much to-day, that the animal is not forgotten.[131]

For its part, the RSPCA seemingly highlighted the role of animals in the British Armed Forces and Civil Defence when drawing attention to its pledge to combat cruelty towards animals. "We must not forget," began an article in the June 1945 edition of *Animal World*, "that the public owes a deep debt of gratitude to animals for their help in various ways towards victory. For this reason, if for no other, our efforts on their behalf should be unflagging."[132]

The decision by the British Armed Forces to utilise canine pets of civilians at times hindered the British military dog scheme of the Second World War. Many military and Civil Defence dog handlers and other servicemen perceived of trained canines as both working animals and pets, a tendency recognised by contemporary training instructions. Such a perception could lead to declining performance on the part of canines. Yet despite the difficulties associated with utilising pet dogs in the Second World War, many dogs entered the post-war British Army and the RAF Police upon being donated by civilians. In contrast to the 1940s, however, dogs donated by their owners constituted permanent rather than short-term donations.[133] As recently as 2009, the British Armed Forces appealed to dog owners to turn over their pets. As in

128   Rose, *Which People's War?*, pp. 21-25, 33, 62-70.
129   Calder, *The People's War*, p. 545.
130   'Brave New World', *Tail-Wagger Magazine*, March 1945, p. 56.
131   M.E. Dickin, 'New Thought about Animals', *P.D.S.A. News*, January 1942, p. 2.
132   'The Work Ahead', *Animal World*, June 1945, p. 41.
133   War Office, *Training of War Dogs* (1952), p. 32 and War Office, *Training of War Dogs* (1962), p. 34 and Davies, *RAF Police Dogs on Patrol*, pp. 68, 101, 127, 163-164 and RAF

the Second World War, the British Army and the RAF Police continued to publish advertisements in national and local newspapers, as well as the RAVC magazine *Chiron Calling*.[134] With the development of the world-wide-web, the British Armed Forces gained another medium for reaching potential donors. Harkening back to the patriotic reasons dog owners gave their animals to the military in the 1940s and the "figurative demobilization" considered in this and earlier chapters, the now defunct web address declared in its title: "Your Country Needs Your Dog."[135]

Museum: R016420, *Royal Air Force Police Dogs*, undated and RAF Museum: 007253, *Royal Air Force Police Dog Training*, May 1974.

134 'The Challenges Facing Dog Procurement Section at DAC, *Chiron Calling*, Summer/ Autumn 2009, p. 23 and 'Dog Recruits Required' Advert in *Chiron Calling*, Winter 1998/1999, p. 24.

135 'Challenges Facing Dog Procurement', *Chiron Calling*, Summer/Autumn 2009, p. 23.

7

The Training and Employment of British Military and Police Dogs After the Second World War

A century after E.E. Bennett's 1889 speech on military dogs at the Royal United Services Institution, Lieutenant Colonel John Bleby of the RAVC delivered an address on the same topic. In his address, also presented at the Royal United Services Institution, Bleby summarised the contributions of military dogs to the British Armed Forces and emphasised the ongoing importance of canines in military roles in the late 20th century. In closing, he told his audience:

> Dogs provide a compact, mobile, flexible aid of proven capability. It is true that technological advances have provided alternative aids, particularly in the areas of explosives and drug detection. Nevertheless, while no-one would claim infallibility for dogs, they remain potent weapons and willing servants in the continuing struggle for supremacy in low-intensity operations and in the fight against terrorism and subversion... We live in a time when change is occurring at an exponential rate. Technology... will lead to the realisation of undreamt of advances... And yet there are no signs of diminishing demand for dogs – quite the reverse.[1]

As Bleby predicted, the British Armed Forces have continued to utilise military dogs even into the 21st century. The First World War represented a crucial step in the history of the British military dog, but it was the Second World War which marked the onset of a permanent military dog scheme in Britain. Many of the training methods, as well as the preferred breeds, espoused by military dog trainers and handlers at the wartime Army's War Dogs Training School and the MAP Guard Dog Training School were carried over into the post-war period.

---

1   Museum of Military Medicine: Box 26, Lecture Notes, Lt. Col. J. Bleby, 'Employment of Dogs for Military Purposes', 15 March 1989, pp. 16-17.

The Post-War Employment of Military Dogs

Although most of the Army's War Dogs Training School's wartime personnel returned to the United Kingdom in late 1945, the training facility in Sennelager survived the immediate post-war period.[2] Moreover, in 1947, the British Army founded a separate Army Dog Training School as part of the RAVC compound in Melton Mowbray, Leicestershire.[3] Within five years of the Second World War, the Army maintained canine training facilities in West Germany, Austria, the United Kingdom, the Middle East and Southeast Asia.[4] In 1949 and 1950, the British Army turned out nearly 330 trained dogs, and by early 1951, it maintained a force of some 1,060 canines.[5]

That the Army's War Dogs Training School in West Germany would survive the immediate post-war period was not entirely clear at the time, however. The demobilisation of servicemen after the war, as well as an influx of civilian staff, led to a significant decline in the ratio of military personnel at the school.[6] While some wartime trainers and handlers remained,[7] the loss of several trainers, as the Assistant Director, Veterinary and Remount Services (BAOR) Lieutenant Colonel W.M. Rouse put it, was "cause for anxiety" since new personnel lacked the maturity and experience of their predecessors. In late 1947, he expressed concern over the future of the school, noting that it was unlikely it could "continue to function satisfactorily" without sufficient personnel.[8]

Another problem which put the future of the Army's War Dogs Training School at risk in the late 1940s was the limited availability of dogs in West Germany. Although local governments in West Germany were compelled to assist the British Army in turning over canines, German breeders were reluctant to furnish animals since greater profits could be fetched through private sale.[9] As a result of insufficient numbers of

---

2   Hunt, 'The War Dogs Training School', p. 11.
3   Gilbert King, 'Our Heritage: RAVC Camp, Melton', *Melton Times*, 24 March 1989, p. 25.
4   TNA: WO 32/14142, 40A, Appendix C, Training of War Dogs at V&R Units, 1949-1950. See Appendix IX for a list of RAVC training facilities which offered military dog instruction in 1949-1950, as well as the total number of canines instructed at each facility.
5   TNA: WO 32/14142, 40A, Use of Guard Dogs Minute Sheet, 9 February 1951 and Appendix C.
6   TNA WO: 267/588, Veterinary and Remount Services Quarterly Historical Report, 31 December 1947 and TNA: WO 267/589, Veterinary and Remount Services Quarterly Historical Reports, 31 March 1948 and 30 June 1948.
7   IWM: 94/1219, Hunt, 'A Brief Look', Book 2, p. 83. Mine detection dog handler Don May, for example, served as an instructor at the training facility in Sennelager after the war. In 1947, he took up a role at the newly-established Army Dog Training School in Melton Mowbray.
8   WO 267/588, Veterinary and Remount Services Quarterly Historical Report, 31 December 1947.
9   TNA: WO 267/588, Veterinary and Remount Services Quarterly Historical Report, 31 March 1947 and TNA: WO 267/589, Veterinary and Remount Services Quarterly Historical Report, 31 March 1948 and Appendix A, Jim Childs to Maintenance Branch,

canine trainees, the school had a mere 26 guard dogs available for deployment as of mid-1948.[10] In an effort to expand its dwindling canine population, the school sought to breed canines using former guard dogs. Although multiple litters of puppies were safely delivered in 1947 and 1948, few animals survived long enough to complete training.[11]

The use of guard dogs in the immediate post-war period seems to have guaranteed the survival of the school in West Germany. As Rouse acknowledged, the widespread demobilisation of human guards ensured the continued use of guard dogs, which in turn prevented the closure of the school. In March 1948, he explained:

> The demand for Guard Dogs [from the Army's War Dogs Training School] continues and appears likely to be maintained as a permanent commitment... The retention of the Training School in BAOR has been much under review in the light of the manpower position. It was generally conceded however that as personnel for guard duties were reduced, the need for guard dogs increased, and it was decided that retention of the school was essential though with a much reduced establishment.[12]

The release of War Office Policy Statement No. 16 the following month further ensured roles for canines in the post-war British Army. The Deputy Chief of the Imperial General Staff affirmed: "There is a requirement in peace and war for dogs in the Army" and specified the roles for which canines should be prepared. Guard, patrol, tracker and detection dogs, it was determined, were to be utilised as part of the British Army for "normal peace time duties," as well as to "provide a sufficient nucleus for expansion in war."[13] In re-assessing Policy Statement No. 16 in early 1951, the War Office noted an even greater commitment among Commands to utilise dogs compared to that indicated in current policy.[14] Considering such "increasing interest

Zonal Executive Offices (BAOR), 16 August 1948 and Veterinary and Remount Services Quarterly Historical Report, 31 December 1948.

10   TNA WO 267/589, Veterinary and Remount Services Quarterly Historical Report, 30 June 1948. Although the school possessed 50 guard dogs at the time, around half of these had yet to complete training. Among the many fully-trained canines, many were already employed in the vicinity of the school or utilised on demonstrations.

11   TNA: WO 267/588, Veterinary and Remount Services Quarterly Historical Reports, 30 June 1947 and 30 September 1947 and 31 December 1947 and TNA: WO 267/589, Veterinary and Remount Services Quarterly Historical Reports, 31 March 1948 and 30 September 1948. As of late September 1948, 35 canines had already succumbed to hard pad disease. An additional 37 dogs, according to the 30 September 1948 Quarterly Historical Report, had taken ill with what appeared to be hard pad disease.

12   TNA: WO 267/589, Veterinary and Remount Services Quarterly Historical Report, 31 March 1948.

13   TNA: WO 32/14142, 60A, War Office Policy Statement No. 16, 30 April 1948.

14   TNA: WO 32/14142, Routine Review of War Office Policy Statements, War Office Policy Statement No. 16, 19 February 1951.

in [the] subject [of military dogs], particularly overseas, and enthusiasm of those with experience of dogs at work,"[15] it was felt that "the lukewarm statement of policy" expressed in War Office Policy Statement No. 16 was lacking.[16] As a result, the War Office released a modified, more exhaustive version of Policy Statement No. 16 which called for additional roles for canines.[17] Moreover, in contrast to the years prior to the First World War, when Richardson was obliged to organise informal training exercises with British Army units stationed near his home,[18] the post-war period saw the participation of military dogs on official Field Exercises with the British Army in West Germany.[19]

The second half of the 20th century saw the continued use of canines to guard military establishments in the United Kingdom and overseas. The Army's War Dogs Training School in Sennelager instructed guard dogs and handlers prior to their employment in West Germany, Austria and Southeast Asia.[20] Between January and November 1946, the school turned out nearly 270 guard dogs.[21] While trainers at the school prepared dogs for other roles, including patrol and mine detection, the overwhelming majority of canines utilised by the British Army in the late 1940s were guard dogs.[22] By early 1951, the British Army relied upon nearly 400 guard dogs in West Germany, Austria, Gibraltar and the United Kingdom.[23]

In the decade following the Second World War, the British Army extended its use of canines to Southeast Asia, where guard dog units were instituted in Singapore and Hong Kong.[24] Dogs attached to the Army Guard Dog Unit, Hong Kong assisted

---

15   TNA: WO 32/14142, 44A, Routine Review of W.O.P.S., Summary of Brief, undated.
16   TNA: WO 32/14142, Routine Review of War Office Policy Statement No. 16, 19 February 1951.
17   TNA: WO 32/14142, 59A, War Office Policy Statement No. 16 (Revise), 26 February 1952. Rescue, or "casualty-finding," was included among the roles listed in this version.
18   Richardson, *Forty Years*, pp. 33-34.
19   TNA: WO 267/590, Veterinary and Remount Services Quarterly Historical Report, 31 December 1949. According to this report, it was "the first time the War Dogs have been actively employed with Troops on Field Exercises" in West Germany.
20   TNA: WO 267/588, Veterinary and Remount Services Quarterly Historical Reports, 31 March 1947, 30 June 1947 and 31 December 1947.
21   Young, 'War Dogs Training School', *Journal of the RAVC*, p. 20.
22   Ibid. According to Young, the school "kept in training simply for demonstration and experimental purposes" patrol, mine detection, tracker, messenger and casualty detection dogs. Similarly, in TNA: WO 267/589, Veterinary and Remount Services Quarterly Historical Report, 31 March 1948, Rouse noted that apart from guards "there is no demand for other types" of canines from the Army's War Dogs Training School.
23   TNA: WO 32/14142, 40A, Appendix 'A', World Wide Distribution of Army War Dogs, 1 January 1951. An additional 188 dogs were currently in training or had completed training but had not yet been deployed. Figures are exclusive of military police dogs attached to the RMP.
24   'Army Guard Dog Unit, Hong Kong', *Journal of the RAVC*, 21:4 (1950), p. 189 and Major A.V. Lovell-Knight, *The Story of the Royal Military Police* (London: Leo Cooper, 1977), pp. 263-264.

human guards in the protection of ordnance depots and other installations throughout the British colony, where, according to an RAVC staff sergeant, "commanders [were] keen to have dogs."[25] Eventually, the employment of guard dogs spread beyond Singapore and Hong Kong to the neighbouring colonies of Malaya and Borneo, so that by 1964, the British Army in Southeast Asia possessed some 170 guard dogs.[26]

The Royal Military Police (RMP), as the CMP became known in 1946, also maintained an international canine presence in the years following the Second World War. In addition to their continued use in Egypt, RMP dogs operated in Libya and East Africa during the post-war period. By early 1951, the RMP possessed some 235 canines attached to three military police dog companies in Africa and the Middle East.[27] Moreover, with the formation of additional dog companies in the late 1950s, the RMP extended the employment of canines to Cyprus, Malta and Gibraltar.[28] At the behest of the Army Council, a number of Army Guard Dog Units (RAVC) in the Middle East and Southeast Asia were converted to RMP formations in the late 1950s.[29]

Baldwin continued as Chief Training Officer at the RAF Police Dog Training School until 1953, at which point a former MAP Guard Dog Training School trainer assumed the role.[30] By early 1951, the RAF Police had some 400 canines, including 175 dogs undergoing instruction at the RAF Police Dog Training School. Upon completion of training at the school, which had relocated to Netheravon in Wiltshire, canines were issued to RAF Police units at airfields in the United Kingdom, West Germany, Gibraltar, the Middle East and South East Asia.[31] As shown in Table 4,

---

25 Staff Sergeant Bratley, 'War Dogs in Hong Kong', *Journal of the RAVC*, 25:2 (1954), p. 60.
26 '£1,000 Dogs Aid Army's Jungle Forces', *The Times*, 1 September 1964, p. 10.
27 TNA: WO 32/14142, 40A, Appendix 'A'. It is unclear if these units, designated Nos. 1, 2 and 3 Dog Companies (RMP), were the same units which operated in Egypt, Lebanon and Palestine during the Second World War. The war diaries of Nos. 1, 2, 3, and 5 Military Police Dog Sections (CMP) indicate that they continued to operate until at least June 1946, while No. 4 Police Dog Section (CMP) was likely deactivated in April 1946. See TNA: WO 169/24100, 1 Dog Section, War Diary of No. 1 Military Police Dog Section, June 1946 and TNA: WO 169/24101, 2 Dog Section, War Diary of No. 2 Military Police Dog Section, June 1946 and TNA: WO 169/24102, 3 Dog Section, War Diary of No. 3 Military Police Dog Section, June 1946 and TNA: WO 169/24103, 4 Dog Section, War Diary of No. 4 Military Police Dog Section, April 1946 and TNA: WO 169/24104, 5 Dog Section, War Diary of No. 5 Military Police Dog Section, June 1946.
28 Lovell-Knight, *Story of the Royal Military Police*, p. 263.
29 'Future of the Royal Army Veterinary Corps', *Journal of the RAVC*, 29:1 (1958), p. 2 and 'Future of the R.A.V.C.', *Journal of the RAVC*, 29:3 (1958), p. 109 and 'No. 4 Army Guard Dog Unit RAVC, Hong Kong', *Journal of the RAVC*, 29:3 (1958), p. 118 and TNA: WO 305/1476, 5 Dog Company Singapore, Major S.E. Harrison, Historical Records, 5 Dog Company RMP, 8 December 1959 and TNA: WO 305/1479, 6 Guard Dog Unit, Major H.M. Simpkin, Historical Record, 6 Guard Dog Unit RMP, 27 May 1960.
30 Davies, *RAF Police Dogs on Patrol*, pp. 4, 7, 69.
31 TNA: WO 32/14142, 40A, Appendix 'D', Memorandum on Police Dogs in the Royal Air Force.

nearly 75 percent of dogs utilised by the RAF Police at that time remained in the United Kingdom[32] where they were relied upon to augment the security of maintenance units, radar units, aircraft dispersal areas and airfields.[33]

Table 4 RAF Police Dogs by Theatre of Operations, 1951[34]

Theatre of Operations	Number of Dogs
United Kingdom	291
West Germany	30
Middle East Land Forces (MELF)	35
Far East Land Forces (FARELF)	42
Gibraltar	2

RAF Police dogs in the United Kingdom were provided with an additional duty beginning in the late 1950s, when the British Armed Forces added nuclear weapons to its arsenal. Along with their handlers, RAF Police dogs took part in nightly patrols to prevent unpermitted access to the Special Storage Areas which housed nuclear weapons. Canines were also relied upon to protect the Bloodhound and Thor missiles and the strategic bomber aircraft located at a number of airfields along the North Sea.[35]

In the Middle East, the RAF Police maintained dog sections in Egypt, Iraq and Cyprus in the post-war period. For a short time in the early 1950s, the RAF Police conducted military police dog training in Egypt at RAF Kasfareet. Although the Egyptian-based RAF Police Dog School was disbanded in 1953, a dog section was raised in its place. While the employment of RAF Police dogs in the Suez Canal Zone and in Iraq ceased in 1956 and 1960, respectively, RAF Police dogs continued to operate in Aden, Libya, Sharjah and Cyprus in the second half of the 20th century.[36]

In the years immediately succeeding the Second World War, RAF Police dogs were limited to the United Kingdom, West Germany and the Middle East. In 1947, however, the RAF Police instituted a dog section in Singapore.[37] Eventually, the RAF Police raised additional dog sections in Southeast Asia. By the late 1960s, several airfields in Singapore, Hong Kong, Borneo and Malaya utilised military police dogs. Prior to departing Singapore in the early 1970s, the RAF Police were instrumental in the formation of a Singaporean military dog scheme. Canines utilised by the RAF

32   Ibid.
33   Davies, *RAF Police Dogs on Patrol*, pp. 59-158.
34   TNA: WO 32/14142, 40A, Appendix 'D'. The number referred to in the United Kingdom is inclusive of canines held by the RAF Police Dog Training School.
35   Davies, *RAF Police Dogs on Patrol*, pp. 85, 92-93, 95, 99, 107-109, 132, 143, 201-202.
36   Ibid, pp. 60-63, 67, 72, 83-85, 90, 96, 100, 119, 131, 134, 139, 151, 168-170, 239.
37   'R.A.F. Dogs', *Gloucestershire Echo*, 30 August 1947, p. 3.

Police in the former British colony were left behind for employment by the Singapore Armed Forces.[38]

While acknowledging "the limited use made of patrol dogs" in the Second World War, the 1952 publication *Training of War Dogs* also noted: "It was found [in the war] that rarely, if ever, was a patrol accompanied by a dog fired on first."[39] Thus, it seems that the employment of patrol dogs in the Second World War, albeit on a small scale, was enough to convince the War Office to re-institute the training of patrol dogs in the post-war period. In 1948, less than three years after the war's end, the War Office identified the patrol dog as one of the roles in which canines were to be instructed and utilised by the British Army.[40]

Perhaps equally important to the post-war use of patrol dogs in the British Army was the support shown by senior officers. For his part, the Commander-in-Chief, BAOR was committed to the instruction of patrol dogs in his command. As evidenced by the AVRS Quarterly Historical Report for March 1950, the Army's War Dogs Training School in West Germany offered such a course in early 1950 in an effort to ensure, per a request by the Commander-in-Chief, "that Infantry Patrol Dogs are used to the fullest extent during the ensuing Training Season."[41]

"A sudden revival of interest" in patrol dogs was also noted in Far East Land Forces (FARELF),[42] where a communist revolt against British rule in Malaya allowed for the employment of military canines beginning in the early 1950s.[43] The training schools in the United Kingdom and West Germany supplied trained patrol dogs to the British Army in Malaya until the opening of the Johore-based War Dog Training Wing (RAVC) in 1952, from which point canines were instructed in Malaya before joining Battalion War Dog Sections.[44] In early 1954, the War Dog Training Wing (RAVC) in Johore reported that the sections were "continu[ing] to increase in popularity," a trend attributed to RAVC officers of the units to which canines were attached.[45]

38 Davies, *RAF Police Dogs on Patrol*, pp. 138, 186-187.
39 War Office, *Training of War Dogs* (1952), p. 72.
40 TNA: WO 32/14142, 60A, War Office Policy Statement No. 16, 30 April 1948.
41 TNA: WO 267/591, Veterinary and Remount Services Quarterly Historical Report, 31 March 1950.
42 TNA: WO 32/14142, Routine Review of War Office Policy Statement No. 16, 19 February 1951.
43 Major J.H. Wilkins, 'War Dogs in Malaya', *Journal of the RAVC*, 25:2 (1954), pp. 43-46. According to Wilkins, the British Army first utilised patrol and other military dogs in Malaya approximately two years prior to the time of writing. However, as indicated in TNA: WO 32/14142, 27A, Commander-in-Chief, FARELF to Under-Secretary of State, 24 November 1950, patrol dogs were already present among British forces in Malaya as of late 1950.
44 Wilkins, 'War Dogs in Malaya', *Journal of the RAVC*, p. 43 and 'Melton Camp', *Journal of the RAVC*, 35:1 (1964), p. 13 and War Office, *Training of War Dogs* (1962), pp. 86-88.
45 'War Dog Training Wing (R.A.V.C.), FARELF, Malaya', *Journal of the RAVC*, 25:1 (1954), p. 36.

Accordingly, the number of "operational successes" executed by Battalion War Dog Sections also climbed steadily during the late 1950s.[46]

The employment of patrol dogs also spread to Kenya in the decade following the Second World War. Patrol dogs were first utilised in the colony in 1953; that year, the British Army established the War Dog School near Mount Kenya. The training facility, which opened with just six canines, produced patrol and other military dogs for units within East Africa Command. Within two years, the British Army in East Africa possessed approximately 35 patrol dogs spread among all battalions in the colony.[47]

The continued employment of patrol dogs with parachute battalions was also considered in the years following the Second World War. In the early 1950s, the War Office determined: "As there may be a requirement for infantry patrol dogs for airborne Forces, the technique of dropping dogs by parachute should be kept alive."[48] Although it is unclear if any military dogs parachuted on operations in the years immediately following the Second World War, both the 1952 and 1962 editions of *Training of War Dogs* stressed: "Occasions will arise when war dogs will be required to parachute from aircraft" and included detailed instructions based on those developed by 13th Parachute Battalion during the Second World War.[49] In 2010, over 65 years after canines parachuted over Normandy as part of the Allied invasion, the *Guardian* exposed that the SAS had lately deployed dogs by parachute in Afghanistan. Affixed with video cameras, the dogs were released upon landing to reconnoitre areas controlled by the Taliban.[50]

Not long after the end of the Second World War, a small number of detection dogs were deployed to Palestine to seek out buried arms.[51] In August 1946, the canines, which were originally trained for mine detection, discovered a substantial amount of *matériel* stockpiled at Zionist encampments along the Mediterranean.[52] Although

46   'War Dog Training Wing, Malaya', *Journal of the RAVC*, 27:1 (1956), p. 39 and 'War Dog Training Wing, Malaya', *Journal of the RAVC*, 28:1 (1957), p. 34 and 'War Dog Training Wing RAVC, Malaya', *Journal of the RAVC*, 29:3 (1958), p. 117. The author(s) of these articles, which constituted periodic reports from the War Dog Training Wing (RAVC), did not specify what was meant by an "operational success."
47   'War Dogs in Kenya', *Journal of the RAVC*, 26:1 (1955), pp. 8-10 and TNA: WO 276/89, DADVRS to G (Ops), 26 May 1955. The employment of patrol and other military dogs in East Africa Command was not limited to the British Army. African units also utilised military dogs and provided handlers for instruction at the War Dog School.
48   TNA: WO 32/14142, 59A, War Office Policy Statement No. 16 (Revise), 26 February 1952.
49   War Office, *Training of War Dogs* (1952), pp. 63-64 and War Office, *Training of War Dogs* (1962), pp. 71-72.
50   'SAS Parachute Dogs of War into Taliban Bases', *Guardian*, 8 November 2010, online <http://www.theguardian.com/uk/2010/nov/08/sas-dogs-parachute-taliban-afghanistan> (accessed 4 September 2015).
51   Clabby, *History of the RAVC*, p. 187.
52   'Dogs Help to Search Settlement', *Manchester Guardian*, 27 August 1946, p. 5 and 'Dogs Find Hidden Arms Dump', *Manchester Guardian*, 31 August 1946, p. 5.

information related to the employment of these dogs is limited,[53] it seems to have been on a small scale and of short duration. Nonetheless, an account of their use included in Clabby's *The History of the Royal Army Veterinary Corps* highlighted the similarities between their employment and that of mine detection dogs during the Second World War:

> [The dogs] scented keenly the ground over which they were cast and if they scented or sensed metal they sat down on the spot and were ultimately rewarded with a lump of meat. In two cases where the dogs 'sat' the ground had previously been covered by the Sappers with their mine detectors. At [location redacted] it was a hen house with a floor of concrete slabs in which a cross-bred Labrador 'sat' before unbelieving eyes. The concrete was raised with the aid of a compressor drill and the earth below was dug out to a depth of four-and-a-half feet before the lid of a seven feet deep cache was reached. In it were stored some fifty assorted weapons including heavy mortars and machine guns together with many thousands of rounds of ammunition. They had been there for some considerable length of time and how they were detected at such a depth remained a mystery to all but the dog.[54]

From this account, it may be inferred that British Army dog handlers in Palestine adhered to the "attraction method" of detection dog training adopted during the Second World War. It is also reminiscent of reports on mine detection dogs from the war in that it underscored the advantages of canines over electronic detectors.

In the early 1950s, mine detection dogs instructed at the Army's War Dogs Training School in West Germany were utilised by the Royal Engineers in Korea. As in Palestine, the British Army relied upon a small number of canine mine detectors in Korea.[55] In fact, of the 40 canines instructed at the school in Melton Mowbray in 1949-1950, just six completed training in mine detection.[56] Yet the small-scale employment of detection dogs in the years immediately following the Second World War should not be seen as a renunciation of the mine detection dog by the War Office. Contemporary policy statements and training instructions made clear that the War Office intended for the use of mine detection dogs to continue in the second half of the

---

53 Apart from the account contained in the *History of the RAVC*, the *Manchester Guardian* articles referred to in the previous footnote provide the most detailed description of detection dogs in Palestine.

54 Quoted in Clabby, *History of the RAVC*, p. 187. As Clabby did not provide a source for the account, it is unclear whether it was submitted by a military dog handler or other serviceman. The locations referred to in this account are likely the Dorot and Ruhama encampments worked by dogs in August 1946. See 'Dogs Find Hidden Arms Dump', *Manchester Guardian*, 31 August 1946, p. 5.

55 'His Dog Aids in Korea Mine Detecting', *Hastings and St Leonard's Observer*, 24 May 1952, p. 6 and Clabby, *History of the RAVC*, p. 186.

56 TNA: WO 32/14142, 40A, Appendix C, Training of War Dogs, 1949-1950.

20th century.[57] Indeed, in 1951, the Organization and Weapons Policy Committee went so far as to describe the mine detection dog as "the only really suitable means of detecting scattered mines in rear areas." Thus, the committee deemed "it was important that the technique of training/handling mine-detecting dogs should be kept alive in peace."[58]

In the 1950s, the British Army again turned to mine detection dogs in Malaya and Cyprus, where they sought to contain insurrections by guerrilla forces.[59] Moreover, as the conflict in Northern Ireland escalated in the late 20th century, detection dogs were introduced in an effort to quell Irish Republican Army activity. The employment of dogs in Northern Ireland spanned nearly 40 years during the late 20th and early 21st centuries.[60] Around the time the Army Dog Unit (RAVC) Northern Ireland was raised in 1973, the British Armed Forces already had between 15 and 21 detection dogs, or "search dogs" as they were alternatively known, in the province with additional canines scheduled to arrive after undergoing instruction with the British Army and the RAF in the United Kingdom.[61] By early 1974, this figure had more than doubled,[62] and a report by HQ Northern Ireland indicated "constant demands for yet more search dogs" in the command.[63] During a two year period in the late 1970s, detection dogs in Northern Ireland took part in more than 24,600 assignments which resulted in the discovery of 129 arms, nearly 880 kilograms of explosives and several thousand rounds of ammunition. As in the Second World War, they were also instrumental in clearing sites suspected of containing explosives or other illegal objects.[64]

57   TNA: WO 32/14142, 60A, War Office Policy Statement No. 16, 30 April 1948 and 59A, War Office Policy Statement No. 16 (Revise), 26 February 1952. The updated version reiterated that mine detection dogs were among the British Army canines "require[d] in peace and in war" outlined in the previous version. See also: War Office, *Training of War Dogs* (1952), pp. 72-73 and War Office, *Training of War Dogs* (1962), pp. 82-83.
58   TNA: WO 32/14142, 43A, Extract from the Minutes of the 108th Meeting of the Organization and Weapons Policy Committee, 22 February 1951.
59   TNA: WO 32/14142, Routine Review of War Office Policy Statement No. 16, 19 February 1951 and 'No. 6 Army Guard Dog Unit, RAVC', *Journal of the RAVC*, 27:3 (1956), p. 116 and 'No. 6 Army Guard Dog Unit, RAVC', *Journal of the RAVC*, 28:1 (1957), p. 29 and 'No. 6 Army Guard Dog Unit-Cyprus', *Journal of the RAVC*, 28:2 (1957), p. 78 and 'No. 6 Army Guard Dog Unit, RAVC, Cyprus', *Journal of the RAVC*, 29:2 (1958), p. 92.
60   Sgt. Ackers, 'Arms Explosive Search Dog Course', *Chiron Calling*, Autumn 2012, p. 30.
61   TNA: WO 32/21774, Explosive Detection by Dogs, E125, Annex B, Army Dog Unit RAVC Northern Ireland, 15 June 1973 and E125, Annex A, Search Dogs' Finds, 15 June 1973 and E110, Minutes of a Meeting to Discuss the Use of Dogs for Detection Purposes, 25 April 1973.
62   TNA: WO 32/21878, E50, Minutes of a Meeting to Discuss the Use of Dogs for Detection Purposes, 19 March 1974.
63   TNA: WO 32/21878, E46, HQ Northern Ireland, Army Dog Unit RAVC, 7 March 1974.
64   TNA: DEFE 70/61, Animals: Use of Dogs in Northern Ireland, 25, Annex A, Summary of Specialist Dog Taskings and Results-Year 1977, 27 February 1978 and 66, Annex A, Summary of Specialist Dog Taskings and Results-January-December 1978, 24 January 1979.

A detection dog employed by the Queen's Lancashire Regiment in Northern Ireland, 1977.
© Crown Copyright. IWM (MH 30551))

In the late 20th and early 21st centuries, military dogs performed a number of detection roles in addition to those carried out in the Second World War. In the 1960s and 1970s, the RMP, the RAF Police and the Ministry of Defence (MOD) Police introduced drug detection dogs in an effort to reduce drug use among British and North Atlantic Treaty Organization (NATO) troops stationed in the United Kingdom and overseas.[65] Beginning in the 1970s, the RAF Police Dog Training School prepared dogs for a similar role with Her Majesty's (HM) Customs and Excise. The scheme, which began as an experimental venture comprising two dogs, continued to flourish in the late 20th century. By 1991, HM Customs and Excise relied upon a force of 63 RAF Police dogs.[66] The second half of the 20th century also saw the use of guard and drug detection dogs by HM Prison Service, which possessed some 750 canines by 1999.[67] Prior to the construction of a separate HM Prison Service canine training

65   Museum of Military Medicine: Box 26, Bleby, 'Employment of Dogs for Military Purposes', p. 14 and Davies, *RAF Police Dogs on Patrol*, pp. 152-153, 182-183. The Royal Navy, although without its own drug detection dogs, utilised those of the MOD Police.
66   Davies, *RAF Police Dogs on Patrol*, pp. 186-191 and Hansard: HC Deb 3 December 1984 vol 69 c16W and HL Deb 30 January 1991 vol 525 c764.
67   Hansard: HC Deb 30 June 1975 vol 894 cc339-40W and HL Deb 14 March 1983 vol 440 cc589-90WA and HC Deb 29 June 1999 vol 334 cc99-101W and HC Deb 4 February 1999 vol 324 c764W.

centre in the 1990s, dogs utilised at prisons in England and Wales were instructed at the training school in Melton Mowbray.[68] Thus, the introduction of the mine detection dog, "a brain child of World War II,"[69] marked a turning point in the history of British military dogs. His use encouraged and influenced the employment of dogs in the British Army during the late 20th and early 21st centuries.

Although the British Army instructed a small number of dogs to track persons during the Second World War, they were not utilised on operations.[70] What has been described as "the first serious use of tracker dogs" by the British Army occurred in the two decades following the Second World War.[71] Beginning in the early 1950s, the War Dog Training Wing (RAVC) in Johore turned out tracker dogs for British Army units in Malaya. The dogs, which used olfaction to trace the location of persons for at least three kilometres, were utilised when the enemy was suspected to have recently been in close proximity.[72]

The effective employment of tracker dogs in Malaya also prompted their use in Kenya, where British forces sought to quell the Mau Mau insurgency.[73] Within two years of the first canine trackers arriving in Kenya there were some 60 tracker dogs employed by the British Army throughout the colony.[74] Despite initial reluctance among some units to utilise canines in Kenya, the British Army's War Dog Wing in the colony reported in early 1956 that battalions had begun "asking for all the dogs they can get."[75]

In Northern Ireland, tracker dogs were utilised as part of canine "search teams" that also included detection dogs.[76] Canine trackers were primarily relied upon to locate individuals suspected of carrying out criminal activity, including violence directed towards the British Armed Forces and the Royal Ulster Constabulary.[77] Although a

---

68   'Prison Service Dogs', *Chiron Calling*, December 1991, p. 8.
69   Clabby, *History of the RAVC*, p. 186.
70   Young, 'War Dogs Training School', *Journal of the RAVC*, p. 20. According to Young, that the Army's War Dogs Training School developed tracker dogs during the war stemmed from the need to discover how to prevent the effective employment of German tracker dogs. See also: War Office, *Training of War Dogs* (1952), p. 2 and Lloyd, 'The Dog in War', p. 192.
71   Museum of Military Medicine: Box 26, Bleby, 'Employment of Dogs for Military Purposes', p. 12.
72   Wilkins, 'War Dogs in Malaya', *Journal of the RAVC*, pp. 43-46.
73   Ibid, p. 46
74   TNA: WO 276/89, 77, Tracker Dog State, 10 May 1956. This figure includes canines employed by African units.
75   'War Dog Wing, E.A. Battle School', *Journal of the RAVC*, 27:1 (1956), p. 35.
76   TNA: WO 32/21774, E128, Notes on the Use and Employment of Specialist Dogs (Draft), 22 June 1973.
77   TNA: DEFE 70/61, 51, Annex B, Summary of Significant Dog Tasks, August 1978. For additional examples of the ways in which tracker dogs were employed, see: TNA: WO 32/21774, E48, Appendix 1 to Annex A, Summary of Positive Finds and Successful

A tracker dog with the South Wales Borderers in Malaya.
(© Imperial War Museum (D 88456))

mere seven tracker dogs were utilised in the province in 1972,[78] their numbers were boosted the following year by the turning out of additional canines by civil police.[79] By the end of 1973, the Army Dog Unit (RAVC) in the province possessed 16 canine trackers.[80]

Shortly after leaving London in 1945, Margaret Griffin and other wartime rescue dog trainers began investigating the employment of rescue dogs over a different type of terrain than that of the capital. Instead of searching for air raid victims in war-torn London, the dogs were taught to seek out missing persons in rugged areas.[81] Moreover, following an explosion at a mine in Cumbria in August 1947, Baldwin arranged for the use of three rescue dogs to seek out casualties.[82]

Tracks, 25 October 1972 and TNA: WO 32/21878, E206, Annex B, Summary of Significant Dog Tasks, January 1976.

78   TNA: WO 32/21774, E48, Minutes of a Meeting to Discuss the Use of Dogs for Detection Purposes, 16 October 1972.

79   TNA: WO 32/21774, E54, David Simmons to E. Cowlyn, 15 November 1972 and E76, Assistance by Police in Dog Training for the Army, 16 January 1973.

80   TNA: WO 32/21878, E36, DAVRS Visit to Northern Ireland, 14 December 1973.

81   'Notes & News of the Breeds', *Our Dogs*, 22 June 1945, p. 714.

82   Brown, *Jet of Iada*, p. 25.

Yet the employment of rescue dogs, in comparison to that of guard, military police and detection dogs, seems to have been relatively rare in the decades following the Second World War. Records produced by the AVRS in the late 1940s and early 1950s indicate that the training of rescue dogs did continue in the post-war period, albeit on a limited scale. In 1947, the Army's War Dogs Training School in West Germany turned out two dogs "for ARP work." It is unclear if these dogs, which were posted to the United Kingdom upon completion of instruction in Sennelager, underwent further training or were utilised on rescue operations following their arrival.[83]

Beginning in the late 1940s, there was a concerted effort by personnel at the school in West Germany to produce rescue dogs, or "casualty Detecting dog[s]" for employment with the Royal Army Medical Corps.[84] In early 1950, a dog instructed for such a role took part in a display witnessed by the Director of Medical Services, BAOR. A report submitted by the AVRS (BAOR) praised the performance of the dog as "extremely well done" and noted the rapid speed in which he discovered soldiers posing as casualties. The report, which indicated a "definite need for" casualty detection dogs in the British Army, also highlighted the influence of the Second World War, during which rescue dogs "were employed successfully on several occasions notably in Civil Defence."[85] This suggests that the decision to prepare British Army canines for casualty detection was partly inspired by the use of rescue dogs by the London Civil Defence Region in 1944 and 1945. Furthermore, the War Office, in 1952, reversed its earlier decision to exclude casualty detection dogs among the list of roles in which "there is a requirement in peace and in war."[86]

Despite such efforts, casualty detection dogs do not appear to have been utilised by the British Armed Forces on operations during the second half of the 20th century. In the late 1980s, an RAVC officer noted in the RAVC publication *Chiron Calling* that, although the British Army had not utilised casualty detection dogs "for some years," they were "becoming increasingly recognised as an extremely useful aid to search and rescue organisations."[87] Indeed, during the second half of the 20th century, a number of British police forces and civilian organisations launched rescue dog schemes. In the 1960s, the secretary of the Mountain Rescue Committee for Scotland introduced rescue dogs to recover lost persons after avalanches in the Scottish Highlands. He established the Search and Rescue Dog Association, which in later years spread

---

83   TNA: WO 267/588, Veterinary and Remount Services Quarterly Historical Report, 30 September 1947.
84   TNA: WO 267/590, Veterinary and Remount Services Quarterly Historical Report, 31 December 1949.
85   TNA: WO 267/591, Veterinary and Remount Services Quarterly Historical Report, 31 March 1950.
86   TNA: WO 32/14142, 59A, War Office Policy Statement No. 16 (Revise), 26 February 1952. See also: 60A, War Office Policy Statement No. 16, 30 April 1948. The decision made in 1952 was a reversal of the earlier War Office Policy Statement No. 16, which had determined the British Army had no "future requirement for" casualty detection dogs.
87   Major P.W. Hepworth, 'Casualty Detection Dog', *Chiron Calling*, November 1988, p. 19.

beyond Scotland to include operations in Wales and England.[88] Around the same time, the Lancashire Constabulary launched a similar scheme involving the employment of dogs to recover fatal casualties as part of criminal investigations.[89]

The Leicestershire Fire and Rescue Service also instituted the employment of rescue dogs in the late 20th century. What began as a small-scale venture with one dog developed into a national scheme involving several fire brigades throughout the United Kingdom. As part of the United Kingdom Fire Services Search and Rescue Team (UKFSSART), an organisation established in 1990 "to co-ordinate the response by the British Fire Service to international disasters," the Leicestershire Fire and Rescue Service and 12 other British fire brigades employed dogs to locate victims of earthquakes and other natural disasters in foreign countries. The dogs were also utilised in the aftermath of domestic events, including the 2004 explosion which demolished a factory in Scotland.[90]

The Training and Recruitment of Military Dogs in the Post-War Period

The training of military dogs in the second half of the 20th century was of slightly longer duration compared to that of the Second World War. Whereas the wartime Army's War Dogs Training School turned out mine detection dogs for employment in northwest Europe after just four months,[91] canines selected for mine or arms/explosives detection in the decades thereafter underwent up to six months of instruction prior to use on operations.[92] For guard and patrol dogs, which during the war spent up to two months in training prior to deployment,[93] training in the post-war period lasted between one and three months and three and four months, respectively.[94] Similarly, RAF Police dogs were required to complete six to eight weeks of instruction as opposed to the five week programme offered at the MAP Guard Dog

88   Christopher Brasher, 'Search Cost Rescue Dog His Life', *Observer*, 29 December 1968, p. 4 and Hepworth, 'Casualty Detection Dog', *Chiron Calling*, p. 19. Hamish MacInnes, the founder of the Search and Rescue Dog Association, was trained to handle rescue dogs by a similar organisation in Switzerland. According to the *Observer* article, personnel at the Swiss training centre claimed to have been inspired by the employment of rescue dogs on the British Home Front during the Second World War. This seems unlikely, however, considering rescuers in Switzerland had utilised dogs in a similar role for several centuries prior to the war.

89   John Kerr, 'Led by the Nose', *Guardian*, 21 January 1978, p. 17.

90   Chris Prichard, 'Search and Rescue Dogs in the UK Fire Service', *Chiron Calling*, Winter 2005/Spring 2006, pp. 10-12.

91   NAA: MP742/1, 240/6324, Training of War Dogs, 3 January 1945.

92   TNA: WO 32/14142, 40A, Use of Guard Dogs, 16 February 1951 and TNA: WO 32/21774, E11/1, Loose Minute, Detection of Explosives, 8 March 1972.

93   Murray, 'War Dogs', *Animal World*, September 1944, p. 68.

94   TNA: WO 32/14142, 40, Use of Guard Dogs, 16 February 1951 and War Office, *Training of War Dogs* (1962), pp. 48, 55.

Training School during the war.[95] That military dog training was of longer duration in the post-war period was undoubtedly a consequence of the British Armed Forces no longer being involved in a conflict on a scale comparable to that of the Second World War. Without the operational demands of a global war, British military dog trainers could devote more time to preparing canines before they were required for active duty. Moreover, the continued training of military dogs after 1945 meant that operational demands could be met without having to re-establish training schemes following the onset of each conflict in which the British Armed Forces was involved.

While the duration of instruction was extended in the post-war period, the actual training of canines remained similar to that of the Second World War. This is unsurprising considering that the War Office publication *Training of War Dogs* (1952), the official set of training instructions for military dogs employed by the British Army for much of the second half of the 20th century, was authored by Major George Young. Young served as the first commandant of the Army's War Dogs Training School following its relocation to West Germany in late 1945.[96] The guidelines for military dog instruction laid down in the 1952 and 1962 editions of *Training of War Dogs* were reminiscent of instructions issued to trainers and handlers during the war:

> The fundamental principles of dog training are firmness and kindness… It is the natural desire of a dog to please and advantage is taken of this admirable trait in its training. To enable it to understand that it has carried out its trainer's wishes it should be immediately rewarded when an order has been correctly obeyed. The reward may be either verbal praise, an encouraging pat or a titbit such as a small piece of meat… Physical violence, even for wilful disobedience, must never be resorted to as the dog may become sullen, stubborn or cowed.[97]

In preparing canines for mine detection, for example, British trainers continued to adhere to the "reward system" practised by instructors at the Army's War Dogs Training School in the Second World War.[98]

Furthermore, a number of breeds utilised by the British Armed Forces in the Second World War, including the Boxer and the Collie, remained among those recommended by the post-war British Army. In particular, the Alsatian, which

---

95   TNA: WO 32/14142, 40A, Appendix D, Memorandum on Police Dogs in the Royal Air Force. Although undated, this document was attached to a minute sheet dated 9 February 1951. See also: Davies, *RAF Police Dogs on Patrol*, pp. 108, 118, 128, 165 and 'War Dogs', *Gloucestershire Echo*, 15 June 1944, p. 3.

96   Major R.G. Mares, 'Some Aspects of the Use of Dogs in the Far East', *Chiron Calling*, Winter 2000/2001, p. 24 and Brigadier G.R. Durrant, 'Brigadier George David Young MBE, MRCVS L/RAVC', *Chiron Calling*, Summer 2004, p. 3.

97   War Office, *Training of War Dogs* (1952), p. 33 and War Office, *Training of War Dogs* (1962), p. 35.

98   War Office, *Training of War Dogs* (1952), p. 54 and War Office, *Training of War Dogs* (1962), p. 61.

emerged from the Second World War as the preeminent British military dog, remained among the British Army's favoured breeds. During the two decades following the Second World War, the Alsatian stood out as the sole breed recommended by the Army for guard, patrol, tracking and mine detection.[99] The 1952 and 1962 editions of *Training of War Dogs* emphasised that the breed, being "highly intelligent, [with] well developed senses of smell and hearing, alert, willing and reliable" possessed "all the attributes required for military purposes."[100] It is thus no surprise Alsatians constituted a significant proportion of British Army canines during the colonial insurrections in Malaya and Kenya in the mid-20th century.[101] Similarly, the RAF Police continued to favour the Alsatian and went so far as to solely recruit the breed throughout much of the post-war period.[102] Only in the early 21st century was the Alsatian supplanted by another breed: the Belgian Malinois. That the British Armed Forces came to favour the Belgian Malinois over the Alsatian was due in part to fewer Alsatian pets among the British public. In addition, decades of selective breeding resulted in health complications among Alsatians. Nonetheless, the British Armed Forces did not abandon the use of Alsatians; the breed continues to be utilised in the early 21st century.[103]

Similarly, the Labrador, a breed which gained prominence in mine detection during the Second World War, continued to grow in popularity as a military dog in the 1950s and 1960s. In addition to being among the British Army's preferred breeds for mine detection, the Labrador was recommended for patrol and tracking.[104] In Malaya, in particular, the British-bred Labrador was considered, according to the *Journal of the RAVC*, "*par excellence* a natural tracking dog."[105] The RAF Police abandoned their commitment to exclusively recruit Alsatians beginning in the late 1960s, when a Labrador commenced training at the RAF Police Dog Training School.[106] In the early

99 War Office, *Training of War Dogs* (1952), pp. 3-5, 41-60 and War Office, *Training of War Dogs* (1962), pp. 3-6, 44-66.

100 War Office, *Training of War Dogs* (1952), p. 4 and War Office, *Training of War Dogs* (1962), p. 4.

101 Wilkins, 'War Dogs in Malaya', *Journal of the RAVC*, p. 43 and 'War Dogs in Kenya', *Journal of the RAVC*, 26:1 (1955), p. 8 and Lieutenant P. Sidone, 'Dogs of War', *Journal of the RAVC*, 26:1 (1955), p. 15.

102 Hennessey, *The Story of the Royal Air Force Police*, p. 74 and Davies, *RAF Police Dogs on Patrol*, pp. 127, 152 and RAF Museum: R016420, *Royal Air Force Police Dogs*.

103 Staff Sergeant D. Franklin, 'Keep an Open Mind or Else!', *Chiron Calling*, Summer 2001, pp. 18-19 and Sean Jones, 'European Dog Buys', *Chiron Calling*, Summer/Autumn 2010, pp. 15-16 and *The Defence Animal Centre Open Day* pamphlet, 7 June 2014, p. 5.

104 War Office, *Training of War Dogs* (1952), pp. 6, 48-60 and War Office, *Training of War Dogs* (1962), pp. 6, 52, 59, 66. While the Labrador was listed as one of the recommended breeds for mine detection in both editions, it was noted that purebred Labradors tended to exceed the 20 kilogram weight limit required of mine detection dogs.

105 Wilkins, 'War Dogs in Malaya', *Journal of the RAVC*, p. 43.

106 Davies, *RAF Police Dogs on Patrol*, p. 152.

21st century, the Labrador remains one of the preferred breeds for detection work with the British Army and the RAF Police.[107]

The Post-War Employment of Police Dogs

The employment of military dogs in the Second World War also seems to have encouraged the use of dogs by civilian police forces in post-war Britain. In the spring of 1946, the Commissioner of the Metropolitan Police sought permission from the Home Office to re-institute the employment of police dogs in London.[108] In what the Assistant Commissioner of the Metropolitan Police T.E. Mahir later called "the first real attempt" to employ police dogs in the British capital, the Metropolitan Police acquired six Labradors.[109] Upon completion of training in late 1946, the canines were deployed to west London for use on patrols in an attempt to reduce burglaries and petty crime.[110] Although the scheme initially suffered from lack of direction and scepticism among some Metropolitan Police officials and policemen,[111] the presence of police dogs did seem to result in lower crime rates in the locales in which they were utilised.[112] The assignment of canines in the late 1940s to the Royal Parks, as well as outside Buckingham Palace, required that the Metropolitan Police more than treble its police dog contingent within three years.[113]

The majority of Metropolitan Police dogs were considered "general purpose dogs" and utilised with policemen handlers on patrols, or in some cases, as guards outside

107 *The Defence Animal Centre Open Day* pamphlet, 7 June 2014, p. 5.
108 TNA: HO 45/21004, Assistant Commissioner, Metropolitan Police to Under Secretary of State, Home Office, 29 April 1946.
109 T.E. Mahir, 'The Training of Police Dogs', *Journal of the Royal Society of Arts*, 111:5080 (1963), p. 312.
110 TNA: MEPO 2/6208, 309A, Report on the First Year's Training and Operations of Police Patrol Dogs, 5 June 1947.
111 TNA: MEPO 2/6208, 333A, Notes on the Police Dog Organisation, 4 November 1947. The District Commander, No. 1 Metropolitan Police District noted "the untidiness of the present scheme" and lamented that "in the first place no decision was made as to the basic policy, or what we were really trying to do with these animals." See also: 309D, Assistant Commissioner 'D' to Deputy Commissioner, 14 June 1947. The Assistant Commissioner noted a lack of enthusiasm among the Metropolitan Police, pointing out that "no one else [apart from the District Commander] seems particularly interested" in the scheme. See also: 347A, Arthur Young to K.A.L. Parker, 9 February 1948. Young, the Assistant Commissioner 'D', argued in favour of continuing the scheme in spite of "mixed feelings" regarding the effectiveness of canines.
112 TNA: MEPO 2/6208, 309A, Report on the First Year's Training, 5 June 1947 and 333A, Notes on the Police Dog Organisation, 4 November 1947.
113 TNA: MEPO 2/8218, Police Dogs for Patrolling Hyde Park, District Superintendent 1 to District Commander 1, 22 April 1947 and TNA: MEPO 2/6208, 486A, A.E. Young to the Under Secretary of State, 7 December 1949 and 423A, Police Dogs, undated.

physical structures.[114] The scheme continued to flourish in the early 1950s, so that by 1955, the Metropolitan Police relied upon some 150 canines throughout London.[115] Like the British Armed Forces, the Metropolitan Police also turned out drug and explosives detection dogs in the second half of the 20th century.[116] As of 2016, the Metropolitan Police employed approximately 250 "general purpose" and detection dogs attached to five Dog Support Units in the capital.[117]

Police dog training took place at the Metropolitan Police Mounted Branch Training Establishment in Surrey before the Metropolitan Police Dog Training Establishment in Kent was founded in 1954.[118] There is evidence that in the years following the Second World War, the Metropolitan Police sought to implement a training scheme modelled after that of the wartime Army's War Dogs Training School. Although the Metropolitan Police initially considered having the RAF Police Dog School conduct the training of its canines,[119] the District Commander of the district in which the dogs were to be employed preferred the instructional methods of the Army over those of the RAF. To this end, the Metropolitan Police hired Captain Godfrey Kent, a former Army's War Dogs Training School instructor, to oversee the instruction of police dogs for London.[120] The training of police dogs in London was similar to that of military dogs in the Second World War in a number of ways. Much emphasis was placed on the role of the humans involved, for example. The *Dog Section Handbook*, first published in 1965 as "an Instruction Book for all Metropolitan Police dog handlers," admonished: "A police dog can only be as efficient as its handler allows it to be!"[121] Much like training instructions from the interwar period and the Second World War, the handbook stressed the importance of repetition, association and positive

114 TNA: MEPO 2/6208, 498A, Arthur Young to S.J. Baker, 22 February 1950.
115 TNA: MEPO 2/6208, 509A, A.E. Young to District Commanders, 15 March 1950 and Hansard: HC Deb 7 July 1955 vol 543 cc113-4W.
116 TNA: MEPO 2/10508, 22A, Training and Use of Police Dogs for the Detection of Drugs and Explosives, E. Fletcher to Chief Superintendent, 15 February 1966 and 193B, D.R.W. Randall to J.R.F. Morris, 29 March 1972.
117 'History', online <http://content.met.police.uk/Article/History/1400009457612/1400009457612> (accessed 15 November 2016) and 'Dog Support Unit', online <http://content.met.police.uk/Article/Unit-structu re/1400009457903/1400009457903> (accessed 15 November 2016).
118 TNA: MEPO 2/6208, 309A, Report on the First Year's Training, 5 June 1947 and 'Successes in Use of Police Dogs', *The Times*, 17 June 1954, p. 4.
119 TNA: HO 45/21004, Assistant Commissioner, Metropolitan Police to Under Secretary of State, 29 April 1946.
120 TNA: MEPO 2/6208, 179A, District Commander, Metropolitan Police to Commissioners, 25 May 1946. The District Commander felt "the training given at [the War Dogs Training School] was very similar to that which [the Metropolitan Police] require."
121 TNA: MEPO 4/153, T.E. Mahir, Foreword to Chief Inspector J.A. Morphy, *Dog Section Handbook* (2nd ed), 1966.

reinforcement. Moreover, handlers were directed to "show patience and perseverance" and to "never resort to physical punishment."[122]

For the provincial police forces which had utilised dogs prior to the Second World War, the six year conflict disrupted the use of canines while also serving to encourage their employment in the post-war period. The breeding of dogs owned by the Lancashire Constabulary was disrupted by the war; by early 1946, police in Lancashire possessed just 11 canines. Nonetheless, the experience gained throughout the war, during which dogs attached to the Lancashire Constabulary protected wireless stations and located fugitive POWs, seems to have helped prompt their further employment in the years thereafter.[123] For a time after the Second World War, H.S. Lloyd assisted the Lancashire Constabulary by supplying the police with canines.[124]

Other police forces reinstituted or launched police dog schemes in the years following the Second World War. The Liverpool City Police, the Manchester City Police and the Newcastle-upon-Tyne City Police each introduced canines in the 1950s.[125] The employment of dogs by the Cheshire Constabulary, which began in the 1930s and was adversely affected by the war, also continued in the post-war period.[126] Throughout the 1950s and 1960s, police forces in close proximity to the Army's War Dog Training School in Melton Mowbray relied upon tracker dogs trained by the British Army.[127] By the early 1970s, seven police dog training facilities were in operation in England and Wales, and approximately 2,000 canines were employed by civil constabularies throughout the United Kingdom.[128] Appendix X shows the number of dogs instructed and employed by the British Armed Forces and civil police as of 1972.

122 TNA: MEPO 4/153, Morphy, *Dog Section Handbook*, pp. 2, 8–12.
123 TNA: MEPO 2/6208, 139A, A.F. Hordern to H.W. Stotesbury, 3 January 1946.
124 TNA: MEPO 2/6208, E154A, George DeChair to Sir Harold Scott, 21 February 1946. According to DeChair, it was doubtful the Lancashire Constabulary would continue to rely on Lloyd to instruct dogs or human personnel, as they felt his "motives [were] rather commercial than anything else."
125 'Alsatians on the Beat: Latest Recruits to City Police', *Manchester Guardian*, 26 May 1959, p. 3 and 'Police Dogs for City', *Guardian*, 10 December 1959, p. 14.
126 TNA: MEPO 2/6208, 139B, J. Becke to H.W. Stotesbury, 13 December 1945 and 'The Well-Bred Police Dog: Bites to Order', *Manchester Guardian*, 3 December 1958, p. 9.
127 'R.A.V.C. Training Centre and Depot, Melton Mowbray', *Journal of the RAVC*, 26:2 (1955), p. 51 and 'War Dog Training School', *Journal of the RAVC*, 27:3 (1956), p. 112 and 'Visit, C.I.G.S. to Melton Mowbray', *Journal of the RAVC*, 31:2 (1960), p. 59 and 'War Dog School', *Journal of the RAVC*, 31:3 (1960), p. 168 and 'War Dog Training School', *Journal of the RAVC*, 32:1 (1961), p. 56 and 'RAVC Training Centre and Depot', *Journal of the RAVC*, 35:1 (1964), p. 34.
128 TNA: WO 32/21774, E48, Minutes of a Meeting, 16 October 1972.

The Defence Animal Centre and the British Military Dog in the 21st Century

A combined British Army and RAF military dog training facility was considered as early as 1950, when the War Office approached the Air Ministry with an idea to develop "a joint dog establishment, to serve both the Services."[129] The idea remained under consideration for several years afterwards, but the British Army and the RAF were sceptical of the proposed union until the late 1980s. The situation was further complicated by the Army's instruction of equines, which also took place in Melton Mowbray. An offer by the RAF to form a combined animal training facility at adjacent airfields in the Midlands was rejected.[130] It was not until 1991 that a combined military dog training facility became reality with the creation of the Defence Animal Centre (DAC) in Melton Mowbray. From April 1991 onwards the DAC oversaw the recruitment, instruction and employment of canines held by the British Armed Forces in the United Kingdom and overseas. As it turned out, the Army did have superior status over the RAF following the creation of the DAC as a result of an earlier ruling on the matter by the Ministry of Defence. The roles of commandant and deputy commandant were filled by a British Army (RAVC) officer and an RAF officer, respectively, and Army horses remained on site.[131] By 1995, the same year in which the British Army's sole operational mounted unit was disbanded,[132] the DAC was turning out some 400 canines annually.[133]

In the second decade of the 21st century, the DAC remains committed, per its mission statement, to "deliver[ing] the required number of appropriately trained and highly motivated Military Working Animals and personnel in order to meet the requirements of Defence."[134] While the British Army continues to keep horses, they are used solely for ceremonial tasks. In the early 21st century, dogs are the only animals used by the British Armed Forces on military operations.[135] In 2014, the DAC's Canine Training Squadron turned out some 180 guard and detection dogs. In addition, more than 400 handlers and other personnel representing the British Army, the RAF, the Ministry of Defence Police and a number of foreign militaries

---

129 TNA: WO 32/14142, Minute, D.B.J. Darley, 2 November 1950.

130 Davies, *RAF Police Dogs on Patrol*, pp. 139, 207-213. According to Davies, scepticism stemmed from a fear shared by both the British Army and the RAF Police that the other would have more power if the proposed union became reality.

131 'The Director's View', *Chiron Calling*, June 1991, p. 5 and Lt. Col. PA Roffey, 'Defence Animal Centre', *Chiron Calling*, June 1991, p. 7.

132 'The Last Army Police Horses', *Chiron Calling*, Summer 1995, p. 3.

133 Major N.C. Smith, 'Services Veterinary Hospital', *Chiron Calling*, Summer 1995, p. 17.

134 *Defence Animal Centre Open Day* pamphlet, 7 June 2014, p. 3.

135 Hansard: HC Deb 7 June 2011 vol 529 c5W and HC Deb 10 January 2012 vol 538 cc9-10W. This figure is inclusive of dogs used by the Ministry of Defence Police. In 2011, the Royal Navy also possessed a small number of falcons likely used to discourage the presence of other animals on aircraft runways.

pass through the DAC each year.[136] Instructors at the DAC continue to utilise the "reward system" adopted by British military dog trainers in the Second World War. A pamphlet produced by the DAC for its 2014 Open Day explained: "The foundation of our training is the relationship with the dog, obedience, control of the dog and the reward of desired behaviour."[137]

At present, military dogs employed by the British Army are attached to 1st Military Working Dog Regiment. As of late 2016, the regiment, which includes between 200 and 384 canines, encompassed five Military Working Dog Squadrons stationed in Germany, Cyprus and the United Kingdom.[138] Owing in large part to the conflicts in Iraq and Afghanistan in the early 2000s, the number of military dogs maintained by the British Armed Forces and the MOD Police in the early 21st century has remained constant at between 900 and 1,175.[139] Beginning in 2003, 1st Military Working Dog Regiment supplied guard, patrol and detection dogs to Iraq and Afghanistan, where they were relied upon to defend military establishments, locate improvised explosive devices (IEDs), and perform vehicle searches.[140] In 2007, at the height of the war in Afghanistan, canines employed by 102 Military Working Dog Squadron daily inspected around 100 vehicles entering the military base Camp Bastion.[141]

As indicated in Appendix XI, the majority of British Army canines in the early 21st century are guard dogs, as was the case during the Second World War. However, in contrast to the Second World War and the immediate post-war period, detection dogs constitute a significant proportion of canines employed by the British Army in the early 21st century.[142] In March 2013, Mark Francois of the Ministry of Defence

136 *Defence Animal Centre Open Day* pamphlet, 7 June 2014, pp. 3-5, 14.
137 Ibid, p. 5.
138 '1st Military Working Dog Regiment', online <http://www.army.mod.uk/medical-services/veterinary/30499.aspx> (accessed 18 November 2016). The squadrons stationed overseas as of late 2016 were scheduled to relocate to the United Kingdom before 2018. When accessed in May 2013, the 1st Military Working Dog Regiment webpage on the British Army website maintained that the regiment possessed approximately 200 dogs. When accessed in November 2016, the webpage did not provide a precise figure but noted the regiment has "the ability to surge to a maximum capacity of 384 Military Working Dogs."
139 Hansard: HC Deb 6 March 2003 vol 400 c1154W and Hansard: HC Deb 22 March 2007 vol 458 c1033W and Hansard: HC Deb 16 October 2008 vol 480 c1393W and Hansard: HC Deb 15 June 2010 vol 511 c343W and Hansard: HC Deb 10 January 2012 vol cc9-10W.
140 '1st Military Working Dog Regiment', online <http://www.army.mod.uk/medical-services/veterinary/30499.aspx> (accessed 18 November 2016) and 'Military Working Dogs Deploy to Afghanistan', 12 March 2003, online <https://www.gov.uk/government/news/military-working-dogs-deploy-to-afghanistan> (accessed 18 November 2016).
141 Corporal Charlie Bates, '102 Military Working Dog Support Unit Op Herrick 7', *Chiron Calling*, Summer 2008, pp. 28-29.
142 Hansard: HC Deb 15 December 2008 vol 485 c330W. Approximately 43% of British Army dogs in late 2008 were trained in detection.

told the House of Commons: "Army detection dogs provide an important and valuable service" to the British Army. Reflecting on the use of trained dogs in Iraq and Afghanistan, Francois noted the "significant role" performed by dogs in the location of IEDs.[143]

The RAF Police have also continued to utilise military dogs in the 21st century, and like the British Army, posted military police and detection dogs to Iraq and Afghanistan in the early 2000s. In contrast to the Second World War, RAF Police dogs perform a number of roles in addition to that of the military police dog solely instructed to defend airfields and other installations. During the war in Afghanistan, RAF Police dogs were relied upon to locate IEDs, inspect vehicles and patrol airfields.[144] Nonetheless, most RAF Police dogs in the early 21st century are relied upon to augment the security of physical structures or locations rather than for detection. In 2008, for example, just 32 percent of the dogs attached to the RAF Police were utilised for detection.[145]

In addition to the British Army and the RAF Police, the MOD Police maintains some 200 canines, all of which are instructed at the DAC. While most dogs utilised by the MOD Police are considered "general purpose," others assist MOD Policemen in the location of explosives and drugs. The MOD Police also utilise "tactical firearms support" dogs to subdue perpetrators in particularly violent situations.[146] In addition to being posted to MOD establishments, such as Royal Navy bases, MOD Police dogs are called upon to assist other organisations, including the Home Office.[147]

143 Hansard: HC Deb 7 March 2013 vol 559 c1125W.
144 'From Crufts to Camp Bastion', 15 March 2010, online <http://www.raf.mod.uk/news/archive.cfm?storyid=61804C00-5056-A318-A8F38EF479E5D02C> (accessed 18 November 2016) and 'Wetnose Bravery Awards for RAF Police Dogs', 4 March 2010, online <http://www.raf.mod.uk/news/archive.cfm?storyid=2A2162D4-5056-A318-A856695A038E33E0> (accessed 24 November 2016).
145 Hansard: HC Deb 15 December 2008 vol 485 c330W. See Appendix XI.
146 'Dog Section', online <http://www.mod.police.uk/specialist/dog-section.html> (accessed 24 November 2016) and Ministry of Defence Guidance, 'MOD Police Specialist Units', 21 May 2014, online <https://www.gov.uk/government/publications/mod-police-specialist-units/mod-police-specialist-units> (accessed 24 November 2016).
147 'MOD Police Specialist Units', 21 May 2014, online <https://www.gov.uk/government/publications/mod-police-specialist-units/mod-police-specialist-units> (accessed 24 November 2016) and 'Ministry of Defence Police Top Dog Award', 29 July 2013, online <http://www.royalnavy.mod.uk/news-and-latest-activity/news/2013/july/29/130729-mod-police-top-dog-award> (accessed 24 November 2016).

Conclusions and Suggestions for Further Research

In his study of the Home Guard in the Second World War, S.P. MacKenzie rightly argued that "the Home Guard evolved from below more than it derived from higher authority." He also noted how, in the months following its inception, the Home Guard was characterised by "improvisation and *ad hoc* decision-making."[1] The same was true of the British military dog scheme of the Second World War. The Army's War Dog Training School, and particularly the MAP Guard Dog Training School, also "evolved from below" considering they came about in large part through the efforts of individuals, namely, Lloyd and Baldwin. Aided by urgent representations from Commanders-in-Chief, Home Forces, as well as reports of foreign militaries employing canines in northwest Europe, they were able to successfully lobby the British government to institute the British Army and the MAP schemes.

That the British Armed Forces came to utilise dogs in the Second World War may be explained by two primary considerations. First, the shortage of human personnel to defend airfields and other military installations in the early 1940s was in large part responsible for the implementation of the British Army and the MAP dog schemes and the employment of guard dogs on the British Home Front. The Army's War Dogs Training School and the MAP Guard Dog Training School came about at a point during the war in which the British Army, as the historian David French put it, "could not grow larger because the necessary manpower was not available."[2] A similar situation unfolded in the Middle East, where the CMP responded to a shortage in human personnel by employing military police dogs to protect War Department installations and *matériel*.

Second, the British Armed Forces and the London Civil Defence Region turned to canines in an effort to overcome the disadvantages involved in utilising human or technological means of locating mines and human casualties, respectively. The belief that dogs, owing to their olfactory ability, possessed advantages over both humans and technological apparatuses was the primary motivation behind their employment for mine detection in northwest Europe and as rescue dogs on the British Home Front. As mine detection dogs and Civil Defence rescue dogs were used in relatively

---

1   MacKenzie, *The Home Guard*, p. 52.
2   French, *Raising Churchill's Army*, p. 186.

small numbers, it was this consideration, not the shortage of human personnel, which prompted their employment.

Yet like other wartime organisations, including the Home Guard, the Army's War Dogs Training School and the MAP Guard Dog Training School adapted to specific circumstances brought about by the war. Just as the Home Guard took on varied responsibilities at different points during its five year run,[3] the history of the Army's War Dogs Training School unfolded in response to the perceived needs of the British Army. The school initially focused on turning out patrol dogs for use with the infantry. While guard dogs remained in demand throughout the Second World War, the British Army renounced the employment of patrol and messenger dogs towards the middle of the war and instead concentrated on turning out additional guard dogs. Around the same time, the use of landmines in North Africa prompted the training of mine detection dogs at the Army's War Dogs Training School. Similarly, the MAP Guard Dog Training School, although occupied throughout most of the war with turning out guard dogs, took on another responsibility late in the war when trainers commenced the instruction of rescue dogs for the London Civil Defence Region. This move was in response to the V1 attacks on the capital.

Dogs employed by the British Armed Forces and the London Civil Defence Region contributed to the British war effort in a number of ways during the Second World War. In doing so, they offered advantages over humans and technology. Yet canines were not used in isolation but employed along with humans and technological equipment. Guard and military police dogs were utilised in addition to human guards and military policemen. Similarly, mine detection dogs formed an ancillary means of mine detection utilised alongside humans wielding prodders and electronic detectors. On the Home Front, human rescue workers turned to the use of dogs in addition to other equipment, including sound location sets. Just as humans and technological equipment operated by humans possessed limitations, the use of military and Civil Defence dogs was not without problems.

The effective performance of military and Civil Defence dogs was often influenced by environmental or other factors beyond the control of dogs and their handlers. The effective employment of mine detection dogs, for example, was largely contingent on the depth at which mines were planted, as well as the amount of time which had elapsed between planting and discovery. Similarly, the performance of rescue dogs was impacted by inclement weather, smoke and other environmental factors. It should be recognised, however, that such unfavourable circumstances not only affected the performance of canines but that of human operators and rescue workers.

Furthermore, the performance of canines was dependent on the actions and behaviours of human trainers, handlers and other servicemen. Training instructions from the First and Second World Wars emphasised the importance of the role of humans in military dog operations, and a number of servicemen noted that the use of dogs

3   MacKenzie, *The Home Guard*, pp. 33-156.

influenced or affected their own thinking and behaviour. Although trainers, handlers and servicemen were discouraged from viewing or treating canines as companions so as not to negatively influence their performance, the perception of military and Civil Defence dogs among many British servicemen was that of compeer and pet. Such thinking was emphasised by the press during the war, as well as in the months surrounding the cessation of hostilities when canines were discharged from the British Armed Forces and the London Civil Defence Region. That many military dogs had to be reunited with their civilian owners at the end of the war both complicated the military dog scheme and influenced the way in which canines were obtained in the post-war period.

While the British Armed Forces utilised dogs in the First World War, a much larger force of British canines was assembled during the Second World War. The establishment of the Army's War Dogs Training School and the MAP Guard Dog Training School during the Second World War marked the onset of the permanent employment of military dogs by the British Armed Forces. In contrast to the interwar period, during which the War Office abandoned the use of military dogs and the training of canines was left to a small number of military and civilian trainers operating independently of the British Armed Forces, the immediate post-war period and the decades that followed saw the continued and extensive use of military dogs by the British Army and the RAF Police. It was the successful use of guard, military police and mine detection dogs during the war which spurred the employment of canines in the same or similar roles in the post-war period. Civil police in the United Kingdom, similarly encouraged by the use of military dogs, instituted or re-established the employment of canines in the years following the Second World War. In this way, the Second World War represented a turning point in the history of British military and police dogs.

In part, the continued employment of military dogs after the Second World War stemmed from opportunity. In contrast to the interwar years, during which the British military was primarily engaged in peacekeeping operations, the post-war period witnessed the decline of the British Empire and the conflicts in Palestine, Malaya, Kenya and Northern Ireland, thus providing ample opportunities for the employment of military dogs. The attempt by the British Armed Forces to maintain a crumbling empire and the numerous armed conflicts of the second half of the 20th century allowed for the unceasing use of military dogs in the post-war period. Yet opportunity alone would likely not have ensured roles for military dogs. Perhaps even more significant for the post-war future of British military dogs was the commitment to their use shown by the War Office and senior military officials, particularly in the years immediately following the Second World War. Such support was paramount, as it prevented the Army's War Dogs Training School and other British military dog training facilities from suffering the same fate as the War Dog School of the First World War.

As the first substantial academic study of the employment of British military dogs in the Second World War, this book provides a crucial analysis of an area of Second

World War history largely overlooked by both contemporary and modern day historians. It adds to the expanding historiography on the Second World War, a conflict characterised by many military historians as overwhelmingly technological. Yet even in a war which saw the use of jet aeroplanes, radar and the atomic bomb, canines were relied upon to supplement both technology and humans. This was particularly evident in the employment of mine detection and rescue dogs. While the significance of technology should not be underestimated in military histories of the Second World War, neither should the role of military dogs. It is hoped, therefore, that this study will not only encourage military historians to recognise the contributions of military dogs in the Second World War but to reconsider the ways in which humans, animals and technology intersected in order to meet the demands of war.

This study also contributes to the growing amount of historical scholarship on animals. It emphasises military dogs as historical actors, and in doing so, highlights their actual and perceived roles in the war. The discussion of the ways in which military dogs and pets on the British Home Front were "figuratively mobilized" by the British Armed Forces, dog owners and the press builds upon the works of Skabelund and Kean on dogs on the Japanese and British Home Fronts and allows for a greater understanding of the influence and pervasiveness of wartime propaganda and the perception of dogs prior to and during the Second World War. Furthermore, the analysis of the treatment and depiction of military dogs and pets and the blurred distinction between working animals and companions provides for a more nuanced understanding of British society at war and contemporary human-animal relations. The depiction of military and pet dogs reflected wider contemporary understandings of British society, such as the belief that Britons were uniquely compassionate towards animals and the idea that all Britons – even animals – were carrying out sacrifices to "do their bit" on the Home Front and in active theatres of war.

In showing that the Second World War was a turning point in the history of British military dogs, this study prompts further questions related to the use of dogs in the late 20th and early 21st centuries. Chapter 7 examined the use of canines by the British Armed Forces and civil police in the post-war period in order to evaluate the impact of the Second World War military dog scheme on the employment of British military and police dogs. Although the use of dogs in various roles during a number of conflicts in the second half of the 20th and early 21st centuries was considered, the examples provided do not constitute an exhaustive history of the post-war employment of military and police dogs but serve to highlight the work carried out by canines since the Second World War. Developments in the training and employment of military and civil police dogs in the late 20th and early 21st centuries thus demand greater attention from military historians.

This study also sheds light on the collaboration between the British and American military dog schemes during the Second World War. Like Britain, the United States Armed Forces retained its military dog scheme in the decades following the Second World War. In the early 1950s, the United States Army deployed scout (patrol) dogs to Korea, where they were attached to a unit raised during the Second World War.

Moreover, the United States Army and the United States Marine Corps utilised some 1,700 canines in guard, scout (patrol), tracker and detection roles during the Vietnam War.[4] The wars in Iraq around the turn of the 21st century and the ongoing war in Afghanistan have provided additional opportunities for American military dogs.[5]

The co-operation that developed between the British and the United States Armed Forces regarding the training and employment of military dogs during the Second World War also continued in the post-war period. In the latter half of the 20th century, the United States Air Force (USAF) relied upon the British Army's War Dogs Training School in Melton Mowbray and the RAF Police Dog Training School to instruct dogs and servicemen deployed to the United Kingdom. Moreover, the USAF in the United Kingdom was for a time dependent on the British for canines, which the RAF Police Dog Training School supplied on a temporary basis.[6] The United States was similarly aided by the British in the Vietnam War, during which American military dog handlers were trained by the British Army in Malaya.[7] The extent and significance of co-operation between the British and American military dog schemes in the second half of the 20th century also deserves further study. It is hoped, therefore, that this study serves not only to draw attention to a previously neglected area of Second World War scholarship but to stimulate future research on the subject of British and American military and police dogs.

4   Headquarters, Department of the Army, *Field Manual 20-20*, pp. 4-5.
5   Headquarters, Department of the Army, *Field Manual 3-19.17, Military Working Dogs* (Washington, D.C., 2005), pp. 1-2, online <https://archive.org/details/FM_3-19.17_Military_Working_Dogs> (accessed 5 November 2013).
6   'R.A.V.C. Training Centre and Depot, Melton Mowbray', *Journal of the RAVC*, 26:2 (1955), p. 51 and RAF Museum: R016420, *Royal Air Force Police Dogs* and Davies, *RAF Police Dogs on Patrol*, pp. 73, 125.
7   Lt. Col. P.A. Roffey, Editorial, *Chiron Calling*, Summer 2000, p. 1 and Major R.G. Mares, 'Some Aspects of the Use of Dogs in the Far East', *Chiron Calling*, Winter 2000/2001, p. 25.

Appendix I

Soviet "Explosive Dogs"

In Britain, the National Anti-Vivisection Society spoke out against the employment of "suicide dogs" by the Red Army. The August 1942 edition of the *Animals'
Defender* asserted: "Any normally sensitive conscience must be revolted by this practice of training faithful and innocent creatures to go unwittingly to their deaths."[1] In
the 1947 publication *Animals Were There*, the authors Arthur W. Moss and Elizabeth
Kirby dismissed altogether the existence of such dogs as "enemy propaganda... put
out [by the Germans] to help divide the Allies."[2] However, that "explosive dogs"
were utilised by the Soviet Union during the war was acknowledged by a number of
contemporary military and press reports and perpetuated by historians and authors
during and after the war.[3] The War Office also referred to the employment of such
dogs in the 1952 and 1962 editions of the British Army training manual *Training of
War Dogs*.[4] Thus, it seems likely that the Soviet military did utilise dogs to immobilise
German tanks and other vehicles, or at least the War Office genuinely believed in
their existence. Yet the extent to which Soviet "explosive dogs" were effective against
enemy forces is open to debate. The historian Juliet Gardiner has cast doubt on the

---

1   'Suicide Dogs', *Animals' Defender*, August 1942, p. 13.
2   Moss and Kirby, *Animals Were There*, p. 130.
3   In addition to the aforementioned articles in the *New York Times* (see Chapter 2) and
     Animals' Defender (above) and the aforementioned United States Army report (see
     Chapter 2), other contemporary sources referred to the employment of such dogs. See, for
     example: Going, *Dogs at War*, pp. 168-169 and Charles F. Prudames, 'Soviet Trains Dogs
     to Destroy Tanks', *Our Dogs*, 24 November 1941, p. 1092 and Major J.H. Wilkins, 'Dogs
     in the Modern Army', *Journal of the RAVC*, 26:3 (1955), p. 89. More recent sources which
     mention such dogs include: Lemish, *War Dogs*, p. xi and Gardiner, *Animals' War*, p. 113 and
     Skabelund, *Empire of Dogs*, p. 138 and 'Did You Know?: Anti-Tank Dog', *Chiron Calling*,
     May 1988, p. 25 and Cummins, *Colonel Richardson's Airedales*, p. 156 and Hamer, *Dogs
     at War*, pp. 59-60 and Mary Elizabeth Thurston, *The Lost History of the Canine Race: Our
     15,000-Year Love Affair with Dogs* (Kansas City: Andrews Mcmeel, 1996), p. 188.
4   War Office, *Training of War Dogs* (1952), p. 2 and War Office, *Training of War Dogs* (1962),
     p. 2.

usefulness of such dogs, noting their tendency on operations to race towards Soviet, as opposed to German, tanks.[5]

While the *Animals' Defender* article was undoubtedly clear in its condemnation of the Soviet tactic, it is less clear what purpose the *New York Times* article served. If it was indeed intended as propaganda, it was seemingly not, as Moss and Kirby alleged, aimed to turn civilians of the Allied nations against the Soviet Union. The tactic of utilising canines to "attack German tanks and destroy them" was presented by its author, the well-known war correspondent Ilya Ehrenburg, in a *positive* light. It seems that it was intended to sway the perception of British and American civilians so that they held the Soviet Army in greater esteem. At no point in the article did Ehrenburg provide commentary on the ethics of relying upon canines "to blow up tanks," nor did he present the tactic as an inhumane or desperate exercise. On the contrary, the dogs referenced by Ehrenburg were depicted as gallant animals widely feared by the German Army on the Eastern Front ("Mere barking said to have checked one Nazi unit"). In addition to describing the actions of such dogs, Ehrenburg drew attention to the Soviet employment of rescue, draught and patrol dogs which "have saved thousands upon thousands of lives on the Russian front."[6] Perhaps equally telling, Ehrenburg's article was published at a point during the war when support for the Soviet Union from the British and American press and civilians in both nations was particularly resolute.[7] This supports the idea that if the *New York Times* intended the article to serve as propaganda, it was certainly not meant to be anti-Soviet.

---

5   Gardiner, *Animals' War*, p. 113. According to Gardiner: "Since the dogs had been fed under Soviet tanks [during training], when they encountered the real thing at the front, instead of making for the German tanks, they rushed for the Soviet ones." Similar arguments were made by Cummins in *Colonel Richardson's Airedales* (p. 156) and Hamer in *Dogs at War* (pp. 59-60).

6   Ehrenburg, 'Soviet Using Dogs to Blow Up Tanks', *New York Times*, 24 June 1942, p. 7.

7   P.M.H. Bell, *John Bull and the Bear: British Public Opinion, Foreign Policy and the Soviet Union 1941-1945* (London: Edward Arnold, 1991), pp. 61-77 and Charles C. Alexander, 'The United States: The Good War?', 297-298 and Mikhail N. Narinsky, Lydia V. Pozdeeva, et al., 'Mutual Perceptions: Images, Ideals, and Illusions', pp. 314-320 in David Reynolds, Warren F. Kimball, and A.O. Chubarian (eds.), *Allies at War: The Soviet, American, and British Experience, 1939-1945* (Basingstoke: Macmillan, 1994).

Appendix II

War Establishment of the British Army's War Dogs Training School, June 1944[1]

Human Personnel	Headquarters and Training Wing	Holding Wing	Total, WDTS
Commandant	1		1
Chief Instructor and Tactical Liaison Officer	1		1
Major (RAVC)		1	1
Captain or Lieutenant (RAVC)		1	1
Instructor	1		1
Trainer	1		1
Adjutant and Quartermaster	1		1
Warrant Officer (RAVC)		1	1
Company Quartermaster-Sergeant	1		1
Clerks	1	1	2
Duty Sergeant	1		1
Instructors	4		4
Kennelman		1	1
Trainers	5		5
Sergeant (RE) (for explosives)	1		1
Sergeant (for battle inoculation)	1		1
Battle Inoculation Personnel	4		4
Butchery Dutymen	3		3
Batmen	3		3
Clerks		2	2
Carpenter and Joiner	1		1

1   TNA: WO 32/10800, 24A, War Dogs Training School Home War Establishment, 20 June 1944.

Human Personnel	Headquarters and Training Wing	Holding Wing	Total, WDTS
Dispenser (RAVC)		1	1
Dressers (RAVC)		6	6
General Dutymen	3		3
Kennelmen		32	32
Regimental Police	3		3
Ration Corporal	1		1
Storemen	1	1	2
Sanitary Dutymen	2		2
Trainers	70		70
Telephone Orderly	1		1
Clerks (ATS)	4		4
Kennel Orderlies (ATS)	40		40
Storewomen (ATS)	2		2
Telephone Orderly (ATS)	1		1
Head Trainer	1		1
Officers Under Instruction	2		2
Privates Under Instruction	24		24
Animals			
Dogs	450	300	750

Appendix III

Canine Dickin Medal Recipients[1]

Name	Breed	Year Awarded	Citation
Bob	Mongrel	1944	"For constant devotion to duty with special mention of Patrol work at Green Hill, North Africa, while serving with the 6th Battalion Queen's Own Royal West Kent Regiment."
Jet	Alsatian	1945	"For being responsible for the rescue of persons trapped under blitzed buildings while serving with the Civil Defence Services of London."
Irma	Alsatian	1945	"For being responsible for the rescue of persons trapped under blitzed buildings while serving with the Civil Defences of London."
Beauty	Wire-Haired Terrier	1945	"For being the pioneer dog in locating buried air-raid victims while serving with a PDSA Rescue Squad."
Rob	Collie	1945	"Took part in landings during the North African Campaign with an Infantry unit and later served with a Special Air Unit in Italy as patrol and guard on small detachments lying-up in enemy territory. His presence with these parties saved many of them from discovery and subsequent capture or destruction. Rob made over 20 parachute descents."
Thorn	Alsatian	1945	"For locating air-raid casualties in spite of thick smoke in a burning building."

1   'PDSA Dickin Medal', <https://www.pdsa.org.uk/what-we-do/animal-awards-programme/pdsa-dickin-medal> (accessed 29 January 2018). This appendix is limited to those dogs decorated for work carried out during the Second World War. Through its website, the PDSA maintains a complete list of all Dickin Medal recipients.

Name	Breed	Year Awarded	Citation
Rifleman Khan	Alsatian	1945	"For rescuing L/Cpl. Muldoon from drowning under heavy shell fire at the assault of Walcheren, November 1944, while serving with the 6th Cameronians (SR)."
Rex	Alsatian	1945	"For outstanding good work in the location of casualties in burning buildings. Undaunted by smouldering debris, thick smoke, intense heat and jets of water from fire hoses, this dog displayed uncanny intelligence and outstanding determination in his efforts to follow up any scent which led him to a trapped casualty."
Sheila	Collie	1945	"For assisting in the rescue of four American Airmen lost on the Cheviots in a blizzard after an air crash in December, 1944."
Rip	Mongrel	1945	"For locating many air-raid victims during the blitz of 1940."
Peter	Collie	1945	"For locating victims trapped under blitzed buildings while serving with the MAP attached to Civil Defence of London."
Judy	Pointer	1946	"For magnificent courage and endurance in Japanese prison camps, which helped to maintain morale among her fellow prisoners and also for saving many lives through her intelligence and watchfulness."
Ricky	Welsh Collie	1947	"This dog was engaged in cleaning (sic) the verges of the canal bank at Nederweent, Holland. He found all the mines but during the operation one of them exploded. Ricky was wounded in the head but remained calm and kept at work. Had he become excited he would have been a danger to the rest of the section working nearby."
Brian	Alsatian	1947	"This patrol dog was attached to a Parachute Battalion of the 13th Battalion Airborne Division. He landed in Normandy with them and, having done the requisite number of jumps, became a fully qualified Paratrooper."
Antis	Alsatian	1949	"Owned by a Czech airman, this dog served with him in the French Air Force and RAF from 1940 to 1945, both in N[orth] Africa and England. Returning to Czechoslovakia after the war, he substantially helped his master's escape across the frontier when after the death of Jan Masaryk, he had to fly (sic) from the Communists."

Name	Breed	Year Awarded	Citation
Tich	Mongrel	1949	"For loyalty, courage and devotion to duty under hazardous conditions of war 1941 to 1945, while serving with the 1st King's Rifle Corps in North Africa and Italy."
Gander	Newfoundland	2000	"For saving the lives of Canadian infantrymen during the Battle of Lye Mun on Hong Kong Island in December 1941. On three documented occasions Gander, the Newfoundland mascot of the Royal Rifles of Canada engaged the enemy as his regiment joined the Winnipeg Grenadiers, members of Battalion Headquarters 'C' Force and other Commonwealth troops in their courageous defence of the Island. Twice Gander's attacks halted the enemy's advance and protected groups of wounded soldiers. In a final act of bravery the war dog was killed in action gathering a grenade. Without Gander's intervention many more lives would have been lost in the assault."
Chips	Husky Crossbreed	2018	"For bravery and devotion to duty during the US Army's invasion of Sicily on 10 July 1943."

Appendix IV

Results of Mine Detection Dog Demonstration, Obstacle Assault Centre (OAC), 16 December 1943[1]

	Dogs	Human Operator with Electronic Detector
Exercise 1		
Total mines to find: 8		
Mines Found	6 (75%)	4 (50%)
Time in minutes/seconds	22:15	22:15
Exercise 2		
Total mines to find: 3		
Mines Found	3 (100%)	3 (100%)
Time in minutes/seconds	12:30	11:30
Exercise 3		
Total mines to find: 10		
Mines Found	9 (90%)	4 (40%)
Time in minutes/seconds	32:30	22:30

1   TNA: WO 203/3126, Report on Trials held at O.A.C., 16 December 1943.

Appendix V

Results of Mine Detection Dog Demonstration, 24 March 1944[1]

	Dogs	Human Operator with Electronic Detector
Exercise 1		
Total mines to find: 12		
Mines Found	9 (75%)	–
Time in minutes/seconds	29.30	–
Exercise 2		
Total mines to find: 14		
Mines Found	12 (85%)	–
Time in minutes/seconds	2:14:50	–
Exercise 3		
Total mines to find: 10		
Mines Found	8 (66%)	–
Time in minutes/seconds	25:00	–
Exercise 4		
Total mines to find: 15		
Mines Found	14 (93%)	11 (73%)
Time in minutes/seconds	29:00	32:30
Exercise 5		
Total mines to find: 4		
Mines Found	2 (50%)	–
Time in minutes/seconds	19:00	–

1   TNA: WO 203/3126, Programme of Mine Detection by War Dogs at Claycart Bottom, 24 March 1944.

	Dogs	Human Operator with Electronic Detector
Exercise 6		
Total mines to find: 4		
Mines Found	4 (80%)	–
Time in minutes/seconds	13:00	–

Appendix VI

War Establishment of the British Army's Mine Detection Dog Platoons, May 1944[1]

Human Personnel

Subaltern	1
Sergeant	1
Corporals (Dog Teams)	3
Handlers	10
Batman-Driver	1
Drivers of Vehicles	3
Kennelmen	2
Attached:	
Sergeant (RAVC)	1
Cook (Army Catering Corps)	1

Animals

Dogs	30

1   NAA: MP742/1, 240/6324, Appendix D, A Dog Platoon, R.E. War Establishment, 10 May 1944.

Appendix VII

Letter to Dog Owners from the Officer Commanding, British Army's War Dogs Training School[1]

APPENDIX 'B'

PLEASE READ CAREFULLY

INSTRUCTIONS AND CONDITIONS FOR LOANING DOGS
FOR WAR PURPOSES

It is much appreciated that you are prepared to loan your dog for the duration of the present emergency.

The following conditions are forwarded for your information and instruction:-

(a) THE DOG MUST BE RAILED NOT LESS THAN 10 DAYS AFTER THE RECEIPT OF THIS LETTER.

(b) Collar, lead, muzzle and railway warrant are herewith enclosed. Great care should be exercised in fixing the collar tight enough to avoid slipping. Name of dog and full particulars to be written in block letters on the back of the attached label.
IF FOR ANY REASON YOU CANNOT SEND YOUR DOG, COLLAR, CHAIN MUZZLE AND RAILWAY WARRANT MUST BE RETURNED.

(c) It must be clearly understood that on arrival at the School the dog will be subjected to a Veterinary and preliminary training test. Should he fail in either or both of these he will be returned to you and no other disposal instructions can be entertained unless received in writing, coinciding with the dog's arrival. Should he fail in the more advanced training the same procedure will be adopted.
If your dog fulfills all the necessary requirements it will be enlisted for the duration of the present emergency or as long as his services are needed.

(d) Every care will be given to your dog. Should he become a casualty you will be informed, but no responsibility will be accepted for loss or accident which may be incurred during the persuance of his service.

(e) PLEASE NOTIFY THE SCHOOL OF YOUR CHANGE OF ADDRESS.

(f) If there is any information regarding previous illness or anything appertaining to veterinary attendance it should be reported by letter.

(Sgd)
Major, R.A.V.C.
Officer Commanding,
War Dogs Training School,
(Holding Wing).

Northaw,
nr. Potters Bar,
Middlesex.
B.Y.

1 NAA: MP742/1, 240/6/324. A copy of this letter, sent to owners who provided their pets to the British Army's War Dogs Training School, was given to Australian Army officers when touring the facility in late 1944. Note the ambiguous language used in paragraph (c).

Appendix VIII

Military Dogs Released from Service in BAOR, 1946-1950[1]

Reason for Release	1946*	1947	1948	1949	1950**	Total
Died/Euthanised	41	56***	66	52	30	245
Missing	5	4	7	8	1	25
Sold	11	8	23	16	0	58
Restored to Owners	79	15	4	2	0	100

*July-December 1946

**January-March 1950

*** This figure includes canines listed as "cast and destroyed" and "killed" in addition to those listed as "died or destroyed."

1 TNA: WO 267/587, Veterinary and Remount Services Quarterly Historical Reports, 30 September 1946 and 31 December 1946 and TNA: WO 267/588, Veterinary and Remount Services Quarterly Historical Reports, 31 March 1947, 30 June 1947, 30 September 1947 and 31 December 1947 and TNA: WO 267/589, Veterinary and Remount Services Quarterly Historical Reports, 31 March 1948, 30 June 1948, 30 September 1948 and 31 December 1948 and TNA: WO 267/590, Veterinary and Remount Services Quarterly Historical Reports, 31 March 1949, 30 June 1949, 30 September 1949 and 31 December 1949 and TNA: WO 267/591, Veterinary and Remount Services Quarterly Historical Report, 31 March 1950. The corresponding records for January-June 1946 and April 1950 onwards are not available in the National Archives. As this appendix pertains to dogs released from military service, the figures above do not include military dogs posted to other commands.

Appendix IX

British Army Dog Training, 1949-1950[1]

Training Facility and Location	Theatre of Operations	Total Number of Trained Dogs
War Dogs Training School, Melton Mowbray, Leicestershire	United Kingdom	40
War Dogs Training Wing, West Germany	British Army of the Rhine (BAOR)	116
War Dog Training Wing, Egypt	Middle East Land Forces (MELF)	123
Army Guard Dog Unit, Singapore Army Guard Dog Unit, Hong Kong	Far East Land Forces (FARELF)	39
No. 5 Guard Dog Unit, Austria	British Troops in Austria (BTA)	10

1   TNA: WO 32/14142, 40A, Appendix B, Military and Civilian Manpower for Training and Employment of War Dogs and Appendix C, Training of War Dogs at V&R Units, 1949-1950.

Appendix X

Military and Civil Police Dog Training in the United Kingdom, 1972[1]

Training Facility/Organisation	Approximate Number of Dogs Trained Annually	Number of Dogs Already Employed
Military		
British Army, RAVC Training Centre, Melton Mowbray	200	650*
RAF Police, RAF Police Depot, Debden	200-250	–
Civil Police		
Metropolitan Police (London)		
Durham		
Lancashire		
Nottingham	500	2,000
South Wales		
Staffordshire		
Surrey		

*This figure includes dogs instructed at the RAVC Training Centre but employed by the MOD Police.

1 TNA: WO 32/21774, E48, Minutes of a Meeting, 16 October 1972. The total number of dogs employed by the RAF as of 1972 was not available.

Appendix XI

British Army and RAF Dogs by Role, 2008[1]

Role	British Army	RAF	Total Number of Dogs
Patrol (Guard)*	82	180	262
Infantry Patrol	2	0	2
Tracker	10	0	10
Army/RAF Police**	0	18	18
Arms and Explosive Search	50	36	86
Vehicle Search	20	40	60
Drug Detection	1	18	19

*Although the Parliamentary Under-Secretary of State referred to "patrol dogs" rather than guard dogs, it is clear he meant dogs utilised to protect military installations, as he cited separate figures for "infantry patrol" dogs.

**It is unclear what the Parliamentary Under-Secretary of State meant by "Army/RAF Police" dogs, although he may have been referring to canines instructed in a dual guard/detection role.

1   Hansard: HC Deb 15 December 2008 vol 485 c330W. For similar, although less detailed figures for later years, see: Hansard: HC Deb 15 June 2010 vol 511 c343W and Hansard: HC Deb 10 January 2012 vol cc9-10W.

A Note on Sources

It must be recognised that many records related to the employment of military and Civil Defence dogs in the First and Second World Wars were produced by military dog trainers and handlers. While these records constitute valuable first-hand accounts from those who most often managed and interacted with military and Civil Defence dogs during the war, they unfortunately offer an incomplete picture of their use on operations. It is likely that, when compiling reports on their animals, military dog handlers sought to influence or persuade others as to the usefulness of dogs by high-lighting or exaggerating their positive contributions while downplaying the problems associated with their employment. This is especially evident in the accounts of guard, sentry and messenger dogs collated by Richardson, as well as those of rescue dog handlers in the Second World War. Along with an account by the commandant of the Messenger Dog Service held by the Imperial War Museum,[1] the accounts provided by Richardson form the bulk of primary source material related to the employment of military dogs in the First World War. Reports and correspondence from handlers and other servicemen were not, it seems, collated and maintained by the War Office but sent directly to Richardson, who presented them verbatim in *British War Dogs* and *Forty Years with Dogs*. In analysing the performance of military dogs in the First World War, it must be recognised that Richardson may have omitted negative feedback in an effort to shape his legacy and that of British military dogs. In an effort to counteract such bias, this study relied upon accounts from multiple sources whenever possible. These included reports from servicemen or civilians who witnessed the performance of dogs but were not attached to military or Civil Defence dog units (e.g. members of RE units) and military or civilian leaders (e.g. ARP officials).

As with any history of the Second World War, it is likely that some records related to the use of military and Civil Defence dogs have not survived. It is clear from archival records that the Army's War Dogs Training School produced records pertaining to individual military dogs during the war. Brigadier C.A. Murray, who served as DAVRS until 1943,[2] noted the existence of registration cards distributed

---

1   IWM: 69/75/1, Waley, Messenger Dog Service.
2   Clabby, *History of the RAVC*, p. 225.

by the RSPCA and completed by owners prior to their dogs entering the school.[3] Writing for the RSPCA publication *Animal World* in 1944, Murray informed readers that "careful records are kept of all dogs and their movements, both at home and overseas."[4] According to an Australian officer who toured the school in late 1944, RAVC personnel at the school's Holding Wing were charged with the "compilation and maintenance of records for all dogs" at the facility.[5] Unfortunately, these records seem to have been destroyed or are otherwise no longer in existence.

Lastly, it should be noted that newspapers, magazines and periodicals, particularly those published during wartime, are not unbiased sources and are not treated as such in this study. In addition to delivering information related to contemporary events, the media served as a means of promoting and disseminating propaganda. Reports on the use, perception and treatment of military and non-military dogs by foreign nations, for example, were often clearly intended to sway the British perception of enemy combatants. The treatment of British military dogs, as well as canine pets on the Home Front, was portrayed by the media as more humane than that extended by Germany. Without sufficient archival material on foreign military dog schemes of the First and Second World Wars, this study must rely on contemporary publications, newspapers and periodicals to gain a better understanding of the ways in which foreign militaries utilised canines. It should be kept in mind, however, that the veracity of the figures related to the employment of foreign military dogs in contemporary newspapers and periodicals cannot be ascertained. It is likely that such figures were either estimates made on the part of the Allied press or were exaggerated totals provided by the enemy in a deliberate attempt to deceive the Allied powers.

3   Brig.-Gen. Murray, 'War Dogs', *Animal World*, August 1944, pp. 60-61.
4   Murray, 'War Dogs', *Animal World*, September 1944, p. 69.
5   NAA: MP742/1, 240/6324, Appendix B, Capt. H.O. Bamford, Training of War Dogs, 3 January 1945.

Bibliography

UNPUBLISHED MATERIALS

Archival Sources

1. Official Papers
Airborne Assault Museum Archive, Duxford
Shelf 3F4, Box 4/9/1, Private J. Barringer

Essex Record Office (ERO), Chelmsford
Essex County Council Records
C/W 2/10, Use of Dogs, Rescue Service Group 7

London Metropolitan Archives (LMA), London
London County Council Records
LCC/CL/CD/03/022, London Civil Defence Region–Operations Circulars

National Archives of Australia (NAA), Melbourne, Australia
General and Civil Staff Correspondence Files and Army Personnel Files
MP742/1,240/6324, Training of Dogs for Use in War and 1 Australian Dog Platoon
    Royal Australian Engineers

The National Archives (TNA), Kew
Admiralty Records (ADM)
ADM 1/20854, Quarantine (82): Importation of Dogs into Great Britain

Air Ministry Records (AIR)
AIR 1/619/16/15/354, Watch Dogs for R.A.F. Stations, Ireland
AIR 2/80, Provision of Watch Dogs for Aerodromes and Policy Re: Use of Watch
    Dogs for Aerodromes
AIR 2/8734, Training of Police as Dog Handlers
AIR 23/6002, R.A.F. Police Dogs: Administration Policy

War Cabinet Records (CAB)
CAB 112/1, Protection of Vulnerable Points, History
CAB 112/26, Extracts and Copies of Chiefs of Staff Committee Memoranda on Vulnerable Points

Ministry of Defence Records (DEFE)
DEFE 2/1060, Obstacle Assault Centre: Progress Reports and Summaries
DEFE 70/61, Animals: Use of Dogs in Northern Ireland

Home Office Records (HO)
HO 45/21004, Police: Committee on Training of Police Dogs
HO 186/2572, Rescue Services: Electric Detector Apparatus and Dogs for Locating Trapped Air Raid Casualties
HO 186/2671, Rescue Services: Dogs Used by Rescue Parties to Locate Buried Casualties
HO 186/2955, Regional Organisation: History of Civil Defence, No. 5 London Region
HO 207/166, Region No. 5 (London): Equipment and Stores and Rescue Services: Rescue Parties: Provision of Sound Detecting Apparatus
HO 207/186, Region No. 5 (London): Rescue Services: Miscellaneous Papers

Metropolitan Police Records (MEPO)
MEPO 2/6208, Introduction and Development of Police Dog Scheme
MEPO 2/8218, Police Dogs for Patrolling Hyde Park
MEPO 2/10508, Training and Use of Police Dogs for the Detection of Drugs and Explosives
MEPO 4/153, Dog Section Handbook

Ministry of Aircraft Production Records (AVIA)
AVIA 9/15, Use of Dogs for Factory and Aerodrome Defence
AVIA 22/861, Mine Detectors: Research and Development
AVIA 22/862, Mine Detectors: Research and Development
AVIA 22/871, Detection of Mines by Dogs
AVIA 74/15, UHF Mine Detector for Non-Metallic Mines

War Office Records (WO)
WO 32/10504, General and Warlike Stores: General Weapons Policy Committee
WO 32/10800, War Dogs: General: Provision of War Dogs
WO 32/11100, Tradesmen: General: Trade Test for Dog Handlers
WO 32/14142, Guard Duties: War Dogs
WO 32/14999, War Dogs: Awards of Royal Society for the Prevention of Cruelty to Animals
WO 32/21774, Explosive Detection by Dogs

WO 32/21878, Explosives Detection by Dogs: Military Use of Dogs in Northern Ireland

WO 95/123/7, General Headquarters Troops: Carrier Pigeon Service Messenger Dog Service

WO 163/183, Organization and Weapons Policy Committee

WO 169/13320, Military Police Dog Training School

WO 169/13321, 1 Police Dog Section, 1943

WO 169/13322, 2 Police Dog Section, 1943

WO 169/13323, 3 Police Dog Section, 1943

WO 169/13324, 4 Police Dog Section, 1943

WO 169/13325, 5 Police Dog Section, 1943

WO 169/17751, 1 Dog Section, 1944

WO 169/17753, 3 Dog Section, 1944

WO 169/17754, 4 Dog Section, 1944

WO 169/17755, 5 Dog Section, 1944

WO 169/17757, Military Dog Training School, 1944

WO 169/19439, MP Dog Section, 1944

WO 169/21379, Dog Training School, 1945

WO 169/21383, 3 Dog Section, 1945

WO 169/24100, 1 Dog Section, 1946

WO 169/24101, 2 Dog Section, 1946

WO 169/24102, 3 Dog Section, 1946

WO 169/24103, 4 Dog Section, 1946

WO 169/24104, 5 Dog Section, 1946

WO 170/3604, Dog Sections: 51 Police Dog Section, 1944

WO 170/3605, Dog Sections: 'A' Police Dog Training Establishment, 1944

WO 170/3606, Dog Sections: 'B' Police Dog Company, 1944

WO 170/7032, Provost Companies: 'B' Dog Company, 1945

WO 171/191B, Veterinary and Remount Services, 1944

WO 171/1824, 2 Platoon, 1944

WO 171/1825, 4 Platoon, 1944

WO 171/3937, Veterinary and Remount, 1945

WO 171/5376, 1 Platoon, 1945

WO 171/5377, 2 Platoon, 1945

WO 171/5378, 4 Platoon, 1945

WO 199/416, Employment of Dogs with Guards at Vulnerable Points

WO 199/2061, War Dog Section: Formation in Southern Command

WO 199/2168, Corps of Military Police (V.P.)

WO 199/2537, Employment of Guard Dogs

WO 203/3126, Mine Detection Methods

WO 204/7732, Military Police Dog Units Organisation: Correspondence

WO 205/1173, Mine Detection by Dogs

WO 205/1186, Mine Clearance in the Netherlands

WO 208/1337, Signals: Messenger Dog Units
WO 232/85, Minefield Clearance
WO 267/587, British Army of the Rhine: Quarterly Historical Reports, Veterinary and Remount Services
WO 267/588, British Army of the Rhine: Quarterly Historical Reports, Veterinary and Remount Services
WO 267/589, British Army of the Rhine: Quarterly Historical Reports, Veterinary and Remount Services
WO 267/590, British Army of the Rhine: Quarterly Historical Reports, Veterinary and Remount Services
WO 267/591, British Army of the Rhine: Quarterly Historical Reports, Veterinary and Remount Services
WO 276/89, War Dogs: Distribution and Employment
WO 291/1048, Detection of Mines by Dogs
WO 291/2673, Outlines of Training of Various Types of War Dogs at the War Dogs Training School, British Army of the Rhine (BAOR) Training Centre
WO 305/1476, 5 Dog Company Singapore
WO 305/1479, 6 Guard Dog Unit

National Archives and Record Administration (NARA), College Park, Maryland, USA
Office of the Quartermaster General Records (RG 92)
General Records, 1942-1947
United States Marine Corps Records (RG 127)
Correspondence Files of the Office of the Commandant and Headquarters Support Division Central Files Section, 1939-50
Reports, Studies, and Plans Relating to World War II Military Operations, 1918-56
War Department General and Special Staffs Records (RG 165)
General Records, Office of the Director of Service, Supply, and Procurement, G-4
War Department Special Staff Public Relations Division Branches–News Branch
Adjutant General's Office Records (RG 407)
Central Decimal Correspondence Files, 1940-1945
Departmental Records Branch Reference Collection
Historical Documents of World War II – Microfilm Rolls 3032, 3033, 3034

2. Private Collections
Museum of Military Medicine, Aldershot
Box 14, File of Captain James Rankin Davison, including Reports on No. 2 Dog Platoon
Box 14, Reports and Correspondence between UK and USA on Training and Trials of Use of Dogs as Mine Detectors
Box 14, War Diary of DAVRS, September-October 1939, June 1941-June 1946

Box 14, War Diary, No. 2 Dog Platoon, Monthly Reports, August 1944-October 1945

Box 26, Lecture Notes, 'Employment of Dogs for Military Purposes' by Lieutenant Colonel J. Bleby, RAVC, 15 March 1989

British Institute of Public Opinion (BIPO)
Survey #53
Survey #126

Imperial War Museum (IWM), London
06/26/1, Private Papers of Miss E Cox
07/45/1, Private Papers of A. Knight, *Peter VC 1941-1952*
62/346/1, Private Papers of Captain B N Gaunt
69/75/1, Private Papers of Major A S Waley
94/1219, S.M. Hunt, 'A Brief Look into the Life of the War Dogs Training School, 1941-1946' (3 scrapbooks)
EPH 171, *Instructions for the Use of Messenger Dogs in the Field* (Army Printing and Stationery Services, April 1918)
Misc 162 (2490), Letter Reporting Dog Has Been Killed in Action
Misc 164 (2529), Certificate Recording the Service of an RAF Patrol Dog, Second World War
Misc 289 (3861), Papers Relating to the Second World War Rescue Dog, 'Rex'

Mass Observation Archive, University of Sussex
File Report 804, Dogs in London (Pilot Survey)
File Report 838, Provincial Dogs (Second Survey)
File Report 2256, Report on Dogs and Dog-Health in Wartime
File Report 651, Questions Uppermost in the Public Mind
File Report 2121, A Survey on the Pilotless Planes

National Army Museum (NAM), London
Archives 1987-06-23, War Dog Certificate Awarded to 'Binks' and Letter from Director, Army Veterinary and Remount Services to Mrs Theobald
Archives 2005-05-53, Eric Griffin to Alastair Massie, 5 July 2000

Nuffield College Library, University of Oxford
CSAC 80/4/81, Papers of F.A. Lindemann, Viscount Cherwell of Oxford

Royal Air Force Museum, London
007253, *Royal Air Force Police Dog Training*, May 1974
R016420, Royal Air Force Police Dogs, undated

Royal Society for the Prevention of Cruelty to Animals (RSPCA) Archive, Horsham

Animals–War Dogs
Materials Used in the Production of Animals Were There by A.W. Moss and E. Kirby
    (File 3 of 3)

Unpublished Memoirs
Davies, John, *Recollections of John Gwylim Davies*

PUBLISHED MATERIALS

Documentary Sources

Aberdeen Press and Journal
Animal World
Animals' Defender
Bucks Herald
Burnley Express and News
Cheltenham Chronicle
Chiron Calling
Citizen (Gloucester)
Daily Express
Daily Mirror
Derby Daily Telegraph
Derby Evening Telegraph
Dog World
Dogs' Bulletin
Dundee Courier
Dundee Evening Telegraph
Fife Free Press
First Aid
Glasgow Herald
Gloucestershire Echo
Guardian
Hastings and St Leonard's Observer
Huddersfield Examiner
Hull Daily Mail
Journal of the Potters Bar and District Historical Society
Journal of the Royal Army Veterinary Corps
Journal of the Royal Society of Arts
Journal of the Royal United Service Institution
Journal of the United Services Institution of India
Kennel Gazette
Lancashire Daily Post
Leicester Mercury

Lincolnshire Echo
Manchester Guardian
Melton Times
Morpeth Herald
New York Times
The Nineteenth Century and After
Northampton Mercury
Northern Daily Mail (Hartlepool)
Nottingham Evening Post
The Observer
Our Dogs
P.D.S.A. News
Soldier
Sunday Express (London)
Sunday Post (Lanarkshire)
Sunderland Echo and Shipping Gazette
Tail-Wagger Magazine
The Times
Western Daily Press (Bristol)
Western Morning News
Western Times (Exeter)
Whitstable Times and Tankerton Press
Windsor Magazine
Yorkshire Evening Post
Yorkshire Post

Printed
Army Council Instructions, Issue 931 (1940)
Army Council Instructions, Issue 1090 (1941)
Army Council Instructions, Issue 1505 (1945)
The Defence Animal Centre Open Day pamphlet (7 June 2014)
Headquarters, Department of the Army, *Field Manual 20-20, Basic Training and Care of Military Dogs* (Washington, D.C., 14 July 1972)
Field Manual 3-19.17, Military Working Dogs, Department of the Army (Washington, D.C., July 2005)
War Office, *Training of War Dogs* (1952)
War Office, *Training of War Dogs* (1962)

Photographs
Airborne Assault Museum, Duxford
Betty Fetch and Brian Receiving his PDSA Dickin Medal from Air Chief Marshal Sir Frederick Bowhill, 1947
Pte Emile Corteil with Para Dog Glen, 1944

Members of 13 Parachute Battalion Relax with a Para Dog, 1945
Scout Platoon of 13th (Lancs) Parachute Battalion with Para Dogs, Wismar, Baltic,
    May 1945

Library of Congress, Prints and Photographs Division, Washington, D.C.
LC-B2-3487-3, Lot 10842, George Grantham Bain Collection

Imperial War Museum (IWM) Photograph Archive
B 6499, The British Army in Normandy 1944
B 6496, Animals in War 1939-1945
B 6501, The British Army in the Normandy Campaign, June-August 1944
B 6506, The British Army in the Normandy Campaign, June-August 1944
CH 10287, Royal Air Force Flying Training Command, 1940-1945
CH 20417, Royal Air Force: 2nd Tactical Air Force, 1943-1945
D 88456, The Malayan Emergency 1948-1960
E 15659, The British Army in North Africa 1942
H 28928, The Royal Air Force in Britain, 1939-1945
HU 88803, Damage Caused by V2 Rocket Attacks in Britain, 1945
MH 30551, The British Army in Northern Ireland, 1969-2007
NA 289, The British Army in Tunisia 1942
NA 13611, The British Army in North Africa 1944
PL 6445F
Q 7345, The British Army on the Western Front, 1914-1918
Q 9276, The Royal Engineers Signal Service on the Western Front, 1914-1918

National Archives and Record Administration Still Picture Branch, College Park,
    Maryland
111-SC-140929

The National Library of Scotland
N.405, First World War 'Official Photographs'
N.411, First World War 'Official Photographs'

PDSA, London
Beauty
Beauty in rubble
Bob with Handler CQMS Cleggett
Judy–Japanese Prisoner of War Dog
Rip–Civil Defence Rescue Dog during the Blitz
Rob

Recorded Interviews

Imperial War Museum (IWM) Sound Archive

11542, Interview with Leonard Walter Williams, 21 September 1990, Reel 3

12347, Interview with Stanley James Ledger Hill, 25 November 1991, Reel 1

12412, Interview with John Bernard Robert Watson, 30 January 1992, Reel 3

16497, Interview with Silvester Montague 'Monty' Hunt, 1 February 1996, Reels 1 and 2

19049, Interview with Malcolm Leonard Connolly, 7 June 1999, Reel 4

21192, Interview with James Baty, 14 April 2001, Reels 1 and 3

22087, Interview with Hugh 'Enoch' Weldon, 3 August 2001, Reel 3

Contemporary Books

Lieutenant Colonel J.H. Boraston (ed.), *Sir Douglas Haig's Despatches, December 1915-April 1919* (London: J.M. Dent & Sons, 1919).

Maria Dickin, *The Cry of the Animal* (London: PDSA, 1950).

James Gilroy, *Furred and Feathered Heroes of World War II* (London: Trafalgar, 1946).

Clayton Going, *Dogs at War* (New York: Macmillan, 1940).

L. Lind-Af-Hageby, *Bombed Animals, Rescued Animals, Animals Saved from Destruction: Typical Cases from the Records of the Animal Defence Society's War Work and Some Comment* (London: The Animal Defence and Anti-Vivisection Society, 1941).

H.S. Lloyd, 'The Dog in War', in Brian Vesey-Fitzgerald (ed.), *The Book of the Dog* (London: Nicholson & Watson, 1948), 177-193.

Ian Malcolm, *War Pictures Behind the Lines* (London: Smith, Elder & Co., 1915).

Frederick Montague, *Let the Good Work Go On* (London: Hutchinson, 1947).

Major General Sir John Moore, *Army Veterinary Service in War* (London: H&W Brown, 1921).

Arthur Moss and Elizabeth Kirby, *Animals Were There: A Record of the Work of the R.S.P.C.A. during the War of 1939-1945* (London: Hutchinson, 1947).

Major S. Ogden-Smith, *A Record of the Activities of The Corps of Military Police in the Middle East, 1939-1944* (Printing and Stationery Services, M.E.F., 1945).

Lieutenant Colonel E.H. Richardson, *British War Dogs: Their Training and Psychology* (London: Skeffington, 1920).

Colonel E.H. Richardson and Blanche Richardson, *Fifty Years with Dogs* (London: Hutchinson, 1950).

Lieutenant Colonel Edwin Hautenville Richardson, *Forty Years with Dogs* (London: Hutchinson, 1929).

R. Sharpe, *Dog Training by Amateurs* (London, 1938).

Dorothea St. Hill Bourne, *They Also Serve* (London: Winchester, 1947).

Major R.F. Wall, *Keeping a Dog* (London: A. & C. Black, 1933).

War Office, *Statistics of the Military Effort of the British Empire during the Great War, 1914-1920* (London: His Majesty's Stationery Office, 1922).

Lieutenant Colonel J.H. Williams, *Elephant Bill* (London: The Reprint Society, 1951).

John Woodward, *You and Your Dog* (London: C. Arthur Pearson, 1933).

Parliamentary Debates (Hansard)

House of Commons Hansard

HC Deb 2 June 1919 vol 116 cc1724-5W
HC Deb, 20 July 1926 vol 198 cc1042-3
HC Deb 24 December 1929 vol 233 cc2130-1W
HC Deb 30 January 1930 vol 234 cc1206-7W
HC Deb 9 October 1939 vol 352 c39W
HC Deb 7 May 1940 vol 360 cc1022-3
HC Deb 5 June 1940 vol 361 cc840-1
HC Deb 2 April 1941 vol 370 cc1003-4
HC Deb 30 September 1941 vol 374 c488W
HC Deb 22 October 1941 vol 374 c1786
HC Deb 4 May 1943 vol 389 c33W
HC Deb 6 July 1944 vol 401 c1326
HC Deb 10 November 1944 vol 404 cc1653-4
HC Deb 15 June 1945 vol 411 c1900W
HC Deb 9 April 1946 vol 421 c293W
HC Deb 22 October 1946 vol 427 cc1452-3
HC Deb 7 July 1955 vol 543 cc113-4W
HC Deb 30 June 1975 vol 894 cc339-40W
HC Deb 3 December 1984 vol 69 c16W
HC Deb 4 February 1999 vol 324 c764W
HC Deb 29 June 1999 vol 334 cc99-101
HC Deb 6 March 2003 vol 400 c1154W
HC Deb 22 March 2007 vol 458 c1033W
HC Deb 16 October 2008 vol 480 c1393W
HC Deb 15 December 2008 vol 485 c330W
HC Deb 15 June 2010 vol 511 c343W
HC Deb 7 June 2011 vol 529 c5W
HC Deb 10 January 2012 vol 538 cc9-10W
HC 7 March 2013 vol 559 c1125W

House of Lords Hansard

HL Deb 14 March 1983 vol 440 cc589-90WA
HL Deb 30 January 1991 vol 525 c764

SECONDARY SOURCES

Cecil Russell Acton, *Dogs, their Care and Training* (London: Witherby, 1949).
Martin S. Alexander, 'War and its Bestiality: Animals and their Fate during the Fighting in France, 1940', *Rural History*, 25:1 (2014), pp. 101-124.

Maggie Andrews, Charles Bagot Jewitt and Nigel Hunt (eds.), *Lest We Forget: Remembrance and Commemoration* (Stroud: The History Press, 2011).

Niall Barr, *Yanks and Limeys: Alliance Warfare in the Second World War* (London: Vintage, 2015).

P.M.H. Bell, *John Bull and the Bear: British Public Opinion, Foreign Policy and the Soviet Union 1941-1945* (London: Edward Arnold, 1991).

Lord Brabazon of Tara, *The Brabazon Story* (London: William Heinemann, 1956).

Mike Brown, *Put that Light Out!: Britain's Civil Defence Services at War 1939-1945* (Stroud: Sutton, 1999).

Ron Brown, *Jet of Iada DM, MFV* (Liverpool, 2006).

Angus Calder, *The People's War: Britain 1939-1945* (London: Pimlico, 1992).

Claire Campbell and Christy Campbell, *Dogs of Courage: When Britain's Pets Went to War 1939-45* (London: Corsair, 2015).

Brigadier J. Clabby, *The History of the Royal Army Veterinary Corps, 1919-1961* (London: J.A. Allen & Co., 1963).

Basil Collier, *The Defence of the United Kingdom* (London: Her Majesty's Stationery Office, 1957).

Jilly Cooper, *Animals in War* (London: Corgi, 2000).

Gloria Cottesloe, *The Story of the Battersea Dogs' Home* (Newton Abbott: David & Charles, 1979).

Mike Croll, *The History of Landmines*, (Barnsley: Leo Cooper, 1998).

Bryan D. Cummins, *Colonel Richardson's Airedales: The Making of the British War Dog School, 1900-1918* (Calgary: Detselig, 2003).

Stephen R. Davies, *Fiat Justitia: A History of the Royal Air Force Police* (London: Minerva, 1997)

Stephen R. Davies, *RAF Police Dogs on Patrol: An Illustrated History of the Deployment of Dogs by the RAF, 1942-2004* (Bognor Regis: Woodfield, 2006).

Fairfax Downey, *Dogs for Defense: American Dogs in the Second World War 1941-1945* (New York: Trustees of Dogs for Defense, Inc., 1955).

Peter Downward, *'Old Yourself, One Day': Personal Memoirs of Peter Downward* (Chippenham: Delworth Group, 2004).

Peter Doyle, *ARP and Civil Defence in the Second World War* (Oxford: Shire, 2010).

David Edgerton, *Britain's War Machine: Weapons, Resources and Experts in the Second World War* (London: Penguin, 2012).

Tim Essex-Lopresti (ed.), *A Brief History of Civil Defence* (Matlock: Civil Defence Association, 2005).

David French, *Raising Churchill's Army: The British Army and the War Against Germany 1919-1945* (Oxford: Oxford University Press, 2000).

Juliet Gardiner, *The Animals' War: Animals in Wartime from the First World War to the Present Day* (London: Portrait, 2006).

Juliet Gardiner, *Wartime Britain 1939-1945* (London: Review, 2004).

Isabel George, *Beyond the Call of Duty: Heart-warming Stories of Canine Devotion and Wartime Bravery* (London: Harper Element, 2010).

Laurie Goldstraw, 'The Paratrooper and his Dog', *After the Battle*, 74 (1991), pp. 28-33.

Ernest A. Gray, *Dogs of War* (London: Robert Hale, 1989).

Blythe Hamer, *Dogs at War: True Stories of Canine Courage Under Fire* (London: André Deutsch, 2006).

Patrick Hennessey, *The Story of the Royal Air Force Police* (undated).

Philip Howell, 'The Dog Fancy at War: Breeds, Breeding, and Britishness, 1914-1918', *Society and Animals*, 21 (2013), pp. 546-567.

Jimmy Quentin Hughes, *Who Cares Who Wins: The Autobiography of a World War Two Soldier* (Liverpool: Charico, 1998).

Steven Johnston, 'Animals in War: Commemoration, Patriotism, Death', *Political Research Quarterly*, 65:2 (2012), pp. 359-371.

Hilda Kean, *Animal Rights: Political and Social Change in Britain since 1800* (London: Reaktion, 1998).

Hilda Kean, 'The Dog and Cat Massacre of September 1939 and People's War', *European Review of History*, 22:5 (2015), pp. 741-756.

Hilda Kean, *The Great Cat and Dog Massacre: The Real Story of World War Two's Unknown Tragedy* (Chicago: The University of Chicago Press, 2017).

Robert G.W. Kirk, 'In Dogs We Trust? Intersubjectivity, Response-Able Relations, and the Making of Mine Detector Dogs', *Journal of the Behavioral Sciences*, 50:1 (2014), pp. 1-36.

Evelyn Le Chêne, *Silent Heroes: The Bravery and Devotion of Animals in War* (London: Souvenir, 1994).

Michael G. Lemish, *War Dogs: A History of Loyalty and Heroism* (Washington, D.C.: Brassey's, 1996).

Norman Longmate, *Hitler's Rockets: The Story of the V-2s* (Barnsley: Frontline Books, 2009).

Norman Longmate, *How We Lived Then: A History of Everyday Life during the Second World War* (London: Arrow, 1977).

Major A.V. Lovell-Knight, *Story of the Royal Military Police* (London: Leo Cooper, 1977).

S.P. Mackenzie, *The Home Guard: A Military and Political History* (Oxford: Oxford University Press, 1996).

Brigadier A.D. Magnay, *The Second World War 1939-1945 Miscellaneous 'Q' Services* (London: War Office, 1954).

Rae McGrath, *Landmines and Unexploded Ordnance: A Resource Book* (London: Pluto Press, 2000).

Ian McLaine, *Ministry of Morale: Home Front Morale and the Ministry of Information in World War II* (London: Allen & Unwin, 1979).

Lydia Monin and Andrew Gallimore, *The Devil's Gardens: A History of Landmines* (London: Pimlico, 2002).

Terence H. O'Brien, *Civil Defence* (London: Her Majesty's Stationery Office, 1955).

Richard Overy, *The Air War: 1939-1945* (London: Europa, 1980).

Richard Overy, *The Bombing War: Europe 1939-1945* (London: Penguin, 2013).

H.M.D. Parker, *Manpower: A Study of War-time Policy and Administration* (London: Her Majesty's Stationery Office and Longmans, Green and Co., 1957).

Chris Pearson, 'Dogs, History, and Agency', *History and Theory*, 52 (2013), pp. 128-145.

Chris Pearson, *Mobilizing Nature: The Environmental History of War and Militarization in Modern France* (Manchester: Manchester University Press, 2012).

Neil Pemberton, 'The Bloodhound's Nose Knows? Dogs and Detection in Anglo-American Culture', *Endeavour*, 37:4 (2013), pp. 196-208.

Neil Pemberton and Michael Worboys, *Mad Dogs and Englishmen: Rabies in Britain, 1830-2000* (Basingstoke: Palgrave Macmillan, 2007).

David Reynolds, *Rich Relations: The American Occupation of Britain, 1942-1945* (New York: Random House, 1995).

David Reynolds, Warren F. Kimball and A.O. Chubarian (eds.), *Allies at War: The Soviet, American, and British Experience, 1939-1945* (Basingstoke: Macmillan, 1994).

Sonya O. Rose, *Which People's War?: National Identity and Citizenship in Wartime Britain 1939-1945* (Oxford: Oxford University Press, 2003).

J.D. Scott and Richard Hughes, *The Administration of War Production* (London, 1955).

Aaron Herald Skabelund, 'Breeding Racism: The Imperial Battlefields of the "German" Shepherd Dog', *Society and Animals*, 16 (2008), pp. 354-371.

Aaron Herald Skabelund, *Empire of Dogs: Canines, Japan, and the Making of the Modern Imperial World* (Ithaca: Cornell University Press, 2011).

Alison Skipper, 'The Dog as a National Symbol: All "British Bulldogs" and "German Sausages on Legs"', Paper delivered at the World Association for the History of Veterinary Medicine and the UK Veterinary History Society, 12 September 2014.

Lieutenant Colonel C.E.E. Sloan, *Mine Warfare on Land* (London: Brassey's, 1986).

Charles F. Sloane, 'Dogs in War, Police Work and on Patrol', *The Journal of Criminal Law, Criminology, and Police Science*, 46:3 (1955), pp. 385-395.

Mary Elizabeth Thurston, *The Lost History of the Canine Race: Our 15,000-Year Love Affair with Dogs* (Kansas City: Andrews Mcmeel,1996).

Stanley Tiquet, *It Happened Here: The Story of Civil Defence in Wanstead and Woodford 1939-1945* (Borough Council of Wanstead & Woodford).

John K. Walton, 'Mad Dogs and Englishmen: The Conflict over Rabies in Late Victorian England', *Journal of Social History*, 13:2 (1979), pp. 219-239.

Graham Winton, *Theirs Not to Reason Why: Horsing the British Army 1875-1925* (Solihull: Helion & Company, 2013).

Andrew Woolhouse, *13–Lucky for Some: The History of the 13th (Lancashire) Parachute Battalion* (Amazon Createspace, 2013).

Philip Ziegler, *London at War 1939-1945* (London: Pimlico, 2002).

Websites

British Army <www.army.mod.uk> (accessed 18 November 2016)

Guardian <http://www.theguardian.com> (accessed 4 September 2015)

Internet Archive <https://archive.org> (accessed 5 November 2013)

Metropolitan Police <http://content.met.police.uk/Home> (accessed 15 November 2016)

PDSA <www.pdsa.org.uk> (accessed 29 January 2018)

Ministry of Defence <https://www.gov.uk/government> (accessed 18 and 24 November 2016)

Royal Air Force <http://www.raf.mod.uk> (accessed 18 and 24 November 2016)

Royal Navy <http://www.royalnavy.mod.uk> (accessed 24 November 2016)

UK Data Service–British Institute of Public Opinion (Gallup) <https://discover.ukdataservice.ac.uk> (accessed 29 September 2016)

Index

Lightning Source UK Ltd.
Milton Keynes UK
UKHW022005121122
412093UK00010B/122